Sports in African American Life

D1453694

Sports in African American Life

Essays on History and Culture

Edited by DREW D. BROWN

McFarland & Company, Inc., Publishers
Jefferson, North Carolina

This book has undergone peer review.

ISBN (print) 978-1-4766-6964-9
ISBN (ebook) 978-1-4766-3766-2

LIBRARY OF CONGRESS AND BRITISH LIBRARY
CATALOGUING DATA ARE AVAILABLE

Library of Congress Control Number 2019056105

Front cover: football player by Mike Orlov
(Shutterstock); Minnesota Lynx small forward
Maya Moore by Lorie Shaull

Printed in the United States of America

McFarland & Company, Inc., Publishers
Box 611, Jefferson, North Carolina 28640
www.mcfarlandpub.com

Table of Contents

Introduction

DREW D. BROWN

For many African Americans, sports are a way of life, a spaceship out of the pitfalls of poverty, a platform for cultural heroes, and/or a display of African aesthetics. For others, it is a neo-colonial institution that perpetuates self-destruction. For African Americans, sport has functioned as a backpack that has weighed heavily on the lives of many but also provided tools for ostensible advancement. It has fashionably been a cultural staple among African Americans, some might say to a fault. The study of this phenomenon has proven that, in many ways, sport has been one of the most influential traditions in African American life and culture.

The analysis of sports in the lives of African Americans has grown tremendously over the past 30 years. Since the first major text by Harry Edwards, *The Rise of the Black Athlete*, scholars have engaged with this subject to varying degrees. The inclusion of race to the dynamics of sports research provided a new perspective and called for a re-examination of the definition, function, and operation of sport. The most common and singular theme among research in the 1990s focused on the denigration of African American athletes (Sailes). Many scholars highlighted the racist treatment of African American professional athletes throughout history or the poor academic achievements among collegiate athletes. However, there was a need for work that did not degrade African American athletes by simply perpetuating stereotypes about them. Around the 2000s, the advent of new scholarship speaks to the various experiences and patterns that exist among the wide range of African American athletes by scholars like Louis Harrison, Ben Carrington, Charles Ross, Thabiti Lewis, and others. Their focus was not only on the negative treatment of African American athletes but also how African Americans have used sport to their benefit and progress. In addition, more research has emerged regarding the intersectional aspects of sport that seek to analyze the overlapping and in-between areas of race, class,

1

gender, and sexuality. While most studies remain dedicated to understanding the dynamics of African American male athletes, there has been a call for more work around African American women that has been answered by some researchers like Akilah R. Carter-Francique and Jennifer H. Lansbury. Today, there are scholars that approach the subject of African Americans in sports from many different yet connected themes, including art, media, history, and gender. This speaks to the robust engagement between African Americans and sports.

This edited collection of fresh and critical essays identifies and examines the strong relationships between sports and African Americans. The volume contains research that sits at the forefront of intellectual thought. This interdisciplinary text carries a multitude of themes including social, cultural, historical, economic, and structural. Although this collection is bonded by the general theme of race and sports, it is by no means an exhaustive examination of the connection between sports and African Americans. Structurally, the text is broken into four parts. It starts with a historical theme that places African Americans in sport mostly during the mid–20th century. Then, it looks at the activism and struggle of African American athletes. It also focuses on the athletic and gender identities of contemporary athletes before finally ending with a look at athletes through media and art.

Part I contains several historical explorations of African American athletes. Stanley Keith Arnold discusses pioneering women who would challenge the racial and gender boundaries of the Olympic movement and reshape the character of the modern Olympic Games. He focuses on athletes such as Tidye Pickett, Audrey Patterson and Alice Coachman to argue that, while their individual and collective feats were extraordinary, their success was bolstered by the support of the Black community. In addition, Arnold claims that the Black press, historically Black institutions of higher learning and the athletes themselves have created a sporting culture quite distinct from white America.

Derrick E. White's essay posits a theory of HBCU football and athletics to explain Black cultural and communal attraction. He argues that Black communities' relationship to HBCU football was rooted in a history of slavery and emancipation, similar to Black churches. By looking at the idea of congregation, coaches' extracurricular and extra-athletic role, and a close examination of HBCU recruiting pitches during desegregation, White is able to show that HBCU football programs developed a cultural role that has been undone, in part, by integration.

Kevin Hogg examines the participation of African Americans in professional wrestling and finds that for at least 135 years, their roles were limited. He claims they were given stereotyped gimmicks and unflattering nicknames; sometimes treated as sideshow entertainment in "tar and feather" matches that brought back memories of slavery and Ku Klux Klan attacks; saddled with gimmicks like pimp, street thug, cannibal, or Voodoo practitioner; and forced to compete on the "Chitlin' Circuit," in segregated venues.

Part II focuses on sports activism and social movements in sports that illustrate African American athletes' struggle against oppression and responsibility to their racial community. Demetrius W. Pearson analyzes archival, sociocultural, and historical data to highlight the triumphs and travails of arguably the two most significant figures in the evolution and development of amateur basketball in the African American community: E.B. Henderson and John McLendon. Pearson explores the respective legacies of Henderson and McLendon, and their social justice efforts both on and off the basketball court.

Fritz G. Polite and Jeremai E. Santiago look at the work and impact of activist and sports sociologist Harry Edwards while examining the attitudes of social responsibility of university athletes and administrators as it relates to Black athletes. They challenge the perceived roles of students and administrators within institutions of higher learning regarding the institution's failure in addressing many of the social and economic issues that many of their recruited Black athletes inhabit.

Joseph N. Cooper, Michael Mallery, Jr., and Charles D.T. Macaulay outline the intersection between broader social movements in the U.S. and the history of African American sport activism. They look expansively at various African American sport activists to show sport as a site for contesting and shifting social ideologies and arrangements related to power, access, resources, and property.

Miciah Z. Yehudah uses the theoretical frame of Franz Fanon, the actions of Paul Robeson, and an African-centered analysis to interrogate questions regarding agency and self-determination among African American athletes. His essay proposes a new endeavor that is controlled and ethically guided by people of African descent, which will shatter psychological shackles and equally disrupt the colonial moneymaker that is the sports industry.

Part III is a dynamic contribution to the discussion and struggles surrounding gender and identity. F. Michelle Richardson and Akilah R. Carter-Francique contribute an important essay that illuminates Black sportswomen's contributions beyond the arena, court, or field of play. They use sport as a platform to elucidate Black sportswomen and their political, charitable, and organizational efforts to support and empower Black women as well as other women and people of color.

Drew D. Brown and Christina Kanu analyze the narratives of Boobie Miles and Rysheed Jordan to illustrate the structural hindrances that continue to challenge Black male athletes throughout their sporting careers. They use identity foreclosure theory to show how many Black male athletes are unprepared to successfully face life after sports.

Bruce Lee Hazelwood uses a critical anti-racist and masculinity studies framework to interrogate the question, "What does it mean to be a man in the context of sports?" He uses examples from sport to explore both formal and informal strategies that educators, community members, and/or family members can implement for productive and meaningful conversations regarding issues of race, gender, and masculinity in African American communities.

Finally, Part IV has three essays that expand the conversation of African Americans and sports to the media and visual arts. Travis R. Bell uses a tenant of critical race theory called "interest convergence" to examine recruiting websites that feature the height, strength, and speed of mostly African American football players, but provide little-to-no recognition of academic success for a prospective recruit. He argues that the recruiting websites and the coaches who utilize them further thrust the athletics-over-academics mentality into the psyche or identity of young African American athletes.

Nathan Kalman-Lamb explores the way in which narratives and documentary films represent sport as a mechanism that produces the false narrative of a post-racial society in the United States. While many sports films promote the promise of the American Dream for African Americans, he claims that sports films such as *Remember the Titans, Friday Night Lights, Glory Road, Hoop Dreams,* and *Through the Fire* reveal that sports can be seen as instruments for enhancing racial conflict, structural racial inequality, and racialized poverty.

Lastly, the work of Daniel Haxall illustrates the way African American artists exploit advertising devices, fan behavior, memorabilia and fashion trends, and societal expectations to interrogate the commodification of the Black athlete and historical associations produced by their intersection. He uses the work of Rashid Johnson, Hank Willis Thomas, and Kehinde Wiley to redress the historical fetishism of sports and Black athletes in contemporary society.

REFERENCE

Sailes, Gary A. *African Americans in Sports.* Routledge, 2017.

PART I

History

We Were Better Runners

African American Women
and the Summer Olympics, 1932–1948

STANLEY KEITH ARNOLD

As America endured the Great Depression in the summer of 1932, the opening of the Summer Olympics provided a badly needed distraction. On July 30, more than 105,000 spectators watched athletes and coaches from 37 nations participate in the opening ceremonies. However, few in the crowd were aware that the United States (U.S.) women's team included the first female black Olympians, Theodora "Tidye" Pickett and Louise Stokes.

This work explores the emergence of this tradition from urban playgrounds and black college tracks to the 1948 London Summer Olympics. These athletes challenged the boundaries of race, class and gender and in the process transformed American sports. Their efforts served as a rallying cry for the black community whose support was crucial to their success on the cinder paths. The rising participation of black women emerged as blacks endured the Great Depression and continued to migrate from the South to other regions of the nation. In addition, the modern civil rights movement began to take shape during this period and it is important to view these athletes as participants in this struggle.

Track and field events for women had their origins in the late nineteenth century. Inspired by female physical educators, elite northern women's colleges developed an interest in athletics. Their goal was not to create a competitive forum; they focused on improving women's health through vigorous exercise. In 1895, Vassar College sponsored the first women's track and field event. Twenty-two students participated in the 100-yard dash, the 120-yard hurdle, the running high jump and the 220-yard dash. Over the next two decades, women's colleges and coed institutions began to sponsor meets.[1]

Despite criticism from doctors, social scientists and journalists about the physical and moral damage of competitive athletics, track and field increased in popularity among women.[2] By the early twenties ethnic athletic clubs and industry teams were also holding meets. The nation's major track and field organization, the American Athletic Union (AAU) decided to sponsor competitions for women. However, they limited the participation of women to specific events. Citing concerns that sustained running would inhibit future childbearing, the AAU limited women to races that were less than a mile.[3] Thus they could capitalize on the growing interest in field and track and yet at the same time maintain gender mores. The qualified inclusion of women's track and field by the nation's most powerful athletic body signaled increasing interest. Yet women were not allowed to compete in track and field events at the Olympic Games. These contests were considered the most prestigious of Olympic events and female athletes were viewed as too weak to compete.[4]

Concerned about this exclusion from international competition, Alice Milliat, a French rower organized the Federation of Sportive Feminine International (FSFI). Milliat sought to highlight the potential of female athletes, especially those in the all-male preserve of track and field. In 1922, the FSFI staged the Women's Olympic Games in Paris with 65 women from Great Britain, the United States, Switzerland, Czechoslovakia and France.[5] After years of protest and pressure, the first female track and field athletes competed at the 1928 Games in Amsterdam. American Betty Robinson won a gold medal in the 100-meter. Robinson hailed from Harvey, Illinois, a suburb of Chicago and honed her skills with the Illinois Women's Athletic Club track team. The Windy City was home to one of the nation's most vibrant women's track and field cultures. In addition to a multitude of high schools, colleges and athletic clubs, the Chicago Park District, a municipal recreational institution, sponsored a series of track and field meets on a regular basis.[6]

In the 1920s, Chicago also had one of the nation's fastest growing black populations. During World War I, hundreds of thousands of blacks left the South, seeking employment in northern factories and also fleeing Jim Crow discrimination, endemic racist violence and declining opportunities in agriculture. They settled in the urban industrial centers of the Northeast and Midwest. Born in 1914, Theodora "Tidye" Pickett hailed from Chicago's emerging black working-class community and attended Englewood High School, an integrated institution on the city's South Side. Since the city's high schools did not sponsor interschool competition for girls, Pickett found opportunities in the Chicago Park District's recreation programs. At barely 5'3" and 100 pounds, she distinguished herself as a member of the South Park track team. Her potential attracted the attention of future Olympian John Brooks. Brooks, an African American long jumper and University of Chicago undergraduate, soon became her trainer and mentor. Brooks would later participate in the 1936 Berlin games, competing against Jesse Owens. Pickett became an outstanding hurdler and broad jumper.[7] By 1931, she was competing and winning on a national level, and some observers argued that Pickett be considered for the upcoming 1932 summer games in Los Angeles.[8]

As Pickett rose to prominence, a similar story was taking place in New England. Louise Stokes was born in 1913 in Malden, Massachusetts, and she too hailed from a working-class family. She began competing as a student athlete at Beebe Junior High in Malden and recruited by the local Onteora Track club. In addition to establishing a reputation as a determined sprinter, Stokes began competing in jumping events. In December 1931, the "Malden Meteor" broke the world record in the standing broad jump. Like Pickett, she was urged to try out for the Olympics.[9]

Although African American men had been competing in the Olympics since 1904, the Northwestern qualifying trials represented a milestone for black women. Both Pickett and Stokes qualified for the 400-meter relay. Eager to highlight any signs of racial progress, the black press provided extensive coverage of the trials. The *Chicago Defender* had been following the rise of Pickett for several years and hailed the inclusion of the two black runners as a blow against Jim Crow. The paper declared "The prejudiced South would not have permitted these two stars to enter a race with their white sisters."[10] In the next decade, the support of the black press would be crucial in raising and maintaining interest in the black community.

In an era of unrelenting racism, the significance of Pickett's and Stokes' accomplishment cannot be understated. They would compete not as representatives of their track clubs or schools, but as representatives of the United States. For African Americans, the desire to be included equally in all aspects of the American experience was extremely important. Pickett and Stokes had chipped away at the monolithic wall of segregation.

While they had made the team, Pickett and Stokes faced discrimination from fellow athletes and officials. On the train to Los Angeles, they were doused by water by Mildred "Babe" Didrikson, the team's star and the nation's most famous woman athlete.[11] Although this incident was described as a harmless prank, the Texas-born Didrikson had been dismissive of black athletes. The two black sportswomen encountered more racism at the Brown Palace Hotel in Denver. Pickett and Stokes were excluded from a banquet held in the team's honor and assigned a room near an upper floor service area. Years later Pickett recalled "All the other girls had private rooms, went to the banquet, were interviewed by the reporters. Louise and I ate upstairs in the attic on our trays."[12]

In Los Angeles, Pickett and Stokes attended all social and press engagements yet would confront a more serious obstacle when the Games commenced.

On August 7, the runners were scheduled to compete in the 4 × 100 relay. Both Pickett and Stokes had been enthusiastic about running this event and had excellent qualifying times at Evanston. However, they were replaced before the race. Although coach George Vreeland made the final decision, there had been a closed-door meeting of the United States Olympic Committee (USOC) before the runners were selected. In addition, Vreeland had received a telegram from the National Association for the Advancement of Colored People (NAACP) prior to his announcement, so he certainly understood the gravity of his decision.[13] In his defense, some teammates recounted that he was more concerned about factors such as passing and speed. However, Tidye Pickett disagreed. In a 1984 interview, the Chicago track star maintained that; "Times were different then. Some people just didn't want to admit that we (Louise Stokes and I) were better runners."[14]

Although they did not run in their events, the conditional inclusion of Pickett and Stokes represented a hopeful sign for many African Americans. One such supporter was Cleveland Abbott, the athletic director at Tuskegee Institute. Born in South Dakota, Abbott had been a star athlete at South Dakota State University and had served as an officer in the all black 369th Infantry in World War I.[15] After the war, he was offered a job as an assistant football coach at Tuskegee. Tuskegee had a rich history of track and field dating from the 1890s, and Booker T. Washington's institution had been one of the founding members of the Southern Intercollegiate Athletic Association (SIAA), a consortium of black colleges and universities. At the time, the AAU had restricted interracial competition and the SIAA provided African American athletes opportunities to compete. Increasingly aware of the potential of women's track and field, he included women in the Tuskegee Relays in 1927. Inspired by Abbott, the university launched its track team two years later. The *Tuskegee Messenger* reported that "The girls voted very heartily in favor of it. Some of the young women had already been participated in the spiked shoe sport and have shown satisfactory progress in track work."[16] Although some administrators and professors were reluctant to support the team, Abbott's wife, Jessie reported that male undergraduates were strident in their opposition to the creation of the team.[17]

While the team competed locally and in the Tuskegee Relays, Abbott believed that he could transform the team into a strong intercollegiate powerhouse. As Abbott worked to build his team, both Pickett and Stokes looked forward to the 1936 Games and continued to train and compete. In 1933, Stokes became the Northeast Amateur Athletic Association (NEAAU) champion in the 40-yard dash on 5.6 seconds. The next three years would witness the evolution of Stokes as one of the nation's most outstanding athletes. She would retain her title in the 50-meter and won the 25-yard sprint, 100-meter, 100-yard, 200-meter, 220-yard, broad jump and the high jump.[18] With these statistics, Stokes' place on the next Olympics was fairly certain. Pickett took more time to return to form. In the summer of the 1934, Pickett dominated the annual meet sponsored by the *Evening American* a Chicago daily, winning the 100-meter, 80-meter hurdle and the broad jump.[19]

Both Pickett and Stokes looked forward to the next Olympiad. They continued to train and compete. In addition, they became stars in the eyes of the African American community and progressive whites. Pickett was feted by Chicago's black elite and Stokes received financial support from both white and black backers in her hometown. Yet it was not clear whether American athletes would compete in the next Summer Olympics. The 1936 Games had been awarded to Berlin, the capital of Nazi Germany. The increasing anti–Semitism of the Nazi regime had sparked calls for a boycott of the Olympics, a campaign which was underway by summer 1935. Jewish organizations, labor unions and leftists argued that the Olympiad would only serve as a propaganda device for Hitler. Avery Brundage, the president of the United States Olympic Committee (USOC), maintained that politics should not affect the participation of American athletes. However, Brundage's support for the games was undermined by his increasingly public praise of Hitler. The USOC president believed that Hitler had established a bulwark against the rise of communism in Europe. African Americans were divided over participation and the black press reflected this division. For example, the *Amsterdam News* of Harlem urged black athletes to boycott the games while the *Pittsburgh Courier* maintained that the victories of African America would eviscerate the racist theories of Aryan supremacy propagated by the Nazis. The games represented an opportunity to strike a blow against Nazi racism and by extension, racism in the United States. While USOC did not permit them to vote, the majority of the athletes supported competing in the games. Although the final vote was extremely close, Brundage and his allies were victorious.[20]

Both women qualified at the Olympic trials at Brown University with Pickett being selected for the hurdles and Stokes for the 400-meter relay. Along with Jesse Owens, Ralph Metcalfe and other members of the U.S. Olympic team, Pickett and Stokes traveled to Germany via luxury ocean liner. In contrast to 1936, the two runners were not excluded from any activities. Stokes recalled sitting so close to Hitler at a banquet that she could touch his neck.[21]

Tidye Pickett became the first African American woman to compete in the Olympics. She was slated to run in the hurdles and the 100-meter. Although in great form, her strength had been affected by constant seasickness on the ten-day voyage to Germany. In addition, the hurdles in Berlin were stationary while the ones Pickett was familiar with were not. As she began the race, Pickett caught her foot on one of the hurdles and fell on the side of track. Pickett also broke her foot, thus ending her chances of competing at the games.[22]

As she saw her teammate carried off the field on a stretcher, Stokes vowed to win a medal in the 400-meter relay. Once again, her hopes were dashed. In a tragic repeat of 1932, she was denied a berth on the relay team after a closed-door meeting by U.S. Olympic officials. She remained in the stands as her teammates won the gold medal.[23] It is difficult to ascertain the reasons for the exclusion of Stokes. Her trials were not as good as Pickett's, yet they were better than many of her white teammates. Racism within the U.S. Olympic hierarchy contributed to the treatment of Stokes. In addition, Brundage's concern over offending Nazi hosts might have been a factor. Although U.S. officials promised to not to accede to anti–Semitism, the two Jewish members of the men's relay squad, Marty Glickman and Sam Stoller were replaced prior to the final race.

Like most African Americans, Abbott had followed the exploits of black Olympians through the pages of the African American press. He believed that this was the time to capitalize on the potential of black female athleticism. By the mid–1930s, white female participation in this sport had steadily declined. Increasingly, physical educators had voiced concern over the masculine nature of track and field events. The nation's most famous female competitors Stella Walsh and Babe Didrikson faced criticism for their "manly" appearance.[24] Abbott believed that as white women retreated from track and field, black female athletes would have more opportunities to compete. In the aftermath of the Berlin Games, Tuskegee created an enhanced women's track and field program. Abbott argued that the program should become more ambitious and searched for opportunities to compete. Most importantly, he reached out to organizations and colleges outside the South, thus propelling Tuskegee into the national spotlight. He also launched an ambitious recruitment drive. Since most prospective athletes came from impoverished backgrounds, Abbott was prepared to offer work-study opportunities to assist with tuition expenses. For many of his recruits, this was their first time away from small towns in the segregated South. As Lansbury has argued, a college education offered the promise of a better future for African American women.[25] Abbott's efforts were not in vain. Through his recruitment efforts and training regimen, Tuskegee's Tigerettes emerged as a major force in women's track and field. Christine Evans Perry, a former tennis star and veteran of the Tuskegee Relays served as the team's coach from 1936 to her death in 1942.[26] One of the first stars was the dynamic Lula Hymes from Atlanta's Booker T. Washington High. A multi-talented athlete, Hymes excelled in 50 and 100-meter sprints, the broad jump and 400-meter relay. An increasing number of observers believed that Hymes would medal at the next Olympics scheduled for Tokyo in 1940.[27]

Hymes emerged as Tuskegee's fortunes began to rise. In 1936, Tuskegee came in second in their first trip to the AAU national outdoor championship.

With the exception of 1943 when they placed second, Tuskegee would retain their championship position until the 1950s. Tuskegee's influence soon extended across the black academic community. Historically black colleges such as Florida A & M, Alcorn A & M, Prairie View A & M, Alabama State created track and field programs for female students. Some of the more prominent black universities such as Fisk and Howard refrained from starting similar programs. Like their white counterparts, these institutions shared a more conventional view of womanhood.[28]

Under Abbott Tuskegee continued their recruiting efforts. In 1939, he signed a promising high school student to the Tuskegee squad. Hailing from rural southwest Georgia, Alice Coachman was the fifth of ten children and had spent some of her youth picking cotton. Coachman joined a team already deep with talent. She quickly distinguished herself in the 50-meter sprint and as the anchor on the 400-meter relay. As graduating seniors departed, Coachman and others filled that void. While they looked to the future, opportunities for international competition were uncertain. The outbreak of World War II had led to the cancellation of the scheduled 1940 Tokyo Games.[29] Although the war brought unprecedented challenges to the nation, many African Americans viewed the conflict as an opportunity to transform race relations. Encouraged by the black press and civil rights organizations, African Americans initiated a sustained effort to argue for equality in all aspects of American life. While segregation remained both on a de facto and de jure basis, the modern civil rights movement was emerging to challenge the nation's racial status quo.

As the war raged, the AAU meet represented the major opportunity for track and field athletes to compete. While Tuskegee's prominence rose, Betty Jean Lane of Wilberforce University emerged as a rising star. In 1940, the seventeen-year-old Lane defeated Walsh in the 100-meter and defeated Tuskegee's Lucy Newell in the 50-meter. The *Chicago Defender* hailed her as "the newest sensation on the cinder path" who ran roughshod over her opponents.[30] Lane's winning streak continued in 1941 when she won both the 100 and 200-meter. The Wilberforce star was expected to defend her titles but dropped out of the 1942 meet and withdrew from future competition. Coachman and the Tuskegee team were also covered by black sportswriters. The *Baltimore Afro-American* referred to Coachman as "National Sprint Queen" after her 1945 victory over Walsh in the 100-meter. The previous year, Sam Lacy, the *Afro-American*'s sportswriter had interviewed Walsh who described Coachman "as the toughest opponent I have ever met," and "the finest runner I've ever raced against"[31] While the black press praised these athletes, there was scant coverage in white dailies such as the *New York Times* and the *Chicago Tribune*.

After Perry's untimely death in 1942, Abbott assumed daily operation of the team.[32] Coachman and others credited Abbott and the Tuskegee community for creating a nurturing and supportive environment. "We were family" claimed Coachman.[33] While training was rigorous, Tuskegee's demanding regimen was moderated by a strong mentoring program. Senior runners assisted and advised their younger counterparts on an ongoing basis. In addition, the athletes engaged in a full range of activities from attending lectures and participating in choir and other. While they were exposed to a larger intellectual world, most of the athletes majored in traditionally female fields. For example, Coachman majored in dressmaking at Tuskegee and later earned a BS in home economics at Albany State in Georgia.

Abbott's influence had an immediate impact on Nashville's Tennessee State University, then known as Tennessee Agricultural and Industrial College. In 1943, his daughter Jessie began her coaching career there. Despite her best efforts, the team struggled, and Tom Harris, Lane's former coach from Wilberforce replaced her in 1946. Like Abbott, Harris realized that recruiting was essential to the success of the team. His most promising addition was sprinter Audrey "Mickey" Patterson of New Orleans. The wiry Patterson had competed in the 200-meter for Wiley College in the 1947 AAU Outdoor Championship. Located in Texas, the historically black college was better known for its nationally renowned debate team than for its athletic program. A short time after the race Patterson had fallen ill with acute appendicitis and denied treatment at a local white hospital. Her decision to transfer to Tennessee State was in part shaped by this potentially life-threatening incident. Patterson also was eager to join a program that had a promising future.[34] In addition to running the 400-meter relay, the wiry Patterson shined in both the 100 and 200-meter races.

Since 1940, African American women had emerged as the dominant force in American women's track and field, therefore it was not surprising that nine of the twelve women on the 1948 team were black. Edward Bancroft Henderson, director of physical education for the District of Columbia's segregated schools and the foremost authority on black sports praised "the Tuskegee and other colored girls" and predicted that these athletes would medal in all of their races. However, Henderson reassured his readers that "Colored girl athletes are as rule, effeminate. They are normal girls. This is not true of the women champions who have made records who have made records that compare with marks set by men."[35]

As the athletes sailed to England, the American presidential race reflected a growing concern over race relations. The Democratic Party had split over several issues, one of which was civil rights. The incumbent, Harry S. Truman had been the first president to address the NAACP. In addition, Truman had desegregated the American military through an executive order. In response to Truman, white southern Democrats established the States

Rights Party. Known as Dixiecrats, they nominated segregationist South Carolina Senator J. Strom Thurmond to run for president. They were not the only Democrats disenchanted with Truman. Liberal Democrats believed that Truman had abandoned FDR's New Deal and was too bellicose toward the Soviet Union. Moreover, they argued that Truman's civil rights policies were far too moderate. Under the banner of the Progressive Party, they selected Henry Wallace, one of FDR's vice presidents to run for the Oval Office. While other concerns occupied the minds of Americans, civil rights had emerged as a potent issue in American politics.[36]

In addition to their male colleagues, the nine African American women who marched under the American flag in London signified a new postwar reality. Like Jackie Robinson who had broken the color line a year earlier, these athletes represented a growing realization that African Americans would confront and overcome racial boundaries. However, with the eyes of the world upon them, symbolism would not suffice. They had to perform. While there were high expectations for the team, some officials expressed concern. American women had not competed in an Olympiad since Berlin and there had been few opportunities to face foreign competitors in the postwar period.

The somber mood among the team matched the somber tone of the London games. Dubbed the "Austerity Olympics," the games took place as Great Britain struggled to recover from the ravages of the Second World War and the decline of its once mighty empire. Athletes were housed in drab former military barracks and complained regularly about the quality of the food. The fickle English climate also added to the melancholy mood. American hopes were buoyed when Audrey Patterson won the bronze in the 200-meter, losing to Audrey Williamson of the United Kingdom and the indomitable Francina "Fanny" Blankers Koen of the Netherlands. Patterson became the first African American woman to win an Olympic medal.[37]

Inspired by Patterson's success, Coachman set her sights on a medal. She faced Dorothy Tyler of Great Britain and Micheline Ostermeyer of France. In a drizzling rain in front of 65,000 spectators, Coachman cleared the bar at the record height of 5'6⅛" and thus became the first African American woman to win gold at an Olympic event. The Tuskegee Flash was in disbelief until she peered at the stadium's scoreboard. Years later Coachman recalled the moment: "I saw it on the board; Coachman USA number one."[38]

Coachman's victory represented a milestone in the emerging civil rights struggle. She had demonstrated that despite segregation, an African American woman could reach the apogee of her sport. Like Robinson, Coachman's triumph would open the door for others. After returning to America, Coachman, Patterson and six of their African American teammates met President Harry S. Truman at the White House. President Franklin Roosevelt had not greeted Owens after the 1936 Olympics, so Truman's invitation had important symbolic meaning. His gesture acknowledged the skill and endurance of these athletes yet other welcoming ceremonies revealed the limitations of Olympic victories for black women. When Coachman returned home to Albany, Georgia, city leaders celebrated her with receptions and a parade. Both *Time* and *Life* magazines provided coverage of Albany's "Alice Coachman Day." Although both blacks and whites celebrated, the crowds remained segregated. Coachman even recalled that some white officials refused to shake her hand.[39] For Audrey Patterson, there was no official celebration in her hometown of New Orleans. Friends and family organized a testimonial and invited Mayor deLesseps Morrison.[40] In a 1976 interview, Patterson stated: "Mayor Morrison sent a telegram saying I was a credit to my race, and that was the extent of it. Morrison was known as a fair man, but he couldn't find it in him to come, I felt I was getting the cold shoulder from New Orleans. I felt I'd done something for the city, and it wasn't appreciated. I was bitterly disappointed."[41]

The victories of Coachman and Patterson marked an important turning point in the history of the modern Olympic Games. African American women had emerged as a dynamic presence in the world of international track and field competition. By 1960, black athletes were vital to American success in Olympic competition as the Games became another battleground in the Cold War. Under the direction of coach Ed Temple, Tennessee State's Tigerbelles made an important contribution to Olympic victories in the 1950s and beyond.

While their contribution to American athletic power cannot be understated, the impact of black female Olympians on the growing civil rights movement is far more important. Although they did not lead marches or make speeches during their Olympic careers, their struggles and triumphs constituted both a real and symbolic victory. These black women made their mark in the international arena, demonstrating that they could compete and win against the best in the world. For African Americans, the participation of Coachman, Patterson and their teammates in the Olympics represented the possibility that the nation was transforming, albeit slowly. Despite the prevalence of Jim Crow segregation and other forms of discrimination, the rise of African American women in Olympic competition exemplified grace and excellence and the hopes of a better tomorrow.

NOTES

1. Louise Mead Tricard, *American Track and Field* (Jefferson, NC: McFarland, 2006), 17–37.

2. *Ibid.*, 50–59.

3. *Ibid.*, 68–90.

4. Cecile Houry, "American Women and the Modern Summer Olympic Games: A Story of Obstacles and Struggles for Participation and Equality," PhD diss., University of Miami, 2011, 48–54.

5. Mary Leigh and Therese Bonin, "The Pioneering Role of Madame Alice Milliat and the FSFI in Establishing International Track and Field Competition or Women," *Journal of Sport History 4 (no.1 1977)*, 73–78.

6. John Keilman, "Betty Robinson: The Greatest Chicago Olympian You've Never Heard Of," *Chicago Tribune*, August 18, 2016, 1–4.

7. Robert Pruter, "Tidye Pickett: The Unfulfilled Aspirations of America's Pioneering African American Female Track Star," in *Before Jackie Robinson: The Transcendent Role of Black Sports Pioneers,* ed. Gerald Gems (Lincoln: University of Nebraska Press, 2017), 238–239.

8. Doris H. Pieroth, *Their Day in the Sun: Women of the 1932 Olympics* (Seattle: University of Washington Press, 1996), 32.

9. Chris Caesar, "Louise Stokes Fraser," *Malden (MA) Mirror,* February 14, 2012, https://patch.com/massachusetts/malden/black-history-month-louise-stokes-fraser.

10. "Sprint Stars Win in Olympic Tryouts," *Chicago Defender,* July 23, 1932.

11. Pieroth, *Their Day in the Sun,* 46, and Pruter, 244.

12. *Ibid.,* 46–47.

13. Pruter, "Tidye Pickett," 244–246.

14. Pieroth, *Their Day in the Sun,* 111.

15. Anne Blaschke, "Southern Cinderpaths: Tuskegee Institute, Olympic Track and Field, and Regional Social Politics, 1916–1955," essay submitted to the Boston University African American Studies Program, 5–10, https://www.bu.edu/afam/files/2016/03/Anne-Blaschke-Southern-Cinderpaths.pdf.

16. "Girls to Have Track Team," *Tuskegee (AL) Messenger,* March 9, 1929.

17. Blaschke, "Southern Cinderpaths," 10.

18. "Louise Stokes File," Malden (MA) Public Library.

19. Pruter, "Tidye Pickett," 246–248.

20. David K. Wiggins *Glory Bound: Black Athletes in a White America* (Syracuse: Syracuse University Press, 1997), 61–72; Gena Caponi Tabey, *Jump for Joy: Jazz, Basketball, and Black Culture in 1930s America* (Amherst: University of Massachusetts Press, 2008), 39–44.

21. "Louise Stokes Fraser" *Massachusetts Hall of Black Achievement.* Item 30 http://vc.brigw.du/hoba/30

22. Pruter, "Tidye Pickett," 249–252; Deborah Riley Draper, *Olympic Pride: American Prejudice,* Documentary, 2016.

23. Matt Osgood, "Sports History Forgot About Tidye Pickett and Louise Stokes, Two Black Olympians Who Never Got Their Shot," *Smithsonian* (online), http://smithsonianmag August 10, 2016.

24. Jennifer H. Lansbury, *A Spectacular Leap: Black Women in Twentieth-Century America* (Fayetteville: University of Arkansas Press, 2014), 50–51.

25. Blaschke, "Southern Cinderpaths," 10–15.

26. Lansbury, *A Spectacular Leap,* 52–61.

27. *Ibid.,* 62; Sandra Collins, *The 1940 Games: The Missing Olympics, Japan, the Asian Olympics and the Olympic Movement* (London: Routledge, 2007), 158–168.

28. "African American Women Make Their Marks in Sport," in *The Unlevel Playing Field: A Documentary History of the African American Experience in Sport,* eds. David Wiggins and Patrick Miller (Urbana: University of Illinois Press, 2003), 115–116.

29. Lansbury, *A Spectacular Leap,* 70–71.

30. "A New Star Streaks Across Athletic Horizon, *Chicago Defender,* May 25, 1940.

31. Lansbury, "'The Tuskegee Flash' and 'The Slender Harlem Stroker': Black Women Athletes on the Margin," *Journal of Sport History 2,* no. 28: 239.

32. Lansbury, *A Spectacular Leap,* 66–72.

33. Lansbury, "Alice Coachman: Quiet Champion of the 1940s," in *Out of the Shadows: A Biographical History of African American Athletes,* ed. David Wiggins (Fayetteville: University of Arkansas Press, 2006), 152.

34. Lyons Yellin, "New Orleanian Audrey 'Mickey' Patterson-Tyler's Olympic Achievement Was Greatly Unnoticed," *Times-Picayune/NOLA.com.* February 22, 2013.

35. Susan Cahn, *Coming on Strong: Gender and Sexuality in Twentieth Century Women's*

Sport (New York: Free Press, 1994), 117; Cindy Himes Gissendanner, "The Impact of Race, Gender, and Class Ideologies," *Research Quarterly for Exercise and Sport* 67, no. 2 (June 1996): 178–179.

36. Steven Lawson, *Running for Freedom: Civil Rights and Black Politics in America Since 1941* (New York: McGraw Hill, 1997), 29–37.

37. Lansbury, *A Spectacular Leap*, 66–72.

38. Richard Goldstein, "Alice Coachman, 90, Dies, First Black Woman to Win Olympic Gold." *New York Times,* July 14, 2014.

39. Lansbury, *A Spectacular Leap,* 70–71.

40. Yellin, "New Orleanian Audrey 'Mickey' Patterson-Tyler."

41. *Ibid.*

Sporting Congregations

The Foundation of Black College Football

Derrick E. White

"Who will be the wrongest guy?" With this 1934 headline Eric "Ric" Roberts and twelve colleagues at the *Atlanta Daily World*, the first Black daily newspaper, announced a new feature in which the writers would select the winner of every major black college football game.[1] With the support of the several African American insurance companies, the best and worst prognosticators earned prizes at season's end. The journalists dubbed their group the 100 Percent Wrong Club, because of the fickle ways that football turned sure victories into defeats. The Club's founding predated the rise of Jesse Owens and Joe Louis by a year, as Roberts recalled he "saw the handwriting on the wall.... Black sports phenoms are incomparable."[2] Over time, the 100 Percent Wrong Club highlighted the games, the stars, the teams, and the coaches of the segregated gridiron, courts, and fields.[3] Roberts observed that the segregated white daily newspapers overlooked black sports and the African American weekly newspapers at the time had limited coverage of black college athletics. Roberts reflected on his rationale to start the Club, "I said to myself, somebody should honor us for what we've done. I was a halfback at Clark [College in Atlanta, Georgia now called Clark Atlanta University]. I thought that Ga. [*sic*] Tech was playing well. They beat Notre Dame, and their reward was the [1929] Rose Bowl Game. I became convinced that sports gifts were going un-rewarded, and I knew some black teams were the best in the nation.... Better than anybody."[4]

The 100 Percent Wrong Club valued black college athletics outside of the quest for integration. On sports pages throughout the 1930s, black sportswriters called for the integration of professional baseball, lamented the growing color line in professional football, and highlighted the exploits of racial pioneers on the gridirons and hardwoods of predominately white colleges in

19

the North.[5] Jesse Owens at the 1936 Olympics and Joe Louis's knockout of Max Schmeling in their 1938 rematch epitomized the possibility of black athletes to gain support from across racial lines. However, the creation of the 100 Percent Wrong Club signaled something else. The Club was an appreciation of the hard work and community support needed for successful black college athletics. The creation of the 100 Percent Wrong Club points to a growing sporting congregation that served as the foundation for the black college football dynasties of the 1950s and 1960s.

The concept of sporting congregation counters the prevailing narrative of race and sports as a means to combat the racial prejudice and to achieve racial integration. An examination of sporting congregations allows one to evaluate Historically Black Colleges and Universities (HBCUs) sports beyond integration by studying the functions of a black sporting community—a network of athletes, administrators, coaches, sportswriters, and fans. Scholars of African American life and history have provided a theoretical frame to comprehend the broader implications of the sporting communities. Notably, historian Earl Lewis has described how African Americans in Norfolk, Virginia, "modified the political language so that segregation became congregation" thereby creating "a certain degree of autonomy and, by extension, power." Although white supremacy circumscribed the power created by the congregation, Lewis's theoretical intervention provides an alternative framework to grasp the creation of Black college sports outside the integration narrative.[6]

The failure to acknowledge the sporting congregational network reflects a broader lack of scholarship on black college athletics. John Sayle Watterson's *College Football* speaks for much of the scholarship when he states: "Inevitably, this book had to deal with the problem of race, notably the slow influx of African Americans players into football at major state institutions. As a result, *I have not tracked the history of African Americans in football at predominately black institutions, a story that needs to be told.*"[7] Even the growing scholarship on black college athletics has only captured parts of the sporting network without showing the intricate connections. Thus, the significant work on athletes, coaches, HBCU conference formation, and teams unsuccessfully ties these formations to one another or larger issues in African American life and education.[8]

This essay will briefly look at three components of the sporting congregation—the black press, college administrators, and coaches—to show how each contributed to a black college football community. The result of the combined efforts would be two decades of high-quality football that was on par or better than its white collegiate counterparts. Many of these examples will come from Florida A&M (FAMU), which the black press named the team of the 1950s and in the first five seasons of the 1960s had a record of 45 wins against 5 losses. In fifteen seasons, FAMU won or shared six national titles. The Rattlers were the quintessential example in developing a sporting congregation that led to a dynasty.

The Black Press

In the early twentieth century, the African American press promoted integrated college sports often at the expense of the games played at HBCUs. Robert Abbott founded the *Chicago Defender* with a desire to make "his newspaper a force to combat the pervasive racism of the era."[9] The role of sports in achieving this goal was unclear to Abbott. Frank "Fay" Young, who joined the paper in 1907, convinced Abbott to dedicate an entire page to sports after a special issue on the Jack Johnson-Jess Willard fight in April 1915 became the newspaper's biggest seller.[10] Young became the first black sports editor in the country, and he called for athletic integration on the sports page, as well as covering boxing, the Negro Leagues, and local athletics.[11] Black college athletics received scant attention in the early years of the *Defender's* sports page. Beginning in 1927, Abbott paid Ric Roberts for columns on black college football.[12] Despite Robert's columns, more space was devoted to the actions of racial pioneers on northern college teams. Although Young was the first sports editor, his belief in the importance of integration, especially in college athletics echoed the work of Edward Bancroft Henderson, the father of African American sports history.[13]

Henderson was the most critical journalist and historian of African American athletes in the early twentieth century. He cataloged the successes of black athletes in the pages of black newspapers and magazines for more than six decades. He penned *The Negro in Sports* in 1939, the first African American sports history.[14] Henderson believed that athletics represented an opportunity for African Americans to lessen racial prejudice and hasten integration. In 1911 he wrote, "The colored college athlete of the past and present bears an enviable reputation. His athletic skill and courage have gained for him the respect and admiration of thousands, and it is impossible to overestimate the effect of his career on the minds of thousands of Americans who have seen him perform or read of his doings."[15] Henderson's firmly believed black athletes were vital in moving the country toward integration.

Born in Washington, D.C., in 1883, Henderson graduated from the famed M Street High School (later renamed Dunbar) in 1902, where he was a star athlete in baseball and football.[16] He attended Miner Normal School, an HBCU in Washington, D.C., earning his teaching credentials. Desiring to teach sports to the thousands of African American youth in Washington, he attended the Harvard Summer School of Physical Education in 1904, becoming the first black male physical education student in America and the first African American physical education teacher in public schools.[17] His educational experience at Harvard solidified his belief that sport could lessen prejudice. As the first director of physical education for the segregated schools in Washington, he would push some student-athletes to attend predominately white institutions (PWIs) in the Northeast. He would write in 1926, "But our boys on white teams competing with other white teams are finding themselves and gaining the respect or at least the tolerance of thousands. We need more athletes in competition with the rest of American just as we do in all other lines to make for understanding."[18] One of Henderson's students at Dunbar High School was famed surgeon Charles R. Drew who starred in football and track at Amherst College. Despite facing racism on and off the field, Drew felt a "debt of gratitude" to Henderson for supporting his athletic and educational goals at the small liberal arts school in Western Massachusetts.[19]

Henderson believed in HBCUs as well, but his goal for black colleges was for them to develop physical education programs and organize. Henderson promoted eligibility requirements and supported the creation of the conferences such as the Colored Intercollegiate Athletic Association (CIAA). Whereas student-athletes at PWIs were at the forefront of fighting racial prejudice, black colleges needed to teach "through the physical ... the ideals of law and order, honesty, and good sportsmanship" which "in the long run mean more to America and to the Negro race."[20] Thus, black college sport needed to promote discipline in its athletes. Despite Henderson's continual support of HBCU sports, black colleges, in his interpretation, played a less immediate role in promoting racial equality.

The 100% Wrong Club would come to reject Henderson's perspective on black college sports, especially football. Founded in 1934 as an "insignificant backroom tribute where members draped up the season with blended spirits in Auburn Avenue clubs," the Club by the 1940s named the black college football champion by awarding W.A. Scott II Trophy.[21] The 100 Percent Wrong Club lauded black athletics. Co-founder Ric Roberts made sure that celebration, not racial reform, governed his coverage of black college football. Roberts saw the club as reflecting a "black world." He recalled, "When Howard and Lincoln played a football game in front of 20,000 people ... there was no such thing about Harvard or Yale; they were just something to read about in the paper." He added, "Our heaven and our glory was ... not at Harvard, but at Howard and Lincoln and it motivated south were Morehouse and Atlanta University and Clark and Morris Brown and Tuskegee and Alabama State and finally Florida A&M and other schools west of the Mississippi ... all joined the passion [of the] black world."[22] These athletic passions were the subject of the club, and ultimately of sports pages of the black press.

In addition to the 100 Percent Wrong Club based at the *Atlanta Daily*

World, the *Pittsburgh Courier* promoted black college football, as well. The *Courier,* founded in 1910, began its coverage of black college football in 1911 when Wilberforce College traveled to Pittsburgh to play the Delany Rifles, "a colored organization of the Hill district." The Rifles defeated Wilberforce in that opening Thanksgiving game.[23] With the growth of the Howard University and Lincoln University Classic, the *Courier* increased its coverage of black college football in 1923.[24] In 1927, the *Courier* released its first black college All-American Team, featuring Tuskegee's Ben Stevenson the most dominant player of the 1920s.[25] By the 1930s, the *Courier* was a leading newspaper covering black college football, naming mythical national title winners and All-Americans annually. Ric Roberts joined the *Courier's* sports section in the early 1940s.[26]

The coverage of Florida A&M's first classic game exemplified the importance of sports pages of the black press. In 1933, Florida A&M announced its inaugural Orange Blossom Classic (OBC) against Howard University in Jacksonville. The intersectional game was an ambitious venture that defied the norms of established "classics." The OBC was played on the first weekend in December, after the traditional big games that took place during the week of Thanksgiving. Game organizer J.R.E. Lee, Jr., FAMU's business manager, envision "the biggest intersectional contest Florida has ever witnessed."[27] Adding to the game's risk, was FAMU's perennial status as a losing program. The Rattlers had only won 11 games in the decade before the first OBC. The school's ability to schedule Howard was a public relations coup. Most important, FAMU's administration convinced Chester Washington, sports editor for the *Pittsburgh Courier,* to attend the game. Washington was instrumental in selection the *Pittsburgh Courier* All-American team, thus getting Washington to a FAMU game for the first time was a significant public relations victory for the program. "From every section comes word that Famcee [sic] will be at Durkee Field in the largest number ever assembled to witness a football contest," reported Washington.[28] When FAMU upset Howard 9 to 6, he expressed the game's importance for the Rattlers. He wrote that Florida A&M's win was "one of the greatest triumphs in the history of Sunshine State elevens."[29] Florida A&M won on the field and in the news columns. The news coverage was the first step in making the Orange Blossom Classic the most attended black college game in the 1950s and 1960s.

The vast distances between the black media hubs in Atlanta, Chicago, Pittsburgh, New York, Norfolk, and Washington prohibited sports writers from attending every game in the far-flung corners of the South. FAMU, Grambling, Wiley, and other HBCUs that desired successful football programs had to provide black newspapers with game coverage and statistics. In the modern parlance, the schools employed sports information directors (SIDs). In this way, the black press followed the path developed by white newspapers in covering college football. By the 1930s, the *Atlanta Daily World*, the *Chicago Defender*, the *Pittsburgh Courier*, the *Norfolk Journal and Guide*, and the *Baltimore/Washington Afro-American* devoted two or more pages a week to sports. In the fall, college football stole headlines from baseball and boxing on the sports pages with game reports, editorial columns, and pictures of teams.[30]

Colleges' sports publicity departments made sure that the black press had game summaries, accurate statistics, and the key quotes needed to support the growing sports coverage. For instance, FAMU's Arthur L. Kidd was key to building support for the Rattler football program and the Orange Blossom Classic. Kidd arrived in Tallahassee in 1925 after graduating from the University of Michigan in 1924 and working a year at Tuskegee University. He spent nearly five decades in Tallahassee holding numerous positions, including the principal of the Florida A&M High School, registrar, and dean. A year after Florida A&M inaugural Orange Blossom Classic, Kidd stepped into the role of promoting the Rattlers in the black press.[31] Kidd's game summaries ensured that every Rattler game was reported in the major black newspapers. His coverage took on additional meaning when the Rattlers hired former Ohio State star William Bell in 1936 and assistant Alonzo "Jake" Gaither in 1937. Kidd's told readers of Henry Butler, the Rattlers "nimblefooted" star quarterback.[32] He vividly described the greatness of the Rattlers' players and coaches as the school won its first conference title in 1937. His description of that year's OBC in which Florida A&M defeated Hampton 25 to 20 is illustrative. "A game that saw both teams resort to a wide open brand of football with passes flying thing and fast—with interceptions—with scores chalked up in every quarter of the game by one or the other team—with beautiful long runs of 80 and 57 yards—and with a last minute rally by Hampton to lessen the scoring advantage of the Rattlers, the Florida classic-conscious crowd of approximately 3500 was afforded thrills galore in reward for their magnificent support of this farewell bid to the 1937 football season."[33] Kidd's colorful narration of the game ensured that those who could, would not miss the next Orange Blossom Classic.

FAMU's longtime coach Jake Gaither described the importance of Kidd to the Rattler program. Although Kidd's primary job at Florida A&M was as a registrar, Gaither noted, "He used his spare time to serve as a statistician, sports publication director and publisher of the Orange Blossom Classic Bulletin." He added, Kidd "never received any remuneration for his work with athletics, yet after every game he could be found in his office, typing the game reports, and sending game information to the press."[34] His sacrifice was essential for the development and growth of the FAMU football program and in building the school's sporting congregation. Kidd was representative of men and women who worked behind the scenes to generate interest in what was happening on the field. When fans arrived at Bragg Stadium in Tallahassee or at the Orange Blossom Classic in Miami, supporters knew the names of star players Willie "the Wisp" Galimore, or Bob "China Doll" Paramore, or "Bullet" Bob Hayes.

Sports information directors at black colleges developed narratives of greatness for programs, and no one was more effective than Grambling University's Collie Nicholson. Grambling University hired Eddie Robinson as its head football coach in 1941. The Tigers had little success until after World War II ended. In 1947, Grambling defeated archrival Southern for the first time behind Tank Younger, Robinson's first star player. The following year Grambling president, Ralph Waldo Emerson Jones, hired Collie Nicholson to publicize the Tigers. He sent upwards of two hundred press releases to black newspapers weekly. Nicholson earned the nickname "the man with the golden pen" for his prolific and vivid writing. In an article on Eddie Robinson, for instance, Nicholson wrote, "Glum Eddie Robinson, the air-minded professor of football at Grambling College, who used to dote on passing pyrotechnics during his early years in the Tigers' lair, will keep his feet braced on solid earth this campaign and stress power football."[35] In Nicholson's first season he let the world know about Paul "Tank" Younger, who became the first HBCU player in the NFL when he signed with the Los Angeles Rams.[36] His descriptions of Younger's exploits drew the attention of pro scouts leading to his signing by the Rams.

The black newspapers, magazines, organizations like the 100 Percent Wrong Club, and sports information directors narrated black college football for fans. The celebration of black college football was not compared to the other side of the color line; instead, a large segment of the black press promoted the quality of the "sepia" leagues. By choosing the black national champion, and black college All-Americans, the media was vital in establishing the sporting congregation beyond campus. It allowed alumni to maintain their rooting interests, drew the attention of local communities, and sparked the imagination of young black athletes, who wanted to be Tank Younger or Willie Galimore just as much as they wanted to be Jesse Owens, Jackie Robinson, or Joe Louis.

College Administrators

While the black press fostered a sporting congregation outside of HBCU campuses, campus presidents and administrators determined whether athletics would be an essential component of the black college experience. Through the hiring of coaches, support for travel, and even work-study and scholarship programs, HBCU administrators shaped the direction of sports, especially football, on their campuses.

College faculty and administrators followed E.B. Henderson's suggestion to control player eligibility. In the fall of 1911, Ernest Jones Marshall, head football coach and chemistry professor at Howard University, mailed letters to every Black college asking them to come together and form an intercollegiate athletic association. Only four schools answered Marshall's clarion call. Disappointed, but determined, Marshall organized a meeting in February 1912, with the four respondents: Lincoln University (PA), Shaw University (NC), Hampton University (VA), and Virginia Union University. These five colleges, including Howard University, formed the Colored Intercollegiate Athletic Association (CIAA) in 1912. CIAA organizers imagined creating a Black version of the NCAA, establishing rules and regulation for the Black colleges, including a four-year eligibility rule.[37] The proposed eligibility rules, while well-meaning, threatened many black college teams, because the schools reflected a range of educational missions—teaching (normal) schools, church-sponsored liberal arts schools, and public schools that emphasized vocational education. Not to mention HBCUs had seminaries and medical schools. Many of these schools had primary and secondary education schools attached where high school players joined the varsity team. Thus, many schools opposed the CIAA's eligibility rules, because they eliminated a high number of players at many schools, especially in the deep south. Since Black colleges offered secondary, normal, collegiate, and industrial curriculums, team rosters contained players from multiple academic levels. Student-athletes not enrolled in college courses or playing for a team for more than four years was often a source of criticism from reformers. W.E.B. Du Bois suggested that Tuskegee's dominance on the gridiron in the late 1920s was because "The name [Ben] Stevenson has appeared in Tuskegee's lineup for no less than six years."[38] For Du Bois, this was emblematic of the problems in black college football. However, Stevenson's time at Tuskegee was easily explained by his enrollment in Tuskegee's high school and later its college.

Tuskegee was not the only school that used high school students on its varsity college teams. The small numbers of students taking college courses often necessitated putting prep players on the college team. For example, Florida A&M had a student population of nearly 350 in 1916, but only twelve of the secondary education students were taking college subjects, instead of high school, industrial, or normal education classes. The marginal difference between secondary and higher education posed unique problems for HBCUs in determining player eligibility. Marshall acknowledged this "second objection has more weight, especially with those institutions whose work is, by necessity, mostly for preparatory departments." Considering the minuscule number of responses to Marshall's call for the creation of a Black athletic commission, most Black colleges refused to limit preparatory school players from the varsity, as the CIAA wanted.[39]

Despite these challenges, college administrators led the call for increased order in college sports. In December 1913, Presidents John Milton Putnam Metcalf of Talladega College and John Hope of Atlanta Baptist College called a meeting of southern Black colleges to address issues surrounding player eligibility in football and other sports. Atlanta Baptist (Morehouse), Clark, Fisk, Florida A&M, Morris Brown, and Talladega joined to form the Southern Intercollegiate Athletic Conference (SIAC). A similar process led to the formation of the Southwestern Athletic Conference in 1920, and the Midwest Athletic Conference in 1924.[40]

While administrators brought organization to black college athletics, they could also undermine programs. Howard University's Mordecai Johnson failed to support the football program because it exhibited the problems of commercialization and excess. Howard had won three mythical national titles between 1920 and 1926. After a controversy over player eligibility in a game against rival Lincoln University, Howard withdrew from the CIAA in 1925. As a result, no other CIAA team could schedule the Bisons. Alumni and fans blamed Howard's white president Stanley Durkee for the embarrassment. Durkee resigned, and Howard University selected Mordecai W. Johnson as its next, and first African American president. Although Johnson had played football at Atlanta Baptist College (now Morehouse College), he ended financial support for the sport in 1927. By 1929, the once-dominant Howard football team went winless.[41] Mordecai Johnson thought that football's popularity undermined Howard's academic purpose.

Athletic and football success required black college administrators to believe in the importance of the sport as part of the broader mission of the college. A college president's support of athletics, concerning the best coaches, financing teams, and expanding opportunities, was essential in shaping the dominant programs of the 1950s and 1960s. The president's role was more acute for public HBCUs that lacked the prestige of Fisk, Howard, Morehouse, and Tuskegee. The presidents at public HBCUs recognized that sports could provide their schools valuable publicity. Presidents believed that sports recognition would increase the number of students and alumni supporting the college.

Despite being a founding member of the SIAC, Florida A&M's football team was a perennial loser for the first two decades of the twentieth century. In 1924, the Florida Board of Control named J.R.E. Lee the third president of Florida A&M. Upon his arrival, he announced that sports were going to take a more critical role at Florida A&M. He declared, "No school in this day can expect to attract promising men or women that does not give organized athletics a foremost place. Where there are no athletics, it is very likely true that only deadheads are attracted. Young men and women of promise desire to be connected with an institution that has spirit and force."[42] Lee made several decisions that changed the trajectory of the athletic program and the university. In 1925, he changed the school's nickname from Tigers to Rattlers, because Lee wanted "his team to be as deadly to opponents as a rattlesnake was to [its] victims."[43] In 1926, Lee hired former Lincoln University star, Franz "Jazz" Byrd as head coach. By hiring Byrd, Lee eliminated student-led football at FAMU and announced that the school was serious about football. Ric Roberts described Byrd as building the "foundation of a rip-snortin' team which will entertain any team in the country."[44] It was under Lee's leadership that Florida A&M began the Orange Blossom Classic, later hired William "Big Bill" Bell and Jake Gaither, and won the school's first national championship in 1938. Lee used sports to make FAMU the primary destination for the state's African American high school graduates.

President Lee was not the only president who viewed sports as playing a pivotal role in the advancement of the university. Tennessee State University (TSU) president Walter Davis also saw sports as vital to the growth of Tennessee's only public HBCU. Davis held numerous positions at TSU including professor, dean, and football coach before rising to the president's office in 1943. He understood that hiring the best coaches was essential to athletic success. He appointed Jessie Abbott, the daughter of the Tuskegee coach and athletic director Cleve Abbott, to lead the women's track and field program. The hiring of Abbott signaled that TSU was serious about women's athletics.[45] The result of this approach to women's track and field would manifest after Ed Temple took over the women's program in 1950, leading the Tigerbelles as the most dominant women's track program in the 1950s and 1960s. Temple and TSU would win 34 national titles and produce 40 Olympians. Davis's support for women's athletics differentiated him from other black college presidents. He also poured money into the football program. In 1944, he lured Henry Arthur Kean from the Kentucky State University. Davis announced, "He is a great coach, and we are expecting Tennessee to regain the high place it once held in the college football world."[46] Kean led the TSU Tigers to three titles from 1944 to 1954.

Presidents Lee and Davis's belief in the importance of college athletics provided an infrastructure that benefited from the expansion of HBCU budgets. Florida A&M and Tennessee State developed robust sporting congregations as the federal and state governments increased financial support to public HBCUs. FAMU gained, albeit unequally, from the New Deal, receiving $19,000 in 1940 to enclose the football field.[47] Also, both schools received additional state money, as Florida and Tennessee rapidly increased funding to public HBCUs during the 1950s in an attempt to stave off desegregation. State appropriations for Florida A&M's biennial budget grew from $2.4 million for 1948–1950 to $3.6 million for 1950–1952.[48] These changes were also reflected in the renaming of the schools. Tennessee State Agriculture and

Industrial College became a university in 1951. The state of Florida changed the name of Florida A&M College to University in 1953 signaling the school's recently established graduate programs, including a College of Law in 1949.

Public HBCUs controlled the athletic landscape over private black colleges. Only Morris Brown College won a black college football title between 1950 and 1980. Larger enrollments, increased financial support from southern states, and the elimination of two-way football led to public black colleges' dominance after World War II. Black college administrators' commitment to the sporting congregation in the 1930s and 1940s resulted in dynasties in the 1950s, 1960s, and 1970s. Still, athletic success revolved around the coaches who were the giant figures of black college athletics.

Black Coaches

If an HBCU sporting congregation is represented by a pyramid with the black press as the base and college administrators forming the centroid, then the apex was established by the coaches. Black college coaches, like their white counterparts, were indispensable to cultivating supporters in the media, university, and community. Coaches such as Florida A&M's Jake Gaither or Grambling's Eddie Robinson became spokesmen for their programs and black college athletics. Moreover, they used their popularity to grow and defend sports on their campuses. The head mentors were the object of discussion for the black press, among the most critical hiring decision for college presidents, and the representative of their athletic programs to the broader public. The ability to transform a robust sporting congregation into an athletic dynasty hinged on a coaches' ability to motivate student-athletes and communicate to the public the importance of black colleges.

The founding generation of HBCU coaches from the late 19th century through the interwar period was dominated by men who learned the game at predominately white colleges. In early college football for instance, Tuskegee's Cleveland Abbott (a graduate of South Dakota State), Howard's Edward Morrison (Tufts), Wiley's Fred Long (Milikin), Wilberforce's Harry Graves (Michigan State), and Clark's Sam Taylor (Northwestern) transferred the hard lessons learned as racial pioneers in the Northeast and Midwest to novice black college programs. This first generation of coaches laid the foundation, and some, like Abbott, even developed the first HBCU dynasty at Tuskegee.[49]

Black college sporting congregations intensified with the second generation of black college coaches who often learned the game from these racial pioneers while studying at private HBCUs. Coaches such as Morgan State's Eddie Hurt (a graduate of Howard University), Southern's Arnett "Ace" Mumford (Wilberforce), Tennessee State's Henry Arthur Kean (Fisk), Prairie

View's Billy Nicks (Morris Brown), Grambling's Eddie Robinson (Leland), and FAMU's Jake Gaither (Knoxville). The majority of these coaches took over public HBCUs in the 1930s and 1940s. These coaches had been reared on black college campuses; thus, they understood the unspoken ways that HBCUs affirmed black humanity in the storm of racial turmoil and hatred. They were both the products and promoters of a black college education. The dual perspective, as a former student and a coach, situated the very best of second-generation coaches as the most significant supporters of black colleges. Gaither, Mumford, Robinson, and others translated this support into wins, often more than the white college coaches within their states.

The coaches benefited from the rapid changes to higher education after World War II. While the depression of the 1930s impacted all colleges, the economic catastrophe nearly devastated private black colleges. In 1935, Tuskegee was running a deficit of $50,000 a year. Overall the income of black colleges decreased by 15 percent and donations were down 50 percent between 1930 and 1943. Several private black colleges closed.[50] However, public HBCUs, like FAMU, survived the downturn due to the New Deal.[51] Public HBCUs also took advantage of the post-war boom. The Serviceman's Readjustment Act, better known as the G.I. Bill, sent millions of veterans to college campuses. One million Black men and women benefited from the bill by returning to college and vocational schools. Black colleges that had traditionally struggled for enrollments during the war were now over capacity. Fisk University in Nashville, for instance, announced a record enrollment in 1946 with 900 students including 230 veterans, but the school had to turn away more than a thousand applicants because of the lack of facilities. Given the limited resources regarding faculty, dormitory and classroom space at Black colleges nearly 20,000 Black vets could not enroll. Despite the limitations facing HBCUs, the increasing number of student meant Black college athletic coaches had a full complement of players, included a significant number who had played football in the military. FAMU was no different from its contemporary Black colleges, as it saw its post-war enrollment double from nearly 900 in 1940 to more than 1,800 in 1949.[52]

Public HBCUs and its football teams, backed by state money, expanded. Black college football teams immediately after the war added veterans to its rosters. The war had led to the suspension of two-way football, meaning that post-war teams were nearly double the pre-war size. Some of the returning players played on military teams such as Tuskegee War Hawks coached by former Florida A&M coach and former Ohio State All-American William Bell. African American veterans, finding their benefits went further at public HBCUs, returned to college and the gridiron. As a headline in the *Norfolk Journal and Guide* stated, "Enter King Football: Returning GIs Form Backbone of College Teams."[53]

As America entered the Atomic Age, the war changed labor require-ments. Education and racial management were seen as essential to winning the Cold War and becoming the "leader of the free world." When the NAACP launched a campaign to equalize teacher salaries across the South, the region responded by increasing the teaching requirements as justification for inequitable salaries. Some HBCUs anticipated these changes. In the mid–1930s, FAMU president J.R.E. Lee convinced the State Board of Education that it needed a Department of Health and Physical Education. Lee stated, "The only teachers capable of teaching physical education are those who have been trained in physical education."[54] In the years after World War II, the State Board of Control and the Florida State Legislature passed the Minimum Foundation Program, which among its provisions increased the teacher requirements. In the enhanced conditions there was a stipulation that high school coaches have college credit in physical education.[55]

To meet the new requirements, HBCU coaches offered courses that were mutually beneficial to high school coaches and their program. HBCU coaches transformed the expanding post-war enrollments into a sporting congrega-tion that served as the backbone to player recruitment. For instance, Jake Gaither developed a coaching clinic, as part of the school's summer school curriculum. Attendees, black coaches from across Florida and Georgia, would earn graduate credits that allowed them to navigate the changing require-ments. The combination of FAMU's growing size and the effectiveness of the coaching clinic led Gaither to regularly brag that 85 to 90 percent of the Florida high school coaches were Florida A&M graduates.[56] By pulling coaches into the Rattler network, Gaither developed a near monopoly on recruiting in-state black athletes.

Recruiting was, and is, the lifeblood of dominant athletic programs. For FAMU, the coaching clinic addressed the needs of coaches and those of the programs. Over time, the high school coaches, often Rattler alumni, used a similar playbook. The best football players in football were ushered to Tal-lahassee with the understanding that Gaither would look out for their best interests and the team would win. Rattler pride trickled down to local com-munities who watched proudly as the former prep stars, played for the Rat-tlers. Other HBCU coaches used different tactics, with similar results. In track and field, Tuskegee's Cleveland Abbott and Tennessee State's Ed Temple used regional track meets to scout the best high school talent laying the foundation for Olympians Alice Coachman, Wilma Rudolph, and others. In basketball, Tennessee State organized a national high school basketball tour-nament to determine the best black team in the country in the 1930s. Henry Arthur Kean and later John McLendon used the competition to recruit the best African Americans high school basketball players.[57]

The development of sporting congregations led to the separation of public from private HBCUs, by translating manpower advantages into financial ones. For instance, the Rattlers' roster nearly doubled in size from the 1930s to 1950s. The unlimited substitutions rule, implemented because of the effects of the war on available players, was the chief cause of the increasing size of teams. Before 1941, players played both ways in single-platoon football. Substitutions only occurred because of injury. This kept roster sizes small. In 1941, the NCAA allowed unlimited substitutions and allowed freshmen to play varsity to help teams whose rosters had been reduced World War II. Unlimited substitutions, two-platoon football, and returning players on the G.I. Bill permitted coaches to expand their rosters at all levels including HBCUs. Many of these roster spots were funded by scholarships, thereby increasing athletic budgets.[58]

Rule changes created athletic economies of scale in which larger schools had distinct financial advantages over smaller, private schools. The larger student populations and state support for public HBCUs created a shift in its sporting futures over private Black colleges. Church-supported black colleges, like Fisk University, Morris Brown College, and Xavier University often struggled in the wake of the expansion of college football, while traditionally weaker football programs like Alabama State, Alabama A&M, and South Carolina State dramatically improved in the 1950s. Unlimited substitutions and two-platoon system led to increasing dominance by Florida A&M, Grambling, Southern, and Tennessee State. Between 1945 and 1970, Wiley College, in 1945, and Morris Brown College, in 1951, were the only private HBCUs to win a national title.[59] Tuskegee's Cleveland Abbott, the orchestrator of the first HBCU football dynasty, lamented the effect of big-time football on private colleges. Abbott noted, "The change in the rules during the last few years … made it mandatory to maintain large squads in order to match strength with opponents." He added, "It seems that the private colleges no longer can afford to finance the great squad required under the free substitution rule. Neither can it pay the expensive coaching staffs required to teach the platoons."[60]

These recruiting strategies allowed legendary black college coaches to build a network of supporters. These coaching networks, the growing cadre of alumni, the media attention, and the coaches' personality consolidated the sporting congregation. The black college football dynasties were a product of the planned development of a sporting congregation.

Conclusion

Beginning with the creation of 100 Percent Wrong Club, Ric Roberts was the de facto historian of black college football.[61] In 1960 he outlined the greatest coaches of the previous decades. He named Tuskegee's Cleveland

Abbott (1920s), Morgan State's Edward Hurt (1930s), and Tennessee State's Henry Arthur Kean (1940s) as the best of the previous three decades. The contenders for the 1950s were Jake Gaither, Morris Brown's Edward (Ox) Clemmons, Prairie View's Billy Nicks, Tennessee State's Henry Gentry, and Southern's Arnett Mumford. Roberts concluded that Gaither's seventy-three wins, winning 89 percent of his games against high-level competition made the FAMU leader the best of the decade. "When the stocky-legged, square-jawed A.S. (Big Jake) Gaither played his last game at his post as a sturdy end for dear old Knoxville College 30 years ago, there was no way of knowing at the time that he would win indelible glory as a coach. Yet there, he towers— on the brink of claiming this ... decade of football as his very own."[62] Gaither, in football, had developed the most robust sporting congregation, leading to his dominance for more than two decades.

Gaither's superiority was ultimately undone by desegregation. As southern universities integrated their teams, sportswriters, black and white, rushed to celebrate the changes on the gridiron, courts, and diamonds. Few worried about the future black colleges. The desegregation of secondary education teachers led to the loss of 38,000 jobs for African American teachers.[63] Many were HBCU graduates. The legendary coaches could not turn back the tidal wave that integration unleashed. Advances in race relations weakened the sporting congregations that had buttressed HBCU programs. In mid–1960s Gaither noted that fewer talented players were becoming Rattlers. "We don't get the best blacks anymore.... We get black leftovers." When FAMU's much-celebrated white recruit did not return for the 1969 season, Gaither surmised, "We're a black team that's being done in by integration."[64]

The 100% Wrong Club, too, could not survive the decline of the sporting congregation. In 1985, the organization celebrated its 50th anniversary by honoring Roberts and presenting the Jake Gaither Award for the best player from a historically black college to Jerry Rice.[65] The Club survived into the next century; however, the economic downturn in 2007–2008 led the Club to end its awards banquet after 77 years.[66] The loss of a valuable promoter of black college athletics signals a declining sporting congregation. Any desire to tell the story of the glory days of black college football must start by paying attention to the creation and maintenance of the sporting congregation.

NOTES

1. Ric Roberts, "'Hundred Percent Wrong' Club Makes Debut This Week End," *Atlanta Daily World*, September 30, 1934, 5.

2. Ric Roberts, "Jamborees Celebrate Excellence," *Atlanta Daily World* January 11, 1985, 7.

3. Ric Roberts, "Introducing '100 Percent Wrong' Club," *Atlanta Daily World,* September 30, 1934, 5.

4. George M. Coleman, "100% Wrong Club Cites Sports Stars; 50th Fete: Eric (Ric) Roberts; Founder of the Club," *Atlanta Daily World*, January 11, 1985, 7.

5. David K. Wiggins, "Wendell Smith, the *Pittsburgh Courier-Journal*, and the Campaign to Include Blacks in Organized Baseball, 1933–1945," in *Glory Road: Black Athletes in a White America* (Syracuse: Syracuse University Press, 1997), 80–103. Thomas G. Smith, "Outside the Pale: The Exclusion of Blacks from the National Football League, 1934–1946," *Journal of Sport History* 15, no.3 (Winter 1988): 255–281. "Bell Scores Win for Ohio: Bell Blocks Kick for Ohio Grid Win," *Chicago Defender*, November 21, 1931, 8.

6. Earl Lewis, *In Their Own Interests: Race, Class, and Power in Twentieth-Century Norfolk, Virginia* (Berkley: University of California Press, 1991), 90.

7. John Sayle Watterson, *College Football: History, Spectacle, and Controversy* (Baltimore: Johns Hopkins University Press, 2000), xii. Emphasis mine. Robin Lester, *Stagg's University: The Rise, Decline, and Fall of Big-Time Football at Chicago* (Urbana: University of Illinois Press, 1995); Michael Oriard, *Reading Football: How the Popular Press Created an American Spectacle* (Chapel Hill: University of North Carolina Press, 1993); Oriard, *King Football: Sport and Spectacle in the Golden Age of Radio and Newsreels, Movies and Magazines, the Weekly and the Daily Press* (Chapel Hill: University of North Carolina Press, 2001); Oriard, *Bowled Over: Big-Time College Football from the Sixties to the BCS Era* (Chapel Hill: University of North Carolina Press, 2009); Charles H. Martin, *Benching Jim Crow: The Rise and Fall of the Color Line in Southern College Sports, 1890–1980* (Urbana: University of Illinois Press, 2010). See also, Lane Demas, *Integrating the Gridiron: Black Civil Rights and American College Football* (New Brunswick: Rutgers University Press, 2010); Raymond Schmidt, *Shaping College Football: The Transformation of an American Sport, 1919–1930* (Syracuse: Syracuse University Press, 2007); Kurt Edward Kemper, *College Football and American Culture in the Cold War Era* (Urbana: University of Illinois Press, 2009); David K. Wiggins, "'The Future of College Athletics Is at Stake:' Black Athletes and Racial Turmoil on Three Predominately White University Campuses, 1968–1972," *Journal of Sport History* 15, no. 3 (1988): 304–333.

8. Thomas Aiello, *Bayou Classic: The Grambling-Southern Football Rivalry* (Baton Rouge: LSU Press, 2010). Samuel G. Freedman, *Breaking the Line: The Season in Black College Football That Transformed the Sport and Changed the Course of Civil Rights* (New York: Simon and Schuster, 2013). Angela Lansbury, *A Spectacular Leap: Black Women Athletes in Twentieth-Century America* (Fayetteville: University of Arkansas Press, 2014). David K. Wiggins and Chris Elzey, "Creating Order in Black College Sport: The Lasting Legacy of the Colored Intercollegiate Athletic Association," in *Separate Games: African American Sport Behind the Walls of Segregation*, eds. David K. Wiggins and Ryan A. Swanson (Fayetteville: University of Arkansas Press, 2016), 145–164.

9. Ethan Michaeli, *The Defender: How the Legendary Black Newspaper Changed America* (Boston: Houghton Mifflin Harcourt, 2016), 22.

10. *Ibid.*, 54–56. Frank A. Young, "In the World of Sports," *Chicago Defender*, April 24, 1915, 7.

11. See for example, "Football Stars with Eastern Schools," *Chicago Defender*, December 18, 1915, 7. Michaeli, *The Defender*, 55–56.

12. Eric Roberts, "Dixie Doings," *Chicago Defender*, October 29, 1927, 11.

13. David K. Wiggins, "Edwin Bancroft Henderson, African American Athletes, and the Writing of Sport History," in *Glory Bound: Black Athletes in a White America* (Syracuse: Syracuse University Press, 1997), 222.

14. Edwin B. Henderson, *Negro in Sports*, 3rd edition (Washington: ASALH Press, 1939, 2014).

15. Edwin B. Henderson, "The Colored College Athlete," *The Crisis*, July 1911, 115.

16. Alison Stewart, *First Class: The Legacy of Dunbar, America's First Black Public High School* (Chicago: Lawrence Hill Books, 2013).

17. Bob Kuska, *Hot Potato: How Washington and New York Gave Birth to Black Basketball and Changed America's Game Forever* (Charlottesville: University of Virginia Press, 2004), 11, 15.

18. Edwin B. Henderson, "Sports," *The Messenger*, 8, no. 5 (May 1926): 149.

19. Drew quote in Kuska, *Hot Potato*, 7. Spencie Love, *One Blood: The Death and Resurrection of Charles R. Drew* (Chapel Hill: University of North Carolina Press, 1996), 110–111.

20. Henderson, *Negro in Sports*, 306.

21. "Awards and Citations Winners to Attend All-Sports Jamboree: 100 Per Cent Wrong Club Organized 25 Years Ago," *Atlanta Daily World*, January 29, 1960, 7.

22. Black Journalist Project Columbia University, Interview with Ric Roberts, July 2, 1971.

23. "Football Game at Exposition Park," *Pittsburgh Courier*, December 2, 1911, 1.

24. "Money Realized from 'Grid Classic," *Pittsburgh Courier*, January 13, 1923, 5. David K. Wiggins, "The Biggest 'Classic' of Them All: The Howard University and Lincoln University Thanksgiving Day Football Games," 1919–1929," in *Rooting of the Home Team: Sport, Community, and Identity*, ed. Daniel A. Nathan (Urbana: University of Illinois Press, 2013), 36–53. "Outlook Bright for CIAA Grid Teams this Season," *Pittsburgh Courier*, September 2, 1923, 7.

25. J.C. Chunn, "Spotlighting Southern College: All-Southern Squad," *Pittsburgh Courier*, December 24, 1927, 17.

26. "Ric Roberts Honor Guest at Farewell Tribute Tonight," *Atlanta Daily World*, March 14, 1941, 5.

27. "Howard-Fla. Outfits in Post Season Contest," *Philadelphia Tribune*, November 20, 1933, 10.

28. "Howard to Invade Florida Rattlers' Stronghold," *Pittsburgh Courier*, December 2, 1933, A4. Florida A&M University was Florida A&M College until 1953. I have used FAMU for consistency.

29. Chester Washington, "Florida A&M Upsets Howard, 9–6, in Thriller," *Pittsburgh Courier*, December 9, 1933, A5.

30. Michael Oriard, *Reading Football*, 57–133.

31. A.L. Kidd, "Maroon Tigers Bow to FAMCEE," *Norfolk Journal and Guide*, October 13, 1934, 18.

32. "Fla. Rattlers Sting Alabama State, 7–0," *Pittsburgh Courier*, October 6, 1937, 18.

33. A.L. Kidd, "Florida A and M Eleven Wrecks Hampton 25–20," *Chicago Defender*, December 11, 1937, 9.

34. "Eight Men of Excellence," *Strike!: The Official Magazine of Rattler Football*, November 21, 1981, 15.

35. Collie J. Nicholson, "Coach Eddie Robinson Seeks Power at Grambling," *Pittsburgh Courier*, September 18, 1948, 12.

36. Eddie Robinson with Richard Lapchick, *Never Before, Never Again: The Autobiography of Eddie Robinson* (New York: St. Martin's Press, 1999), 79–85.

37. Bob Kuska, *Hot Potato*, 41–46. David K. Wiggins and Chris Elzey, "Creating Order in Black College Sport, 145- 164.

38. W.E.B. Du Bois, "Athletics in Negro Colleges," *The Crisis* 37 (June 1930): 209.

39. Kuska, *Hot Potato*, 43–44. Thomas Jesse Jones, *Negro Education: A Study of the Private and Higher Schools for Colored People in the United States,* vol. II (Washington: Department of Interior, Bureau of Education, 1916), 171. Adam Fairclough, *A Class of Their Own: Black Teachers in the Segregated South* (Cambridge: Harvard University Press, 2007), 11.

40. "SWAC History," http://www.swac.org/ViewArticle.dbml?ATCLID=205246152. Accessed January 24, 2017. Dennis C. Dickerson, *Militant Mediator: Whitney M. Young Jr.* (Lexington: University of Kentucky Press, 1998), 27.

41. Raymond Schmidt, *Shaping College Football,* 137–141. Patrick B. Miller, "To Bring the Race Along Rapidly: Sport, Student Culture, and Educational Mission at HBCUs During the Interwar Years," *History of Education Quarterly* 35, no.2 (Summer 1995): 125–130.

42. Leedell W. Neyland and John W. Riley, *Florida Agricultural and Mechanical University*: A Centennial History (Tallahassee: Florida A&M University, 1963, 1987), 79–85, 126–28.

43. Bill Berlow, "How 'Bout Them Pinheads? It Didn't Have to Be Seminoles and Rattlers, You Know," *Tallahassee Democrat*, October 14, 1983, 1A, 2A.

44. Eric Roberts, "Southern Sportsdom," *Chicago Defender*, December 11, 1926, 11.

45. Carroll Van West, "The Tennessee State Tigerbelles: Cold Warriors on the Track," in *Separate Games: African American Sport Behind the Walls of Segregation*, eds. David K. Wiggins and Ryan Swanson (Fayetteville: University of Arkansas Press, 2016), 61.

46. "Kean Quits Ky. State for Tennessee," *Pittsburgh Courier*, September 9, 1944, 12. Fay Young, "Through the Years," *Chicago Defender*, September 9, 1944, 7.

47. Leedell W. Neyland, and John W. Riley, *Florida Agricultural and Mechanical University*, 77–112, 151, 158, 171–72.

48. *The Biennial Report for Florida Agriculture and Mechanical College, 1948–1950*, 52. http://palmm.digital.flvc.org/islandora/object/ucf%3A22908#page/488/mode/1up. *The Biennial Report for Florida Agriculture and Mechanical College, 1950–1952*, 81. http://palmm.digital.flvc.org/islandora/object/ucf%3A23477#page/481/mode/1up. Accessed May 2, 2017.

49. Ric Roberts, "What Is Negro Football?" *Pittsburgh Courier*, December 24, 1966, 11A.

50. Marybeth Gasman, *Envisioning Black Colleges: A History of the United College Fund* (Baltimore: Johns Hopkins University Press, 2007), 15, 18.

51. Neyland and Riley, *Florida Agricultural and Mechanical University*, 147–170.

52. "Negro Colleges Open Peak Year," *Chicago Defender*, September 28, 1946, 3. Hilary Herbold, "Never a Level Playing Field: Blacks and the GI Bill, " *Journal of Blacks in Higher Education*, no. 6 (Winter 1994–1995), 104–108. Lua S. Bartley, *A Brief History of the Division of Health, Physical Education, and Recreation at Agricultural and Mechanical University from 1918 Through 1978* (Tallahassee: Florida A&M Press, 1978), 14.

53. Lem Graves, Jr., "Enter King Football: Returning GIs Form Backbone of College Teams," *Norfolk Journal and Guide*, September 14, 1946, 13.

54. Quoted in Robert Pete Griffin, *The Historical Development of Athletics at Florida Agricultural and Mechanical College* (Master's Thesis, Ohio State University, 1946), 22.

55. George E. Curry, *Jake Gaither: America's Most Famous Black Coach* (New York: Dodd, Mead, & Company), 29–30. *A Guide to Teaching Physical Education in Secondary Schools: Bulletin No. 3* (Tallahassee: State Board of Control, 1948), 86.

56. Jake Gaither memo to President George W. Gore, March 27, 1956. Jake Gaither Papers, Florida A&M University, Box 1, file 9.

57. Lansbury, *A Spectacular Leap*, 47–48. Milton S. Katz, *Breaking Through: John B. McClendon, Basketball Legend and Civil Rights Pioneer* (Fayetteville: University of Arkansas Press, 2007), 78.

58. Watterson, *College Football*, 202–203.

59. Michael Hurd, *Black College Football, 1892–1992* (Virginia Beach: Donning Company, 1993,1998), 164–165. According to Hurd records, this can be extended until 1992. See also, Marion E. Jackson, "Sports of the World," *Atlanta Daily World*, October 16, 1949, 7.

60. "SIAC Winter Meeting Set for Miami, Florida, December 3–4," *Atlanta Daily World*, November 13, 1951, 5.

61. "Legendary Sportswriter Pic Robert Says He's a Historian By Choice," *Atlanta Daily World*, January 11, 1985, 6.

62. Ric Roberts, "Gaither's Mark of 73-9-2 Paces Decade Begun in '51," *Pittsburgh Courier*, January 9, 1960, 19.

63. Greg Toppo, "Thousands of Black Teachers Lost Jobs," *USA Today*, April 28, 2004. http://usatoday30.usatoday.com/news/nation/2004-04-28-brown-side2_x.htm. Accessed November 6, 2014. Carol F. Karpinski, "Bearing the Burden of Desegregation: Black Principals and *Brown*," *Urban Education* 41, No. 3 (May 2006): 237–276.

64. Associated Press, "Jake Gaither Loves Violence," *Asbury Park Press*, November 13, 1969, 26.

65. Portia A. Scott and Chico Renfroe, "100% Wrong Club Has Capacity at Historic Banquet," *Atlanta Daily World*, January 15, 1985, 1.

66. Hal Lamar, "The Economy's Latest Victim: The 100% Wrong Club of Atlanta," *Onnidanwww*, February 4, 2012. http://onnidan.com/blogs-videos/blogs/hal-lamars-inside-hotlanta/1350-hal-lamars-blog-the-economys-latest-victim-the-100-wrong-club-of-atlanta. Accessed May 22, 2013.

REFERENCES

Aiello, Thomas. *Bayou Classic: The Grambling-Southern Football Rivalry.* Baton Rouge: LSU Press, 2010.

Associated Press. "Jake Gaither Loves Violence." *Asbury Park Press,* November 13, 1969, 26.

"Awards and Citations Winners to Attend All-Sports Jamboree: 100 Per Cent Wrong Club Organized 25 Years Ago." *Atlanta University Press,* January 29, 1960, 7.

Bartley, Lua S. *A Brief History of the Division of Health, Physical Education, and Recreation at Florida Agricultural and Mechanical University from 1918 Through 1978.* Tallahassee: Florida A&M Press, 1978.

Berlow, Bill. "How 'bout Them Pinheads? It Didn't Have to Be Seminoles and Rattlers, You Know." *Tallahassee Democrat,* October 14, 1983, 1A, 2A.

Chunn, J.C. "Spotlighting Southern College: All-Southern Squad." *Pittsburgh Courier,* December 24, 1927, 17.

Coleman, George M. "100% Wrong Club Cites Sports Stars; 50th Fete: Eric (Ric) Roberts; Founder of the Club." *Atlanta Daily World,* January 11, 1985, 7.

Curry, George E. *Jake Gaither: America's Most Famous Black Coach.* New York: Dodd, Mead, & Company, 1977.

Demas, Lane. *Integrating the Gridiron: Black Civil Rights and American College Football.* New Brunswick: Rutgers University Press, 2010.

Dickerson, Dennis C. *Militant Mediator: Whitney M. Young Jr.* Lexington: University of Kentucky Press, 1998.

Du Bois, W.E.B. "Athletics in Negro Colleges." *The Crisis,* June 1930, 209.

"Eight Men of Excellence." *Strike!: The Official Magazine of Rattler Football,* November 21, 1981, 15.

Fairclough, Adam. *A Class of Their Own: Black Teachers in the Segregated South.* Cambridge: Harvard University Press, 2007.

"Fla. Rattlers Sting Alabama State, 7–0." *Pittsburgh Courier,* October 6, 1937, 18.

Florida A&M College. "The Biennial Report for Florida Agriculture and Mechanical College, 1948–1950." accessed May 2, 1950, http://palmm.digital.flvc.org/islandora/object/ucf%3A22908-page/488/mode/1up.

Florida A&M College. "The Biennial Report for Florida Agriculture and Mechanical College, 1950–1952." accessed May 2, 1952, http://palmm.digital.flvc.org/islandora/object/ucf%3A23477-page/481/mode/1up.

"Football Game at Exposition Park." *Pittsburgh Courier,* December 2, 1911, 1.

"Football Stars with Eastern Schools." *Chicago Defender,* December 18, 1915, 7.

Freedman, Samuel G. *Breaking the Line: The Season in Black College Football That Transformed the Sport and Changed the Course of Civil Rights* New York: Simon & Schuster, 2013.

Gasman, Marybeth. *Envisioning Black Colleges: A History of the United College Fund* Baltimore: Johns Hopkins Press, 2007.

Graves, Lem, Jr. "Enter King Football: Returning GIs Form Backbone of College Teams." *Norfolk Journal and Guide,* September 14, 1946, 13.

Griffin, Robert Pete. "The Historical Development of Athletics at Florida Agricultural and Mechanical College." M.A. Master's, Ohio State University, 1946.

Henderson, Edwin B. "The Colored College Athlete." *The Crisis,* July 1911, 115.

Henderson, Edwin B. *Negro in Sports.* 3d ed. Washington, D.C.: ASALH Press. 1939, 2014.

Henderson, Edwin B. "Sports." *The Messenger* 8 (5) (1926):149.

Herbold, Hilary. "Never a Level Playing Field: Blacks and the GI Bill." *Journal of Blacks in Higher Education* (6) (1994):104–108.

"Howard-Fla. Outfits in Post Season Contest." *Philadelphia Tribune,* November 20, 1933, 10.

"Howard to Invade Florida Rattlers' Stronghold." *Pittsburgh Courier,* December 2, 1933, A4.

Hurd, Michael. *Black College Football, 1892–1992: One Hundred Years of History, Education, and Pride.* 2d ed. Virginia Beach: Donning Company. 1992, 1998.

Jackson, Marion E. "Sports of the World." *Atlanta Daily World,* October 16, 1949, 7.

Jones, Thomas Jesse. *Negro Education: A Study of the Private and Higher Schools for Colored*

People in the United States. Vol. II. Washington, D.C.: Department of Interior, Bureau of Education, 1916.

Karpinski, Carol F. "Bearing the Burden of Desegregation: Black Principals and Brown." *Urban Education* 41 (3) (2006): 237–276.

Katz, Milton S. *Breaking Through: John B. McClendon, Basketball Legend and Civil Rights Pioneer* Fayetteville: University of Arkansas Press, 2007.

"Kean Quits Ky. State for Tennessee." *Pittsburgh Courier,* September 9, 1944, 12.

Kemper, Kurt Edward. *College Football and American Culture in the Cold War Era.* Urbana: University of Illinois Press, 2009.

Kidd, A.L. "Florida A. and M. Eleven Wrecks Hampton 25–20," " *Chicago Defender,* December 11, 1937, 9.

Kidd, A.L. "Maroon Tigers Bow to FAMCEE." *Norfolk Journal and Guide,* October 13, 1934, 18.

Kuska, Bob. *Hot Potato: How Washington and New York Gave Birth to Black Basketball and Changed America's Game Forever.* Charlottesville: University of Virginia Press, 2004.

Lamar, Hal. "The Economy's Latest Victim: The 100% Wrong Club of Atlanta." accessed May 22, 2012, http://onnidan.com/blogs-videos/blogs/hal-lamars-inside-hotlanta/1350-hal-lamars-blog-the-economys-latest-victim-the-100-wrong-club-of-atlanta.

Lansbury, Angela. *A Spectacular Leap: Black Women Athletes in Twentieth-Century America* Fayetteville: University of Arkansas Press, 2014.

"Legendary Sportswriter Pic Robert Says He's a Historian by Choice." *Atlanta Daily World,* January 11, 1985, 6.

Lester, Robin. *Stagg's University: The Rise, Decline, and Fall of Big-Time Football at Chicago* Urbana: University of Illinois Press, 1995.

Lewis, Earl. *In Their Own Interests: Race, Class, and Power in Twentieth-Century Norfolk, Virginia* Berkley: University of California Press, 1991.

Love, Spencie. *One Blood: The Death and Resurrection of Charles R. Drew* Chapel Hill: University of North Carolina Press, 1996.

Martin, Charles H. *Benching Jim Crow: The Rise and Fall of the Color Line in Southern College Sports, 1890–1980.* Urbana: University of Illinois Press, 2010.

Michaeli, Ethan. *The Defender: How the Legendary Black Newspaper Changed America* Boston: Houghton Mifflin Harcourt, 2016.

Miller, Patrick B. "To Bring the Race Along Rapidly: Sport, Student Culture, and Educational Mission at HBCUs During the Interwar Years." *History of Education Quarterly* 35 (2) (1995): 111–132.

"Money Realized from 'Grid Classic.'" *Pittsburgh Courier,* January 13, 1923, 5.

"Negro Colleges Open Peak Year." *Chicago Defender,* September 28, 1946, 3.

Neyland, Leedell W., and John W. Riley. *Florida Agricultural and Mechanical University: A Centennial History (1887–1987).* Tallahassee: Florida A&M University. 1963, 1987.

Nicholson, Collie J. " Coach Eddie Robinson Seeks Power at Grambling," *Pittsburgh Courier,* September 18, 1948, 12.

Oriard, Michael. *Bowled Over: Big-Time College Football from the Sixties to the BCS Era* Chapel Hill: University of North Carolina Press, 2009.

Oriard, Michael. *King Football: Sport and Spectacle in the Golden Age of Radio and Newsreels, Movies and Magazines, the Weekly and the Daily Press* Chapel Hill: University of North Carolina, 2001.

Oriard, Michael. *Reading Football: How the Popular Press Created an American Spectacle* Chapel Hill: University of North Carolina Press, 1993.

"Outlook Bright for CIAA Grid Teams This Season." *Pittsburgh Courier,* September 2, 1923, 7.

"Ric Roberts Honor Guest at Farewell Tribute Tonight." *Atlanta Daily World,* March 14, 1941, 5.

Roberts, Ric. "Gaither's Mark of 73-9-2 Paces Decade Begun in '51." *Pittsburgh Courier,* January 9, 1960, 19.

Roberts, Ric. "'Hundred Percent Wrong' Club Makes Debut This Week End," " *Atlanta Daily World,* September 30, 1934, 5.

Roberts, Ric. "Introducing '100 Percent Wrong' Club," *Atlanta Daily World*, September 30, 1934, 7.

Roberts, Ric. "Jamborees Celebrate Excellence." *Atlanta Daily World*, January 11, 1985, 7.

Roberts, Ric. "Southern Sportsdom." *Chicago Defender*, December 11, 1926, 11.

Roberts, Ric. "What Is Negro Football?" *Pittsburgh Courier*, December 24, 1966, 11A.

Robinson, Eddie, and Richard Lapchick. *Never Before, Never Again: The Autobiography of Eddie Robinson* New York: St. Martin's Press, 1999.

Schmidt, Raymond. *Shaping College Football: The Transformation of an American Sport, 1919–1930* Syracuse: Syracuse University Press, 2007.

Scott, Portia A., and Chico Renfroe. "100% Wrong Club Has Capacity at Historic Banquet." *Atlanta Daily World*, January 15, 1985, 1.

"SIAC Winter Meeting Set for Miami, Florida, December 3–4." *Atlanta Daily World*, November 13, 1951, 5.

Smith, Thomas G. "Outside the Pale: The Exclusion of Blacks from the National Football League, 1934–1946." *Journal of Sport History* 15 (3) (1988) :255–281.

Stewart, Alison. *First Class: The Legacy of Dunbar, America's First Black Public High School* Chicago: Lawrence Hill Books, 2013.

"SWAC History." accessed January 24. http://www.swac.org/ViewArticle.dbml?ATCLID= 205246152.

Toppo, Greg. "Thousands of Black Teachers Lost Jobs." *USA Today*, April 28, 2004. Accessed November 6, 2014. http://usatoday30.usatoday.com/news/nation/2004-04-28-brown-side2_x.htm.

Van West, Carroll. "The Tennessee State Tigerbelles: Cold Warriors on the Track." In *Separate Games: African American Sport Behind the Walls of Segregation*, edited by David K. Wiggins and Ryan Swanson, 61–71. Fayetteville: University of Arkansas Press, 2016.

Washington, Chester. "Florida A&M Upsets Howard, 9–6, in Thriller." *Pittsburgh Courier*, December 9, 1933.

Watterson, John Sayle. *College Football: History, Spectacle, and Controversy* Baltimore: Johns Hopkins University Press, 2000.

Wiggins, David K. "The Biggest 'Classic' of Them All: The Howard University and Lincoln University Thanksgiving Day Football Games." In *Rooting of the Home Team: Sport, Community, and Identity*, edited by Daniel A. Nathan, 36–53. Urbana: University of Illinois Press, 2013.

Wiggins, David K. "Edwin Bancroft Henderson, African American Athletes, and the Writing of Sport History." In *Glory Bound: Black Athletes in a White America*, edited by David K. Wiggins, 221–240. Syracuse: Syracuse University Press, 1997.

Wiggins, David K. "'The Future of College Athletics Is at Stake': Black Athletes and Racial Turmoil on Three Predominately White University Campuses, 1968–1972." *Journal of Sport History* 15 (3) (1988): 304–333.

Wiggins, David K. "Wendell Smith, the Pittsburgh Courier-Journal, and the Campaign to Include Blacks in Organized Baseball, 1933–1945." In *Glory Road: Black Athletes in a White America* 80–103. Syracuse: Syracuse University Press, 1997.

Wiggins, David K., and Chris Elzey. "Creating Order in Black College Sport: The Lasting Legacy of the Colored Intercollegiate Athletic Association." In *Separate Games: African American Sport Behind the Walls of Segregation*, 145–164. Fayetteville: University of Arkansas Press, 2016.

Young, Fay. "Through the Years." *Chicago Defender*, September 9, 1944, 7.

Young, Frank. "In the World of Sports." *Chicago Defender*, April 24, 1915.

From Chitlins to Championships

Limited Opportunities for African American Professional Wrestlers

KEVIN HOGG

Combat sports existed in Africa long before European colonization, serving as recreation, entertainment, and practice for hunting and war, in addition to holding cultural and spiritual significance.[1] During the period of American slavery, African Americans participated in organized fights for the entertainment of plantation owners. Although they have since worked their way near the top of the professional wrestling world, very few have held a company's top title, thus becoming the face of the promotion. Along the way, they have faced segregation, discrimination, and offensive stereotypes. African Americans now have far more opportunity in professional wrestling, but world championship status is a door that, more often than not, remains closed.

Due to the scripted nature of professional wrestling, championships are held by wrestlers selected by the promotions. Therefore, it would be wrong to state that African Americans have not succeeded due to lack of ability. Their inability to rise to the top of the profession stems rather from lack of opportunity. For many years, African Americans were simply not permitted to face white wrestlers. Even after desegregation, promoters have rarely given top championships to African Americans. When they have won titles, the victories often come with controversy or circumstances that diminish the achievement. Apart from this discrimination, African American wrestlers have been subjected to overt racism. In 2015, World Wrestling Entertainment (WWE), the world's largest wrestling promotion, took a stand against racism.

However, comments from prominent WWE personnel, both in and outside of storylines, highlight the tension that has existed for almost a century and a half: African Americans have not been treated with respect; rather, they have been portrayed as uncivilized, misogynistic, or criminal, and have been denied opportunities open to their white colleagues. While the no-tolerance approach to racism is a welcome change, it is also important to acknowledge the history of racial tensions and discrimination in both the company and the sport as a whole.

Organized fights between slaves were among the first combat sports in the United States. Former slave John Finnely recalled occasions when plantation owners would pit their slaves against each other, both for betting and for entertainment. Weapons were not permitted, but anything else was fair game. He described a match involving punching, biting, and striking with the knee. The fight was eventually won by Tom, a slave from the same plantation as Finnely, who kicked his opponent in the stomach repeatedly until the other plantation owner conceded defeat and stopped the fight.[2] Even before professional wrestling gained popularity in the United States, African Americans were seen as a form of entertainment, fighting each other for the benefit of their white owners.

After the abolition of slavery, one of the first recorded African American professional wrestlers was former slave Viro Small, who made his debut in New York in the 1870s.[3] Competing under the ring name Black Sam, Small won the Vermont Collar and Elbow Championship twice. Although more prestigious titles existed, he and other African Americans were not permitted to hold these championships. Promoters felt it would be too risky to inflate their pride by allowing them to see themselves as capable of defeating a white man to become the company's preeminent competitor.[4] The 1870s saw the sport transition into predetermined outcomes,[5] which gave promotions significant ability to control the fate of African American employees. Owners could not only control which matches involved African Americans, but also who would win these matches and be featured as a promotion's champion.

Professional wrestling began to emphasize scripted entertainment more than a legitimate athletic competition in the 1920s.[6] However, for the first half of the twentieth century, African Americans remained shut out of mainstream professional wrestling, leading some to find ways around this exclusion. Jack Claybourne left the country and began his career in Mexico, building a reputation that later helped him find work in the United States.[7] Some wrestled far away from the Deep South, in places like the Pacific Northwest, where greater opportunities existed.[8] Others competed in segregated venues on what was known as the "chitlin' circuit," which hosted segregated music, theater, and sporting events.[9] These sites were named for chitterlings, or pig intestines, that were originally given to slaves and later became a part of "soul food" cooking.[10] Tiger Conway, Sr., got his start competing in these venues before being permitted to face white wrestlers later in his career.[11] Even after integration, Conway's only title victory was the Negro Championship while competing for the National Wrestling Alliance (NWA) in Texas.[12] With promoters still able to determine the course of his career, he was allowed to beat several well-known white wrestlers, but never with a championship on the line. The sport's racial bias remained too strong to allow African Americans to be featured among the top white stars, limiting their careers despite their abilities and popularity.

Both on the chitlin' circuit and on interracial shows, African Americans faced each other, sometimes competing for promotions' Negro Championships. Ras Samara is the first person on record holding such a title,[13] and he was followed by Claybourne, Conway, and many others. In integrated shows, African Americans were not featured prominently, and promoters protected them from crowds, who may have turned violent seeing an African American fighting a white man, by refusing to allow them to face white wrestlers.[14] However, much of the segregation was simply due to racist attitudes of promoters and society.[15] While these feelings were undoubtedly shared by some fellow wrestlers, African Americans received support from some of the most famous competitors in the sport's history. Lou Thesz helped train football player Gene Lipscomb for a career in the ring,[16] and Bruno Sammartino offered positive comments to *Ebony* magazine about wrestling newcomer Bobby Hunt.[17] Although Thesz and Sammartino are recognized as two of the greatest wrestlers of all time, their ability to advocate for social change remained limited despite their positive feelings toward African Americans.

Even seating in the arenas was also originally segregated, often with African Americans afforded few seats and forced to watch from a balcony. This likely also served to limit opportunities for African American wrestlers, as promoters would have given the most prominent positions to white wrestlers, who would be thought to hold more appeal for the majority of the audience. Roscoe Brumbaugh, a white wrestler who competed as Sputnik Monroe, had a large African American fan base and helped integrate arenas. He would bribe employees to lie about the numbers and allow more African Americans in, forcing the arena staff to seat them alongside white fans. Although this was not originally received well, the manager of Ellis Auditorium saw the financial benefit to drawing a larger crowd. Other promoters followed suit, which helped desegregate many southern venues.[18] Although this was a step forward for African Americans, it was simply a matter of economics for the companies, who may not have liked African Americans, but were willing to accommodate them if it meant larger profits.

The integration movement also gained momentum as a result of World

War II, when many male competitors were fighting overseas and women's wrestling developed a strong following.[19] This popularity continued into the 1950s. In one respect, African American women had an easier time than men in breaking the color barrier. White female wrestlers, who had faced discrimination due to sexism, were often more empathetic and willing to compete against women of other races.[20] Ethel Johnson debuted in 1951 and often competed both with and against her sisters, Babs Wingo and Marva Scott.[21] Wingo is reported to have competed in the first interracial women's match against Mildred Burke,[22] who was also the trainer and booker for many female wrestlers. African American women were reported to earn an impressive average of $300 per week as wrestlers.[23] Reporting on their success still carried some stereotypical values, with both *Jet* and *Ebony* focusing on how the sport benefited women financially while also being good for their figures.[24]

One of the most famous African American wrestlers, Susie May McCoy, competed as Sweet Georgia Brown. She was trained by "The Fabulous Moolah" Lillian Ellison, who controlled most booking for female wrestlers. McCoy left home and her son Kenny to pursue financial success and provide for her family. Although she was ranked near the top of her profession, she was not allowed to open her own bank account and only made enough money to send $30 to $50 home per month.[25] To earn the money, she not only had to wrestle, but was also expected to perform sexual services for male promoters. During her years on the road, she was raped repeatedly, gave birth to three children, and was forced to take so many drugs that she developed an addiction.[26] Upon her retirement after 15 years, she had no savings and returned home to face the anger and embarrassment of her relatives. Moolah was in the business for herself, and she exploited the women she controlled.[27] She also controlled the booking of women's wrestling and chose to give herself the NWA World Women's Championship in 1956. She held the belt almost uninterrupted for the next 28 years,[28] during which time women's wrestling declined in popularity. Little was written about women in the sport, most likely due to the lack of genuine competition due to Moolah's monopoly on the business.

Even after desegregation, many African American wrestlers, both male and female, still found limited opportunities, as promotions often lacked confidence in their marketability. It is worth noting that professional wrestling at this time was divided into regions, each controlled by different owners. Some of these promotions, such as the World Wide Wrestling Federation (WWWF), later renamed the World Wrestling Federation (WWF) and then World Wrestling Entertainment (WWE), became more powerful, leading to their titles being considered more prestigious. Some other promotions competed under the NWA banner, hosting some of their own championships while also recognizing one NWA World Heavyweight Championship as the most important title in the business.

As federal desegregation efforts moved forward, some states responded by passing their own laws to stall or prevent integration. In 1956, Louisiana passed an "anti-mixing" law that ensured that sports, including in professional wrestling, would remain segregated.[29] Despite these obstacles, several African American wrestlers gained prominence in the 1960s. Two of them, Bearcat Wright and Bobo Brazil, were notable for overcoming racial barriers and winning major titles in integrated promotions. Edward "Bearcat" Wright is sometimes considered the first African American to hold a world heavyweight wrestling championship.[30] Frustrated that he was not permitted to wrestle against white wrestlers, he announced in 1960 that he was no longer willing to wrestle in arenas that enforced segregation. The Indiana State Athletic Commission responded by banning him altogether. He was supported by the National Association for the Advancement of Colored People (NAACP), and the commission chose not to pursue the issue.[31] Wright's successful stand helped open new doors to African American wrestlers.[32] Such trailblazers gave hope that the end of arbitrary discrimination was in sight and proved that African Americans had support for their cause and their careers. In 1961, Wright won the Big Time Wrestling Heavyweight Championship, becoming the first African American to win the top title in any promotion.[33] It is important to remember that Big Time Wrestling was just one of many regional promotions, so Wright was among about two dozen wrestlers holding their promotion's top title at the time.

In August 1963, he gained a better claim as first African American world champion by defeating Fred Blassie to win the World Wrestling Associates World Heavyweight Championship.[34] The WWA was a recognized and respected organization, but it was, to a large extent, another regional promotion, confined primarily to California. While the company had chosen Wright as their champion, they soon decided to have him lose, or "drop," the championship to another wrestler. Unwilling to give up the title, Wright refused to go along with the plan. In the rematch, Blassie states that Wright intentionally punched him in the chin, rendering Blassie legitimately unable to re-enter the ring before the referee's ten count.[35] Unwilling to let Wright continue as champion, the promotion secretly changed his opponent one night, pitting him against Gene LeBell, a well-known tough guy known for "shooting," or actually trying to hurt his opponent. Concerned about his safety, Wright chose not to enter the ring and was stripped of the title as a result.[36] The WWA Championship was the peak of Wright's career, but it ended tumultuously, and Wright never again held a major singles title in North America.

Bobo Brazil, born Houston Harris, was popular with fans for over four decades and won a wide range of titles throughout his career, but his biggest victory also remains surrounded in controversy. He unsuccessfully faced WWWF Champion Bruno Sammartino for the promotion's top title on several occasions, but the highlight of his career came on August 18, 1962, when he defeated NWA Champion Buddy Rogers and was awarded the title belt.[37] An African American finally winning one of the highest honors in the business could be seen as proof that African Americans were truly accepted and were permitted to compete on a level with white wrestlers. However, promoter Willie Gilzenberg, had planned to end the match with controversy to generate fan interest and more revenue from a rematch.[38] Rogers claimed that he had sustained an injury, so Brazil refused to accept the championship. After doctors later determined that Rogers had not actually been injured, Brazil was once again named the winner. Brazil is not included in the title lineage due to the dispute surrounding his victory.[39] Although he was the first African American to win a major world title, the victory is not recognized because it was used as a marketing gimmick rather than a true step forward for African Americans.

Brazil also later won the WWA World Championship, but the title was less prestigious than the ones he had challenged for in the past. He held the title for two weeks in 1966 and won it back in 1968.[40] When the WWA joined the NWA, Brazil's championship was eliminated. He faced NWA Champion Gene Kiniski in a match that brought together the two champions. The bout ended in a draw, allowing Kiniski to keep the belt because the NWA's title took precedence, while Brazil left with nothing.[41] Although he did not lose the match, he had his title taken away. Wright and Brazil were both trailblazers for African American wrestlers, and both enjoyed some success, but their opportunities did not come readily and were often surrounded in controversy.

Because of segregation, there were times that African Americans were unable to find opponents to wrestle. Melvin Nelson, who was given the name Cockleburrhead (later Burrhead) Jones because of his Afro hairstyle, sometimes arrived at shows and found that his appearance had been cancelled. To earn a paycheck for the evening, he was forced to fill an alternative role like referee.[42] This segregation hurt the ability of African Americans to find employment, as the majority of matches featured white wrestlers. African Americans were treated as a "novelty,"[43] not permitted to compete in the main events or be considered for promotions' top titles. Even after the sport was integrated, promoters were hesitant to use African Americans as "heels," or bad guys, because they were afraid the crowds would turn violent.[44] It took many years before true integration opened doors to African Americans to compete in a variety of gimmicks. Even then, however, some found themselves limited by promotion officials' attitudes, including the idea that "being black *is* their gimmick."[45]

One of Nelson's matches in Mississippi generated controversy with the NAACP after he was tarred and feathered.[46] Although tarring and feathering was not limited to African Americans either historically or in the wrestling world, the troubled race relations in Mississippi had led to numerous examples of African Americans being threatened with the punishment in the state's past.[47] The lack of sensitivity demonstrated by replicating racially charged attacks from the Jim Crow era shows a definite lack of understanding of how race relations have shaped the country. Nelson, billed as being from "the cotton fields of Louisiana,"[48] was expected to accept these roles to continue his employment, which allowed promoters to exploit and make light of hurtful incidents in the name of entertainment.

Thunderbolt Patterson also found his career limited by his race. Although he was popular with fans and had a strong influence on the style of fellow wrestlers, he was not given the same opportunities or financial compensation as white wrestlers. Many fans in Texas enjoyed his performances, but Patterson states that a local church pressured promoter Fritz Von Erich to force Patterson out of the territory.[49] Discouraged by his experiences, he hoped to effect change by purchasing part of the promoting rights in Florida. He states that promoter Cowboy Luttrall, citing race as his reason, refused to sell Patterson the rights.[50] Later, Patterson asked to challenge for the championship in Jim Crockett Promotions. This request was rejected, with the explanation that it would be easy to find other African Americans who would be content with the limited opportunities they were offered.[51]

Patterson was essentially pushed out of wrestling altogether in the early 1980s after speaking out against the conditions faced by African Americans and filing a lawsuit against several promotions alleging racial discrimination.[52] He was eventually rehired by Georgia Championship Wrestling on the condition that he drop the lawsuit.[53] Eddie Mansfield spoke out against being paid less than white wrestlers and was soon unable to find any promotion willing to hire him.[54] Patterson and Mansfield's experiences are described in *Choke Holds*, written by Jim Wilson, a white professional wrestler shunned by the industry due to his push for a labor union and his support for the pair. Both Patterson and Mansfield were forced to choose between their need for employment and their desire to end racial discrimination. In both cases, even rival promoters worked together to push African Americans out of the business rather than addressing inequalities in pay and opportunity.

Sylvester Ritter, who performed as Junkyard Dog, was an unusual success story, gaining a large following in the Deep South with his charisma and powerful physique. Promoter Bill Watts, running a promotion in New Orleans, a city in which 70 percent of the population was African American,[55] recognized the financial benefit of featuring a star that people would see as "one of their own."[56] On July 22, 1979, Watts's strategy paid off with a record-breaking crowd attending a match between African Americans Junkyard Dog and Ray Candy.[57] Despite his natural appeal, the promotion tried to build gimmicks for him, including a fondness for white women and a dog collar around his neck.[58] In addition to the obvious racial connotations of placing a chain on a black man, Junkyard Dog's image was also attacked by storyline comments from fellow African American Butch Reed, who criticized him as an "Uncle Tom" figure, subservient to white men.[59] Junkyard Dog's gimmick later evolved into one in which he crawled in the ring and growled and barked during interviews,[60] and he eventually left the promotion for the bigger pay-days of the WWF.

Over time, the WWF purchased not only the top stars from other companies, but the companies themselves, establishing itself as the country's top promotion. When the WWF launched its flagship event, WrestleMania, in 1985, it showcased its product to the largest viewing audience in wrestling history at the time. The event also highlighted the small number of African Americans competing for the company. Although the African American community had shown interest in the event, with Mr. T discussing his match in *Jet* magazine,[61] the number of black participants was noticeably low. African Americans accounted for none of the 10 managers featured, and only 3 of the 22 wrestlers: S.D. "Special Delivery" Jones, Junkyard Dog, and Mr. T. Early in the event, Jones faced King Kong Bundy but, in an inauspicious start for African Americans, lost in a match that the WWF claimed lasted only nine seconds.[62] Jones had objected beforehand to the quick defeat, but WWF owner Vince McMahon assured him it was for the best, as it would benefit Bundy's career.[63] Although Jones was known as a "jobber," or someone whose role is to lose matches and make others look good, he was concerned about how such a one-sided victory would affect his credibility. The victory helped establish Bundy as a top star, leading to a WWF Championship title shot in the main event at WrestleMania 2, while Jones never again appeared on a pay-per-view.

Junkyard Dog, competing for the WWF Intercontinental Championship, was victorious in his match, but because he won by count out, he was not awarded the title. The final African American competitor was Mr. T, who was brought in as Hulk Hogan's teammate in the main event. Unlike the other competitors, Mr. T was not a wrestler by trade, which led to negative feelings among the wrestlers who felt he was not deserving of the spot.[64] He was clearly a secondary attraction, as the pair entered the ring, and later celebrated their victory, to Hogan's theme music. Hogan spent most of the match in the ring and ultimately scored the winning pin. Even Muhammad Ali, brought in as a referee for the main event, was relegated to a secondary role, serving as the "outside" referee while Pat Patterson controlled the match inside the ring. Although commentator Gorilla Monsoon attempted to portray Ali's job as "just as important as being inside, and maybe more so," the statement was clearly false. In the first major opportunity to showcase their top wrestlers, the WWF chose not to give a title to a popular African American wrestler, had a second African American lose in an embarrassing fashion, and brought in a third to serve as the sidekick to a white man.

Mr. T was brought back for the next year's WrestleMania, competing in one of the show's three main events. Although the show was even bigger the second year, aside from a battle royal featuring WWF wrestlers facing NFL players, there were only two African Americans involved: Mr. T and Junkyard Dog.[65] Junkyard Dog teamed with Tito Santana in a tag team loss,[66] indicating that his career was on the decline. At WrestleMania III, he lost to Harley Race, a white man, and was forced to bow to him due to the match stipulation.[67] Junkyard Dog made one final WrestleMania appearance in the following year's battle royal before being released from the promotion,[68] never having held a championship. Although he had overcome racial barriers to become one of the biggest names in a smaller organization, he was unable to gain the same prominence on a national stage.

Following the first WrestleMania, no African Americans were featured in the main event until 1995 when football player Lawrence Taylor was brought in for a match at WrestleMania XI. In the 33 annual WrestleMania shows to date, only Mr. T, Taylor, and The Rock have competed in main events,[69] although, as discussed later, there is disagreement over whether The Rock, the only trained wrestler of the three, is more appropriately described as African American or Samoan.

Although African Americans had some notable roles throughout the second half of the twentieth century, this time period also saw the rise of more outlandish gimmicks, and many were given roles that played upon offensive stereotypes. Lawrence Shreve of Windsor, Ontario, became Abdullah the Butcher.[70] As the "Madman from the Sudan," he beat and bloodied his opponents with unrestrained violence, supposedly speaking little English beyond, "Me beat! Me beat!"[71] James Harris of Senatobia, Mississippi,[72] was repackaged as Kamala, a cannibal and headhunter from Uganda.[73] Anthony White from Roanoke, Virginia,[74] initially gained fame as a bodybuilder, winning the World Bodybuilding Guild's 1979 "Pro Mr. USA" title.[75] As a wrestler, White competed as Tony Atlas; however, the WWF later changed his gimmick to Saba Simba, a tribal warrior.[76] Such gimmicks perpetuated an image of African Americans as wild savages, hopelessly out of place in western society. Because they also appealed more to the spectacle aspect of wrestling rather than the sport, it was also difficult for people with such roles to be taken seriously and rise to the top of their promotion.

It was not until August 2, 1992, well over 100 years after Viro Small's debut, that wrestling had a universally recognized African American world champion. Although some people considered Brazil and Wright as legitimate champions, no doubt remained when Ron Simmons pinned Big Van Vader to win the World Championship Wrestling (WCW) World Heavyweight Championship. Simmons had previously enjoyed success both in football, where he was drafted by the Cleveland Browns,[77] and as a tag team wrestler. He and fellow African American Butch Reed teamed up as Doom and held the WCW Tag Team Championship for the longest reign in the company's history.[78] He made his biggest mark as a singles wrestler, however, when he won the promotion's top title and achieved a first for African Americans.

Although the decision to give Simmons the title was made in advance, the storyline claimed he was picked randomly for the match.[79] An opportunity existed to highlight an African American working his way to the top and achieving a momentous first for his race, but he was portrayed merely as lucky rather than as a top challenger. Neither his title victory nor his reign showed him to be an elite wrestler. As champion, Simmons defended the belt only on two pay-per-views, beating perennial mid-card wrestler The Barbarian, and defeating Steve Williams by disqualification. Although Simmons's title reign was historic, it was otherwise uneventful and unmemorable. He was never able to replicate the success, disappearing from main event status after losing the championship and eventually moving to the WWF. He first appeared as a gladiator in a role that was met with ridicule,[80] and was eventually relegated to comic relief, with his major role being walking into skits and saying, "Damn!"

Michael Jones, who worked in the WWF as Virgil and later in WCW as Vincent, was placed in a role that emphasized his apparent inferiority to a white man. He was the servant of "The Million Dollar Man" Ted DiBiase, who insulted him and ordered him around. Virgil was actually DiBiase's replacement for Hercules Hernandez (portrayed by Ray Fernandez), who DiBiase purchased as a "slave."[81] When Hernandez turned against him, DiBiase decided to replace him with an African American, but to refer to him as a "bodyguard" and a "servant."[82] After three and a half years of humiliation and sacrificing himself to protect DiBiase, Virgil stood up to DiBiase and eventually won his Million Dollar Championship. However, the feud ended with DiBiase winning the belt back,[83] and Jones later surfaced in WCW as the "head of security" for the New World Order, a group that included DiBiase.[84] In both companies, the rich white man was shown coming out on top, offering little hope to fans hoping to see justice prevail with the African American rising up from his mistreatment to succeed on his own.

DiBiase was also the villain in the storyline that saw an African American woman featured on television after they had been long absent. Juanita Wright was brought into the WWF in 1989 as manager to Dusty Rhodes. Wright, who had a legitimate history in the sport and had held a referee's license, was given the name Sapphire.[85] This name has a long history in African American culture and has been used as a reference to a stereotype of loud and obnoxious black women.[86] While Rhodes had been a major star in the NWA, he was fired from the promotion, allowing Vince McMahon to hire a former rival and place him in an unflattering role. He was portrayed as an inept "everyman," performing jobs like fixing a toilet, and was forced to wear black tights with large yellow polka dots.[87] Sapphire, who was overweight and in her fifties,[88] accompanied him to the ring in matching polka dots.[89] At SummerSlam 1990, she was involved in a storyline in which "The Million Dollar Man" Ted DiBiase purchased her,[90] further developing the racially insensitive storyline in which Virgil worked as DiBiase's servant. While more television exposure for an American wrestler could have been a step forward, placing her in a comedy gimmick with a racially charged name before allowing a white man to buy her certainly did nothing to show that the company embraced racial equality or sensitivity.

Charles Wright spent many years in the WWF but was also subjected to insensitive character development. Shortly after his debut, he held the top title in the United States Wrestling Association,[91] a prominent promotion but not on the same level as the WWF or WCW. After joining the WWF, however, he was repackaged as voodoo practitioner Papa Shango. He wore a necklace of animal bones, painted his face like voodoo spirit Baron Samedi, and carried a smoking skull to the ring. He would go into trances, during which he set his opponents' hands or feet on fire. His voodoo curses culminated in a feud with the Ultimate Warrior when Papa Shango caused him to vomit profusely and caused his face paint to melt and run on his face.[92] Despite his rivalry with one of the promotion's top stars, Papa Shango was soon forgotten when the Warrior instead resumed a feud with WWF Champion Randy Savage.

Wright was later brought back with other gimmicks, including The Godfather. Billed from the Red Light District, he wore multiple gold chains, and came to the ring with a cane, a cigar, and often a large feather on his hat. Proclaiming himself a pimp, he led a group of scantily clad women, known as his Ho Train, to the ring.[93] He would sometimes offer the services of these women to his opponent in exchange for forfeiting the match. His gimmick reflected one of the major stereotypes of African Americans described by film historian Donald Bogle. The Godfather was portrayed as a "buck"—a misogynist with an overdeveloped and uncontrollable sex drive.[94] Both of Wright's memorable gimmicks involved offensive African American stereotypes. It is worth noting that he received "pushes," or featured positions in storylines and events, as both Papa Shango and The Godfather, even winning the Intercontinental Championship, a secondary title, in the latter role.[95] However, when his character looked to be taken seriously for his strength or skills, he met with little success. As both Kama, a no-nonsense mixed martial artist, and Kama Mustafa, a black nationalist, he received little attention and was involved only in forgettable storylines.

Booker Huffman, Jr., wrestling as Booker T, was initially saddled with an offensive gimmick, but, once given the opportunity to succeed on his own merit, worked his way near, but never quite, to the top of the profession. Early in his WCW career, competing alongside his brother Lash Huffman (as Stevie Ray), he was reportedly led to the ring in a prison jumpsuit and leg shackles by Colonel Robert Parker, a cigar-chomping Southern gentleman said to have won the brothers in a card game.[96] The gimmick never made it to television, but the team, Harlem Heat, held the company's World Tag Team Championship ten times. While this is more reigns than any other team, it is also worth noting that their average reign length of 47 days is the shortest of any of the top 35 teams ranked by combined reign length.[97] He also held the WCW Television Championship six times, but this was merely a third-tier championship in the promotion, and, once again, his average reign length was the shortest among wrestlers with the top 25 combined reign lengths (a list that only includes one other African American).[98]

Booker T did rise to the top of the promotion, holding the WCW World Heavyweight Championship four times. Even these accomplishments, how-ever, should be viewed with caution. WCW was in a state of decline, having fallen behind the WWF in the Monday Night ratings war in every head-to-head matchup since October 1998.[99] Booker T won all four of his world cham-pionships in the promotion's dying days, from July 2000 to March 2001. The title's credibility had been further tarnished two months earlier, when actor David Arquette won the championship.[100] Even when Booker T was the top wrestler in the company, he still lacked a legitimate claim to being the best in the world. His second reign was particularly unimpressive, lasting only eight days and ending with a loss to Vince Russo, a non-wrestler who was in charge of storylines and determining the winners of matches.[101] In addition, there is speculation that he was chosen to win the championship to counter claims made in two racial discrimination lawsuits brought against WCW.[102] African American wrestler Bobby Walker had filed a suit in 1998,[103] and Sonny Onoo later led a group of wrestlers, including several African Americans, in a lawsuit alleging discrimination.[104] While Walker's suit was dismissed, Time Warner agreed to a reportedly lucrative settlement with Onoo and his fellow plaintiffs.[105]

In 2003, Booker T won the opportunity to compete for the WWE World Heavyweight Championship at WrestleMania XIX. While he was in the ring talking to the crowd the week after qualifying for the match, he was inter-rupted by Triple H. Triple H told him that he seemed to misunderstand his role in the company. He made the observation, "Somebody like you doesn't get to be a world champion....people like you don't deserve it." While there was no direct mention of race in the statement, his subsequent references to Booker T's Ebonics and "nappy hair" emphasized the theme. He said that

Booker T was merely there for comedy and entertainment, and told him repeatedly to dance for him. He wrapped up by telling him, "You're going to do what people like you always do: you're going to lose." These statements rang all too true, as Triple H, soon to marry the boss's daughter in real life, was in a position of power over Booker T. His criticism and disparagement of Booker T can certainly be interpreted with racial overtones, given the history of power and control historically exerted over African Americans. When Booker T lost the match, this reinforced the message that people "like [Booker T]" would never succeed. He went on to win several titles, including the World Heavyweight Championship. However, he never won the WWE Championship, the promotion's top honor. He is one of the most successful African American wrestlers of all time, but his biggest wins came during a period of collapse for WCW, and he was limited to secondary championships in WWE.

Jacqueline Moore is an example of an African American woman who overcame both sex and race barriers to succeed, although her career path was not always smooth. She first gained recognition under the ring name Miss Texas in the United States Wrestling Association by defeating male wrestlers. This led to her being the first female to be included in *Pro Wrestling Illustrated*'s PWI 500, a listing of the top 500 wrestlers in the world.[106] She then entered WCW, where she showed off her power against men both as a manager and a wrestler.[107] She had an extended run in the WWF/WWE and won the Women's Championship twice, becoming the first African American to hold the title.[108] She also won a men's title by defeating Chavo Guerrero for the Cruiserweight Championship.[109] Although the company acknowledged her talent by giving her several title reigns, she was also placed in a group known as Pretty Mean Sisters, often abbreviated PMS as an allusion to premenstrual syndrome. Her time in PMS included a storyline with one of her partners faking a miscarriage and the women forcing a male wrestler to be their "sex slave."[110] Following a match at the Capital Carnage pay-per-view in 1998, her shirt was ripped off in a pre-planned storyline, exposing her breasts to the audience and television cameras.[111] Moore was a trailblazer for African American women, who had never before reached such a level in the story, but she was also portrayed as a sex object and placed in a series of plots better suited for soap operas before she was released from the company.

In the late 1990s, Dwayne Johnson, wrestling as The Rock, became one of the top wrestlers in the world, holding the WWF/WWE Championship seven times from 1998 to 2002. The son of retired professional wrestler Rocky Johnson, he became the first wrestler of African descent to hold the promotion's top championship, recognized by many people as the most prestigious title in professional wrestling. This should be viewed with a few caveats, however. According to a story run by *The Atlantic* in 2014, Dwayne Johnson identifies as Samoan rather than African American (or African Canadian, like his father).[112] Writer Dion Beary further states that, as his maternal grandfather was also a famous and successful wrestler, The Rock was promoted as a third generation wrestler, rather than emphasizing his African heritage.[113] He initially competed in the WWF as Rocky Maivia, combining the names of his father and his Samoan maternal grandfather, High Chief Peter Maivia. Giving him a Samoan surname highlighted the connection to his grandfather, and the resulting ties to the prolific and successful Anoa'i wrestling family. In doing so, his African heritage was given less attention. Regardless of how he was billed, he is unquestionably the first African American to hold the top promotion's primary championship, and the multitude of championships he held in WWF/WWE establish him as one of the top wrestlers of all time. However, he was only allowed to hold the top belt more than 100 days on one occasion. Of the seven reigns prior to his retirement (he returned in 2013 to hold the belt one final time), his longest reign was 119 days, with the rest spanning between 2 and 44 days. These seven reigns average 42 days each, far short of the average reigns of Caucasian wrestlers Stone Cold Steve Austin, Triple H, and Kurt Angle during this period.[114]

Cryme Tyme was an African American tag team that was given a comedy gimmick playing upon racial stereotypes even before entering WWE in 2006. Jayson Paul, known as JTG, and Shad Gaspard portrayed a pair of street thugs. They were introduced by a theme song that began, "Yo yo yo yo. Pop a 40, and check your rollies," playing upon stereotypes of African Americans drinking cheap 40-ounce beer, as well as an ambiguous term referring either to the materialism of African Americans wearing Rolexes or the drug culture represented by rolling papers for marijuana. A later song bragged of "twelve misdemeanors, three felonies." In their role as a comic duo, the team was shown committing small crimes like stealing hubcaps and selling counterfeit goods. Prior to their debut, they were shown in a series of "training videos," demonstrating their skills through muggings, robberies, and a carjacking. In WWE, they appeared in such roles as singing Christmas songs to senior citizens while changing the lyrics to reflect their life on the streets, including "Reggie the Red-Faced Crackhead" and a version of "Silent Night" about "robbin' all the whites." Despite competing for WWE for over three years as a team, Cryme Tyme did not win a championship. They stole the title belts in a storyline, but their gimmick was clearly designed more for laughs than to portray the duo as legitimate stars. If anything, Cryme Tyme was a step backward for African American wrestlers, as it was yet another example of harmful racial stereotyping.

Not all African American comedy gimmicks even involved African Americans. George Gray, a Caucasian wrestler, competed for several years as One Man Gang, a biker gimmick. While men with shields and spears performed a tribal dance around a garbage can in a parking lot, Gray appeared, transformed into Akeem the African Dream, claiming to have "returned to his African roots."[115] He wore bright traditional African colors and danced while speaking jive talk. This persona took racially offensive gimmicks to a new level by using an obvious impostor to further stereotypes. Gray was not the first white wrestler to use this gimmick, as Virgil Runnels, Jr., wrestling as Dusty Rhodes, based his character on the speech and other aspects of Thunderbolt Patterson's character.[116] Rhodes, however, was able to use his adopted African American persona to achieve success that was not available to African Americans themselves.

Mark Henry achieved some success in the WWF, despite never holding the top championship. He competed as a weightlifter in the 1992 and 1996 Olympics, and the WWF offered him a wrestling contract to capitalize on his strongman image. However, he became better known as a sex addict as a result of storylines surrounding his "Sexual Chocolate" gimmick. He was shown visiting a psychiatrist and discussing an incestuous relationship with his sister that began at age eight and had continued up to two days before his psychiatrist appointment.[117] In this role, he was tricked into having a relationship with a trans person,[118] and impregnated the almost 80-year-old former women's wrestler Mae Young, who was later shown giving birth to a rubber hand.[119] Despite spending much of his career as a combination of stereotype and comic relief, he was given two world title victories. However, after WWE purchased WCW as well as ECW, the country's third biggest promotion, they had begun promoting three belts as world titles. The WWE Championship was the company's biggest title, with the WWE World Heavyweight Championship and the ECW Championship, held in lower esteem as the titles of the two defunct promotions. Although Henry won each of the less prestigious belts, he never won the top championship. He was also the victim of direct racism from SmackDown writer Michael Hayes, a white man born Michael Seitz, who told Henry in 2008, "I'm more of a nigger than you."[120] Although Seitz was suspended, he kept his job, despite the fact that this was not the only time he was accused of mistreating African Americans.[121]

According to reports, Seitz was not alone in his attitude toward other races. Trainer Bill DeMott resigned in 2015 after several reports surfaced of him making derogatory comments and using racial slurs toward several wrestlers, including African Americans. While WWE eventually condemned his behavior, their initial investigation led nowhere, as they stated they were unable to verify the reports. It was not until two years later, when more allegations surfaced, that DeMott was pressured to leave the company.[122]

The use of language offensive to minorities has even extended to the top of the WWE power structure. In a scripted segment filmed backstage, John Cena, who formerly portrayed a white rapper, caught Vince McMahon, the owner and chairman of WWE, plotting against him. McMahon tried to brush it off, asking him, "What's good in the hood?" McMahon then told Cena, "Keep it up, my nigga," and walked away smiling. Cena looked baffled, while onlooker Booker T stammered to his wife, "Tell me he didn't just say that."[123] The company owner casually tossing out a racial slur on television highlights the lack of consideration and sensitivity given to race relations. Even in a comedic sketch, the use of this word by a white billionaire, in the presence of an African American, was offensive to both employees and fans. Such an incident cannot help eliminate racism from the company, as there would be little reason to believe that complaints about mistreatment would be taken seriously, as McMahon himself is not opposed to using a racial slur for comic effect.

In July 2015, WWE tried to assert their support for African Americans through public condemnation of Hulk Hogan. A 2007 audio recording of Hogan revealed Hogan using the n-word several times. When the recording surfaced, WWE stated that it "is committed to embracing and celebrating individuals from all backgrounds as demonstrated by the diversity of [its] employees, performers and fans worldwide."[124] Hogan's contract was terminated, and most references to him were removed from the WWE website, including his biography and hall of fame profile.[125] While the WWE statement shows that the company at least intends to support and feature African Americans on a more equal basis, given the history of African Americans in professional wrestling, this statement rings hollow for both WWE and the business as a whole.

African American women have been able to rise to the top of their divisions within WWE, including Victoria Crawford, who held the WWE Divas Championship under the name Alicia Fox[126]; Carlene Moore-Begnaud, a two-time WWE Women's Champion as Jazz[127]; and Trinity Fatu, who competed as Naomi while winning the WWE Smackdown Women's Championship twice.[128] The most prominent example in recent years has been Mercedes Ton, who wrestles as Sasha Banks. She held the WWE Raw Women's Championship four times between 2016 and 2017. This makes her the most successful African American women's wrestler of this century, and arguably of all time. Her talent and personality have made her a favorite of fans, and she will quite possibly join Jacqueline Moore in the WWE Hall of Fame. It should be noted, however, that her first three reigns ended with losses to Charlotte Flair. Banks won the belt from Flair three times, but she never emerged from the feud with a decisive victory, as Flair always came out on top by regaining the belt. Banks's final reign lasted only eight days.[129] The success of these African American women shows that more possibilities than ever are open to them, although it comes in a division that has often been portrayed as a sideshow, or "filler," between the more prominent men's matches.[130]

Professional wrestling, even before it became popular in the United

States, has treated African Americans as lesser beings. Slaves were ordered to fight each other for the enjoyment of white owners with little reward. Once the sport became formalized, African Americans were segregated, both as wrestlers and as fans. Integration has brought them far from their days on the "chitlin' circuit," but equality remains elusive. Top titles in the business are rarely open to African Americans. As author David Shoemaker states, they have often been treated as "the sideshow's sideshow,"[131] portraying and enforcing stereotypes. Wrestlers who have tried to push for equality have been blacklisted; in the words of Eddie Mansfield, promoters "kill you with the eraser."[132] Despite the history of the business, WWE's 2015 statement against racial intolerance is reason for hope. Perhaps this will serve as a wake-up call, leading to a time when African Americans are respected for their abilities rather than portrayed as cannibals, sexual predators, and street thugs.

NOTES

1. Ming Li, Eric W. MacIntosh, and Gonzalo A. Bravo, eds., *International Sport Management* (Champaign, IL: Human Kinetics, 2012), 166; Namulundah Florence, "Guinea-Bissau," in *Africa: An Encyclopedia of Culture and Society*, eds. Toyin Falola and Daniel Jean-Jacques (Santa Barbara, CA: ABC-CLIO, 2016), 593; T.J. Desch Obi, *Fighting for Honor: The History of African Martial Art Traditions in the Atlantic World* (Columbia, SC: University of South Carolina Press, 2008), 74.

2. Norman R. Yetman, ed. *Voices from Slavery: Authentic Slave Narratives* (Mineola, NY: Dover, 2000), 124–5.

3. Sharon Harley, *Timetables of African-American History: A Chronology of the Most Important People and Events in African-American History* (New York: Simon and Schuster, 1996), 165; Scott M. Beekman, *Ringside: A History of Professional Wrestling in the United States* (Westport, CT: Praeger, 2006), 29.

4. Beekman, 28–29.

5. Jonathan Snowden, *Shooters: The Toughest Men in Professional Wrestling* (Toronto: ECW Press, 2012), 4–5.

6. Scott A. Richmond, "Professional Wrestling," in *Encyclopedia of Social Deviance*, eds. Craig J. Forsyth and Heith Copes (Los Angeles: SAGE, 2014), 550.

7. Tim Hornbaker, *Legends of Pro Wrestling: Years of Headlocks, Body Slams, and Piledrivers* (New York: Sports Publishing, 2016), 79.

8. Steven Verrier, *Professional Wrestling in the Pacific Northwest: A History, 1883 to the Present* (Jefferson, NC: McFarland, 2017), 47.

9. Niambi Lee-Kong, "Chitlin Circuit," in *Encyclopedia of African American History, 1896 to the Present: From the Age of Segregation to the Twenty-first Century*, ed. Paul Finkelman (New York: Oxford University Press, 2009), 376.

10. Katharina Vester, *A Taste of Power: Food and American Identities* (Berkeley: University of California Press, 2015), 129.

11. Greg Oliver, "Tiger Conway, Sr. Dead at 74," *Canadian Online Explorer*, last modified November 14, 2006, http://slam.canoe.com/Slam/Wrestling/2006/11/14/2352158.html.

12. Julian L.D. Shabazz, *Black Stars of Professional Wrestling* (Clinton, SC: Awesome Records, 2010), 53.

13. David Shoemaker, *The Squared Circle: Life, Death, and Professional Wrestling* (New York: Gotham, 2013), 133.

14. *Ibid.*

15. Greg Oliver and Steven Johnson, *The Pro Wrestling Hall of Fame: The Tag Teams* (Toronto: ECW Press, 2005), 140.

16. "Wrestling 'Daddy,'" *Ebony* 16, no. 1 (November 1960): 61.

17. "A Pittsburgh Hurricane Roars Into Wrestling," *Ebony* 20, no. 8 (June 1965): 101.

18. James West, "Sputnik Monroe," in *The New Encyclopedia of Southern Culture: Volume 18*, eds. Allison Graham and Sharon Monteith (Chapel Hill, NC: University of North Carolina Press, 2011), 314.

19. Pat Laprade and Dan Murphy, *Sisterhood of the Squared Circle* (Toronto: ECW Press, 2017), 37.

20. Laprade and Murphy, 55.

21. Laprade and Murphy, 55–56.

22. Gai Ingham Berlage, "Robinson's Legacy: Black Women and Negro Baseball," in *The Cooperstown Symposium on Baseball and American Culture*, eds. Peter M. Rutkoff and Alvin L. Hall (Jefferson, NC: McFarland, 2000), 132.

23. "Lady Wrestlers," *Jet* 1, no. 17 (February 21, 1952): 57.

24. "Lady Wrestlers," *Jet*, 58; "Lady Wrestlers," *Ebony* 9, no. 8 (June 1954): 64.

25. Murfee Faulk, "Baby of Sweet Georgia Brown," *Free Times* (Columbia, SC), last modified December 20, 2006, https://www.free-times.com/archives/baby-of-sweet-georgia-brown/article_e82fe915-fb49-5d12-8848-42750f5dc785.html.

26. Faulk.

27. Faulk.

28. Royal Duncan and Gary Will, *Wrestling Title Histories: Professional Wrestling Champions Around the World from the 19th Century to the Present* (Waterloo, ON: Archeus Communications, 2000), 28.

29. Greg Klein, *The King of New Orleans: How the Junkyard Dog Became Professional Wrestling's First Black Superstar* (Toronto: ECW Press, 2012), 5.

30. Shabazz, 184.

31. "Negro Wrestlers," *Ebony* 17, no. 7 (May 1962): 44.

32. Shabazz, 183.

33. Shabazz, 184.

34. Dave Meltzer, *Tributes II: Remembering More of the World's Greatest Professional Wrestlers* (Champaign, IL: Sports Publishing, LLC, 2004), 24.

35. Fred Blassie and Keith Elliot Greenberg, *Listen, You Pencil Neck Geeks* (New York: Pocket, 2003), 111.

36. *Ibid.*

37. Shoemaker, 135.

38. Steven Johnson, Greg Oliver, and Mike Mooneyham. *The Pro Wrestling Hall of Fame: Heroes and Icons* (Toronto: ECW Press, 2012), 91–2.

39. *Ibid.*

40. Duncan and Will, 294.

41. Blassie and Greenberg, 155.

42. Mike Mooneyham, "Burrhead Jones: Legend of the Ring," *The Wrestling Gospel According to Mike Mooneyham*, last modified February 23, 2003, http://www.mikemooneyham.com/2003/02/23/burrhead-jones-legend-of-the-ring.

43. Charles Hughes, "'Tell Them It's What Their Grandfathers Got': Racial Violence in Southern Professional Wrestling," in *Performance and Professional Wrestling*, eds. Broderick Chow, Eero Laine, and Claire Warden (New York: Routledge, 2017), 166.

44. Shoemaker, 134.

45. Shoemaker, 138.

46. Mike Mooneyham, "Local Legend Bound for Big Apple," *The Wrestling Gospel According to Mike Mooneyham*, last modified July 16, 2006, http://www.mikemooneyham.com/2006/07/16/local-legend-bound-for-big-apple.

47. Michael Newton, *The Ku Klux Klan in Mississippi: A History* (Jefferson, NC: McFarland, 2010), 83; Claude H. Nolen, *African American Southerners in Slavery, Civil War and Reconstruction* (Jefferson, NC: McFarland, 2001), 164.

48. Mike Mooneyham, "Q&A with Burrhead Jones," *The Wrestling Gospel According to Mike Mooneyham*, accessed January 2, 2017, http://web.archive.org/web/20070728023954/http://www.mikemooneyham.com/pages/viewfull.cfm?ObjectID=41CAF4E0-5975-42A9-A52C9C1F4E3390AF.

49. Johnson, Oliver, and Mooneyham, 242.

50. *Ibid.*

51. Johnson, Oliver, and Mooneyham, 243.

52. Steven Johnson, "Thunderbolt Patterson Still 'on Top,'" *Canadian Online Explorer,* last modified August 8, 2008, http://slam.canoe.com/Slam/Wrestling/2008/08/08/6392216.html; Jim Wilson and Weldon T. Johnson. *Choke Hold: Pro Wrestling's Real Mayhem Outside the Ring* (Bloomington, IN: Xlibris, 2003), 335.

53. Wilson and Johnson, 342.

54. Wilson and Johnson, 339.

55. Klein, 51.

56. Klein, 14.

57. Klein, 2.

58. Klein, pp. 9, 22.

59. Klein, 101.

60. Klein, 147.

61. "Mr. T Tells Why He Became a Wrestler," *Jet* 68, no. 7 (April 29, 1985): 22.

62. Brian Shields, *WWE in the Raging 80s* (New York: Pocket, 2006), 148.

63. Greg Oliver, "S.D. Jones Dies in Antigua," *Canadian Online Explorer,* last modified October 26, 2008, http://slam.canoe.com/Slam/Wrestling/2008/10/26/7213751.html.

64. Hulk Hogan and Michael Jan Friedman, *Hollywood Hulk Hogan* (New York: Pocket, 2002), 138; Ariel Teal Toombs and Colt Baird Toombs, *Rowdy: The Roddy Piper Story* (Toronto: Random House Canada, 2016), 251.

65. Basil V. Devito, Jr., and Joe Layden, *WrestleMania: The Official Insider's Story* (New York: ReganBooks, 2001), 12.

66. Klein, 148.

67. Klein, 149.

68. Klein, 150.

69. Dave Richard, "Ranking Every WWE WrestleMania Main Event Match from Worst to Best," *CBS,* last modified April 3, 2016, http://www.cbssports.com/general/news/ranking-every-wwe-wrestlemania-main-event-match-from-worst-to-best.

70. Tim Baines, "Man or Madman? Abdullah in Hull," *Canadian Online Explorer,* last modified October 31, 2003, http://slam.canoe.com/Slam/Wrestling/2003/10/31/242993.html.

71. Marty Gervais, *My Town: Faces of Windsor* (Windsor, ON: Bibioasis, 2006), 75.

72. Jerry Lawler, *It's Good to Be the King ... Sometimes* (New York: Simon and Schuster, 2002), 221.

73. Lawler, 222.

74. Maxwell Mogensen, *Legendary Locals of Androscoggin County, Maine* (Charleston, SC: Arcadia, 2013), 92.

75. Hornbaker, 202.

76. Shoemaker, 140.

77. Hornbaker, 510.

78. "World Tag Team Champions and WCW/NWA Title History," *World Championship Wrestling,* accessed December 29, 2016, https://web.archive.org/web/20001110053700/http://www.wcw.com/2000/superstars/tagteam; Duncan and Will, 16–18.

79. Graham Cawthon, "WCW: 1992," *The History of* WWE, accessed November 14, 2016, http://www.thehistoryofwwe.com/wcw92.htm; Ric Flair and Keith Elliot Greenberg, *To Be the Man* (New York: Pocket, 2004), 314.

80. R.D. Reynolds and Blade Braxton, *The WrestleCrap Book of Lists* (Toronto: ECW Press, 2007), 78.

81. Shields, 131.

82. Ted DiBiase, *Every Man Has His Price* (Sisters, OR: Multnomah, 1997), 113.

83. John Milner, "Ted DiBiase," *Canadian Online Explorer,* accessed December 29, 2016, http://slam.canoe.com/Slam/Wrestling/Bios/dibiase.html.

84. Reynolds and Braxton, 113.

85. Harris M. Lentz, III, *Biographical Dictionary of Professional Wrestling* (Jefferson, NC: McFarland, 2003), 307.

86. David Pilgrim, "The Sapphire Caricature," *Jim Crow Museum of Racist Memorabilia*, accessed September 1, 2018, https://ferris.edu/HTMLS/news/jimcrow/antiblack/sapphire.htm.

87. Shaun Assael and Mike Mooneyham, *Sex, Lies, and Headlocks: The Real Story of Vince McMahon and World Wrestling Entertainment* (New York: Crown, 2004), 103.

88. *Ibid.*

89. Shabazz, 145.

90. Ted DiBiase and Tom Caiazzo, *Ted DiBiase: The Million Dollar Man* (New York: Pocket Books, 2008), 170.

91. Lentz, 126.

92. R.D. Reynolds, *WrestleCrap: The Very Worst of Pro Wrestling* (Toronto: ECW Press, 2003), 73.

93. Jon Robinson, *WWE: The Attitude Era* (Indianapolis: DK, 2015), 169.

94. Donald Bogle, *Toms, Coons, Mulattoes, Mammies, and Bucks: An Interpretive History of Blacks in American Films* (New York: Bloomsbury, 2016), 10.

95. Lentz, 126.

96. Shoemaker, 140.

97. "World Tag Team Champions and WCW/NWA Title History"; Duncan and Will, 16–18.

98. Duncan and Will, 19–20.

99. Octavio Fierros, "Lounge Flashbacks: Best & Worst Moments During WWF vs. WCW War," *Pro Wresting Torch*, last modified December 25, 2003, http://pwtorch.com/artman2/publish/font_color_770000_TPFKATL_font_24/article_6520.shtml.

100. Reynolds and Braxton, 202.

101. Beekman, 138.

102. Jamie Peltz, "Radio Review: Sonny Onoo Rips Russo, Says He Wouldn't Work for TNA," *Pro Wrestling Torch*, last modified February 19, 2003, http://pwtorch.com/artman2/publish/Other_News_4/article_2666.shtml.

103. Wade Keller, "WCW News: Discrimination Suit Filed Against WCW—5 Yrs Ago," *Pro Wrestling Torch*, last modified June 28, 2003, http://pwtorch.com/artman2/publish/Torch_Flashbacks_19/article_4337.shtml.

104. Wilson and Johnson, 534.

105. R.D. Reynolds and Bryan Alvarez, *The Death of WCW* (Toronto: ECW Press, 2004), 138.

106. Liz Hunter, "It's a Man's Sport? Yeah, Right," *Pro Wrestling Illustrated* (August 1995): 31.

107. Laprade and Murphy, 202.

108. Shabazz, 71.

109. Laprade and Murphy, 203.

110. Luke Winkie, "The 5 Worst Moments from Professional Wrestling's Attitude Era," *Sports Illustrated*, last modified November 11, 2014. https://www.si.com/extra-mustard/2014/11/11/worst-attitude-era; Reynolds, 222.

111. Laprade and Murphy, 203.

112. Dion Beary, "Pro Wrestling Is Fake, but Its Race Problem Isn't," *The Atlantic*, last modified July 10, 2014, http://www.theatlantic.com/entertainment/archive/2014/07/the-not-so-fictional-bias-in-the-wwe-world-championship/374042.

113. *Ibid.*

114. *Pro Wrestling Almanac & Book of Facts* (Blue Bell, PA: Sports & Entertainment Publications, 2014), 42–43.

115. Reynolds and Braxton, 30.

116. Johnson.

117. Art O'Donnell, "Induction: Mark Henry, Sex Addict: Mark Finds a Way to Spend Even More Time on the Couch," *WrestleCrap*, last modified September 5, 2013, http://www.wrestlecrap.com/inductions/mark-henry-sex-addict.

118. Reynolds and Braxton, 238.

119. Robinson, 185.

120. Shoemaker, 138.
121. Beary.
122. Marissa Payne, "WWE Trainer Bill DeMott Resigns Amid Allegations of Racist, Homophobic and Abusive Behavior," *The Washington Post*, last modified March 6, 2015, https://www.washingtonpost.com/news/early-lead/wp/2015/03/06/wwe-trainer-bill-demott-resigns-amid-allegations-of-racist-homophobic-and-abusive-behavior.
123. Wills Robinson, "Billionaire WWE Boss Who Fired Hulk Hogan for Racist Tirade Once Used N-Word in Awkward Skit with Black Wrestler Booker T," *Daily Mail*, last modified July 25, 2015, http://www.dailymail.co.uk/news/article-3174113/Billionaire-WWE-boss-fired-Hulk-Hogan-racist-tirade-used-N-word-awkward-skit-black-wrestler-Booker-T.html.
124. Danika Fears and Jonathan Lehman, "Hulk Hogan's Race Rant Over His Daughter Dating a Black Man," *New York Post*, last modified July 24, 2015, http://nypost.com/2015/07/24/why-is-wwe-frantically-scrubbing-hulk-hogan-mentions.
125. *Ibid.*
126. "Divas Championship," *WWE*, accessed September 1, 2018. https://www.wwe.com/classics/titlehistory/divas.
127. Shabazz, 74–75.
128. "Smackdown Women's Championship," *WWE*, accessed September 1, 2018, https://www.wwe.com/classics/titlehistory/smackdown-womens-championship.
129. "Raw Women's Championship," *WWE*, accessed September 1, 2018, https://www.wwe.com/classics/titlehistory/raw-womens-championship.
130. Christina Harrell, "Wrestling Revolution in Ring of Honor with Women of Honor," *Miami Herald*, last modified March 4, 2017, https://www.miamiherald.com/sports/fighting/article135076814.html.
131. Shoemaker, 133.
132. Wilson and Johnson, 340.

References

Assael, Shaun, and Mike Mooneyham. *Sex, Lies, and Headlocks: The Real Story of Vince McMahon and World Wrestling Entertainment*. New York: Crown, 2004.

Baines, Tim, "Man or Madman? Abdullah in Hull." *Canadian Online Explorer*. Last modified October 31, 2003. http://slam.canoe.com/Slam/Wrestling/2003/10/31/242993.html.

Beary, Dion. "Pro Wrestling Is Fake, but Its Race Problem Isn't." *The Atlantic*. Last modified July 10, 2014. http://www.theatlantic.com/entertainment/archive/2014/07/the-not-so-fictional-bias-in-the-wwe-world-championship/374042.

Beekman, Scott M. *Ringside: A History of Professional Wrestling in the United States*. Westport, CT: Praeger, 2006.

Berlage, Gai Ingham. "Robinson's Legacy: Black Women and Negro Baseball." In *The Cooperstown Symposium on Baseball and American Culture*, edited by Peter M. Rutkoff and Alvin L. Hall, 123–136. Jefferson, NC: McFarland, 2000.

Blassie, Fred, and Keith Elliot Greenberg. *Listen, You Pencil Neck Geeks*. New York: Pocket, 2003.

Bogle, Donald. *Toms, Coons, Mulattoes, Mammies, and Bucks: An Interpretive History of Blacks in American Films*. New York: Bloomsbury, 2016.

Cawthon, Graham. "WCW: 1992," *The History of* WWE. Accessed November 14, 2016. http://www.thehistoryofwwe.com/wcw92.htm.

Devito, Basil V., Jr., and Joe Layden. *WrestleMania: The Official Insider's Story*. New York: ReganBooks, 2001.

DiBiase, Ted. *Every Man Has His Price*. Sisters, OR: Multnomah, 1997.

DiBiase, Ted, and Tom Caiazzo. *Ted DiBiase: The Million Dollar Man*. New York: Pocket Books, 2008.

"Divas Championship." *WWE*. Accessed September 1, 2018. https://www.wwe.com/classics/titlehistory/divas.

Duncan, Royal, and Gary Will. *Wrestling Title Histories: Professional Wrestling Champions*

Around the World from the 19th Century to the Present. Waterloo, ON: Archeus Communications, 2000.

Fears, Danika, and Jonathan Lehman. "Hulk Hogan's Race Rant Over His Daughter Dating a Black Man." *New York Post*. Last modified July 24, 2015. http://nypost.com/2015/07/24/why-is-wwe-frantically-scrubbing-hulk-hogan-mentions.

Fierros, Octavio. "Lounge Flashbacks: Best & Worst Moments During WWF vs. WCW War." *Pro Wrestling Torch*. Last modified December 25, 2003. http://pwtorch.com/artman2/publish/font_color_770000_TPFKATL_font_24/article_6520.shtml.

Flair, Ric, and Keith Elliot Greenberg. *To Be the Man*. New York: Pocket, 2004.

Florence, Namulundah. "Guinea-Bissau." In *Africa: An Encyclopedia of Culture and Society*, edited by Toyin Falola and Daniel Jean-Jacques, 580–606. Santa Barbara, CA: ABC-CLIO, 2016.

Gervais, Marty. *My Town: Faces of Windsor*. Windsor, ON: Bibioasis, 2006.

Harley, Sharon. *Timetables of African-American History: A Chronology of the Most Important People and Events in African-American History*. New York: Simon & Schuster, 1996.

Harrell, Christina. "Wrestling Revolution in Ring of Honor with Women of Honor." *Miami Herald*. Last modified March 4, 2017. https://www.miamiherald.com/sports/fighting/article135076814.html.

Hogan, Hulk, and Michael Jan Friedman. *Hollywood Hulk Hogan*. New York: Pocket, 2002.

Hornbaker, Tim. *150 Years of Pro Wrestling: Headlocks, Body Slams, and Piledrivers*. New York: Sports Publishing, 2016.

Hughes, Charles. "'Tell Them It's What Their Grandfathers Got': Racial Violence in Southern Professional Wrestling." In *Performance and Professional Wrestling*, edited by Broderick Chow, Eero Laine, and Claire Warden, 165–176. New York: Routledge, 2017.

Hunter, Liz. "It's a Man's Sport? Yeah, Right." *Pro Wrestling Illustrated* (August 1995): 28–31.

Johnson, Steven. "Thunderbolt Patterson Still 'on Top.'" *Canadian Online Explorer*. Last modified August 8, 2008. http://slam.canoe.com/Slam/Wrestling/2008/08/08/6392216.html.

Johnson, Steven, Greg Oliver, and Mike Mooneyham. *The Pro Wrestling Hall of Fame: Heroes and Icons*. Toronto: ECW Press, 2012.

Keller, Wade. "WCW News: Discrimination Suit Filed Against WCW—5 Yrs Ago." *Pro Wrestling Torch*. Last modified June 28, 2003. http://pwtorch.com/artman2/publish/Torch_Flashbacks_19/article_4337.shtml.

Klein, Greg. *The King of New Orleans: How the Junkyard Dog Became Professional Wrestling's First Black Superstar*. ECW Press: Toronto, 2012.

"Lady Wrestlers." *Ebony* 9, no. 8 (June 1954): 64–68.

"Lady Wrestlers." *Jet* 1, no. 17 (February 21, 1952): 56–58.

Lawler, Jerry. *It's Good to Be the King ... Sometimes*. New York: Simon & Schuster, 2002.

Lee-Kong, Niambi. "Chitlin Circuit." In *Encyclopedia of African American History, 1896 to the Present: From the Age of Segregation to the Twenty-first Century*, edited by Paul Finkelman, 375–376. New York: Oxford UP, 2009.

Lentz, Harris M., III. *Biographical Dictionary of Professional Wrestling*. Jefferson, NC: McFarland, 2003.

Li, Ming, Eric W. MacIntosh, and Gonzalo A. Bravo, eds. *International Sport Management*. Champaign, IL: Human Kinetics, 2012.

Meltzer, Dave. *Tributes II: Remembering More of the World's Greatest Professional Wrestlers*. Champaign, IL: Sports Publishing, LLC, 2004.

Milner, John. "Ted DiBiase." *Canadian Online Explorer*. Accessed December 29, 2016. http://slam.canoe.com/Slam/Wrestling/Bios/dibiase.html.

"Mr. T Tells Why He Became a Wrestler." *Jet* 68, no. 7 (April 29, 1985): 22–23.

Mogensen, Maxwell. *Legendary Locals of Androscoggin County, Maine*. Charleston, SC: Arcadia, 2013.

Mooneyham, Mike. "Burrhead Jones: Legend of the Ring." *The Wrestling Gospel According to Mike Mooneyham*. Last modified February 23, 2003. http://www.mikemooneyham.com/2003/02/23/burrhead-jones-legend-of-the-ring.

Mooneyham, Mike. "Local Legend Bound for Big Apple." *The Wrestling Gospel According to*

Mike Mooneyham. Last modified July 16, 2006. http://www.mikemooneyham.com/2006/07/16/local-legend-bound-for-big-apple.

Mooneyham, Mike. "Q&A with Burrhead Jones." *The Wrestling Gospel According to Mike Mooneyham.* Accessed January 2, 2017. http://web.archive.org/web/20070728023954/http://www.mikemooneyham.com/pages/viewfull.cfm?ObjectID=41CAF4E0-5975-42A9-A52C9C1F4E3390AF.

"Negro Wrestlers." *Ebony* 17, no. 7 (May 1962): 43–50.

Newton, Michael. *The Ku Klux Klan in Mississippi: A History.* Jefferson, NC: McFarland, 2010.

Nolen, Claude H. *African American Southerners in Slavery, Civil War and Reconstruction.* Jefferson, NC: McFarland, 2001.

Obi, T.J. Desch. *Fighting for Honor: The History of African Martial Art Traditions in the Atlantic World.* Columbia, SC: University of South Carolina Press, 2008.

O'Donnell, Art. "Induction: Mark Henry, Sex Addict: Mark Finds a Way to Spend Even More Time on the Couch." *WrestleCrap.* Last modified September 5, 2013. http://www.wrestlecrap.com/inductions/mark-henry-sex-addict.

Oliver, Greg. "S.D. Jones Dies in Antigua." *Canadian Online Explorer.* Last modified October 26, 2008. http://slam.canoe.com/Slam/Wrestling/2008/10/26/7213751.html.

Oliver, Greg. "Tiger Conway, Sr., Dead at 74." *Canadian Online Explorer.* Last modified November 14, 2006. http://slam.canoe.com/Slam/Wrestling/2006/11/14/2352158.html.

Oliver, Greg, and Steven Johnson. *The Pro Wrestling Hall of Fame: The Tag Teams.* Toronto: ECW Press, 2005.

Payne, Marissa. "WWE Trainer Bill DeMott Resigns Amid Allegations of Racist, Homophobic and Abusive Behavior." *The Washington Post.* Last modified March 6, 2015. https://www.washingtonpost.com/news/early-lead/wp/2015/03/06/wwe-trainer-bill-demott-resigns-amid-allegations-of-racist-homophobic-and-abusive-behavior.

Peltz, Jamie. "Radio Review: Sonny Onoo Rips Russo, Says He Wouldn't Work for TNA." *Pro Wrestling Torch.* Last modified February 19, 2003. http://pwtorch.com/artman2/publish/Other_News_4/article_2666.shtml.

Pilgrim, David. "The Sapphire Caricature." *Jim Crow Museum of Racist Memorabilia.* Accessed September 1, 2018. https://ferris.edu/HTMLS/news/jimcrow/antiblack/sapphire.htm.

"A Pittsburgh Hurricane Roars Into Wrestling." *Ebony* 20, no. 8 (June 1965): 101–106.

Pro Wrestling Almanac & Book of Facts. Blue Bell, PA: Kappa Publishing Group, 2014.

"Raw Women's Championship." *WWE.* Accessed September 1, 2018. https://www.wwe.com/classics/titlehistory/raw-womens-championship.

Reynolds, R.D. *WrestleCrap: The Very Worst of Pro Wrestling.* Toronto: ECW Press, 2003.

Reynolds, R.D., and Blade Braxton. *The WrestleCrap Book of Lists.* Toronto: ECW Press, 2007.

Reynolds, R.D., and Bryan Alvarez. *The Death of WCW.* Toronto: ECW Press, 2004.

Richard, Dave. "Ranking Every WWE WrestleMania Main Event Match from Worst to Best." *CBS.* Last modified April 3, 2016. http://www.cbssports.com/general/news/ranking-every-wwe-wrestlemania-main-event-match-from-worst-to-best.

Richmond, Scott A. "Professional Wrestling." In *Encyclopedia of Social Deviance,* edited by Craig J. Forsyth and Heith Copes, 550–551. Los Angeles: SAGE, 2014.

Robinson, Jon. *WWE: The Attitude Era.* Indianapolis: DK, 2015.

Robinson, Wills. "Billionaire WWE Boss Who Fired Hulk Hogan for Racist Tirade Once Used N-Word in Awkward Skit with Black Wrestler Booker T." *Daily Mail.* Last modified July 25, 2015. http://www.dailymail.co.uk/news/article-3174113/Billionaire-WWE-boss-fired-Hulk-Hogan-racist-tirade-used-N-word-awkward-skit-black-wrestler-Booker-T.html.

Shabazz, Julian L.D. *Black Stars of Professional Wrestling.* Clinton, SC: Awesome Records, 2010.

Shields, Brian. *WWE in the Raging 80s.* New York: Pocket, 2006.

Shoemaker, David. *The Squared Circle: Life, Death, and Professional Wrestling.* New York: Gotham, 2013.

"Smackdown Women's Championship." *WWE.* Accessed September 1, 2018. "Divas Championship," *WWE*, accessed September 1, 2018. https://www.wwe.com/classics/titlehistory/smackdown-womens-championship.

Snowden, Jonathan. *Shooters: The Toughest Men in Professional Wrestling.* Toronto: ECW Press, 2012.

Toombs, Ariel Teal, and Colt Baird Toombs. *Rowdy: The Roddy Piper Story.* Toronto: Random House Canada, 2016.

Verrier, Steven. Professional *Wrestling in the Pacific Northwest: A History, 1883 to the Present.* Jefferson, NC: McFarland, 2017.

Vester, Katharina. *A Taste of Power: Food and American Identities.* Berkeley: University of California Press, 2015.

West, James. "Sputnik Monroe." In *The New Encyclopedia of Southern Culture: Volume 18,* edited by Allison Graham and Sharon Monteith, 313–315. Chapel Hill: University of North Carolina Press, 2011.

Wilson, Jim, and Weldon T. Johnson. *Choke Hold: Pro Wrestling's Real Mayhem Outside the Ring.* Bloomington, IN: Xlibris, 2003.

Winkie, Luke. "The 5 Worst Moments from Professional Wrestling's Attitude Era." *Sports Illustrated.* Last modified November 11, 2014. https://www.si.com/extra-mustard/2014/11/11/worst-attitude-era.

"World Tag Team Champions and WCW/NWA Title History." *World Championship Wrestling.* Accessed December 29, 2016. https://web.archive.org/web/20001110053700/http://www.wcw.com/2000/superstars/tagteam.

"Wrestling 'Daddy.'" *Ebony* 16, no. 1 (November 1960): 61–66.

Yetman, Norman R., ed. *Voices from Slavery: Authentic Slave Narratives.* Mineola, NY: Dover, 2000.

PART II

Social Justice
and Responsibility

Social Justice
and Black Basketball

Playing the Game On and Off the Court

DEMETRIUS W. PEARSON

Organized sport has traditionally been perceived as an innocuous com-petitive activity representing democratic principles and values, whereby highly skilled athletes test their physical and mental attributes against an opponent and/or course. However, this naïve perception has not necessarily been the case in American sport. Historical circumstances and socio-cultural factors have played a significant role in the growth and development of Amer-ican sport forms. This includes the type of sports sanctioned and embraced, as well as the socioeconomic status and race/ethnicity of the participants. This sociocultural and historical analysis highlights the triumphs and travails of arguably the two most influential figures in the development of basketball in the African American community and their social activism on and off of the court: Edwin B. Henderson and John McLendon.

Before discussing the salient contributions of the aforementioned indi-viduals, it is imperative that a historical overview of the American sport land-scape, during its nascent years, be thoroughly articulated. This is necessary because American sport has always been intertwined with its social, political, and historical aspects. Sport historians (Eisen & Wiggins, 1994) contend that sport is a viable medium for examining the evolution and rapidly developing aspects of society. For example: "Sport and recreational pursuits of ethnic and racial groups represent a slice of life that reflected all the sorrows, hap-piness, and struggles of their lives. They also provide a glimpse of the chang-ing world of ethnic cultures as well as the evolution of a multicultural society" (p. xvi). Coakley (2017) noted that organized sport and various sport forms oftentimes mirror the society that gave birth to them: "This means that the kinds of sports that exist and gain popularity often tell us much about the values and orientations of those who play, watch, or sponsor them. They also tell us who has power in a social world" (p. 8). Therefore, this brief historical overview of American sport, and basketball in particular, will put into context the enormous challenges faced by individuals attempting to change the status quo.

Sport and the Industrial Revolution

According to Zeigler (1988), organized sport forms and recreational pastimes primarily took shape during the height of the Industrial Revolution and coinciding Gilded Age period (1880–1920). They grew out of the industrial workplace, which was the catalyst for America's unprecedented growth and expanding economy during the latter years of the 19th century. "Between 1870 and 1900, some 12 million persons immigrated to the United States. At the beginning of this period, one-third of all U.S. industrial workers were immigrants; by 1900, more than half were foreign-born" (Sage & Eitzen, 2013, p. 29). Because of the massive immigration from Europe, industrialists and capitalists believed pragmatically that sport participation could be used to train immigrant workers to become loyal, efficient, and patriotic citizens (Coakley, 2009). Thus, team sports were employed as an assimilatory agent and value purveyor in hopes that ethnic and cultural ties would be abandoned, and a sense of unity and esprit de corps emerge. "Americanized" team sports such as football, baseball, and basketball were endorsed and sponsored, while soccer was shunned and viewed as a foreigner's game. The systematic utilization of sport as an assimilatory agent and value inculcator was routinely institutionalized in densely populated, lower class ethnic, metropolitan environs.

The acculturation process of new immigrants to America extended beyond the industrial work place. Coakley's (2009) assessment of early American sport contends that the "playground movement" was also a key contributor. Advocates of this corporate-bureaucratic society promoted organized playground programs that used team sports because they could suppress the traditional values of white ethnic groups (i.e., Italians, Irish, Germans, Jews, and others) and replace them with those deemed "American" (Gems, Borish, & Pfister, 2008). The inculcated values were reinforced in state-mandated public schools, adult-sponsored sport programs, and religious-affiliated entities (Rader, 2004). The latter group, most notably the Young Men's Christian Association (YMCA), was the first to play organized basketball in 1891. Although the early players and disseminators of the game were upper class males, several key aspects of the game made it a viable sport of choice for the lower class ethnic. They included nominal startup costs for equipment, facilities, and training, as well as access to public school parks, playgrounds, gymnasiums, and municipal recreation centers (Eisen & Wiggins, 1994).

Sport Disenfranchisement

Unfortunately, all groups were not welcomed to participate in late 19th and early 20th century sport due to federally sanctioned segregation and discriminatory legislation known as Jim Crow laws. These legislative mandates were implemented to thwart the social advances made by African Americans during the post–Civil War and Reconstruction Period (1865–1877). Essentially, they subjugated and restricted their basic civil rights (Ashe, 1988; Rader, 2004). These statutes were routinely passed into law and adherently enforced in the southern states and several in the mid-west well into the mid–20th century. As a result, all aspects of social life were adversely impacted. Thus, laws in certain states prohibited interracial sport competitions. These exclusionary bans limited the sport involvement of other non-white ethnic groups as well (e.g., Hispanics, Native Americans, and Asian Americans).

The Etiology and Growth of Basketball

Basketball was created at the Young Men's Christian Association (YMCA) International Training School at Springfield, Massachusetts, in 1891 by James Naismith, the Canadian born physical educator and coach, who was tasked to develop an indoor winter sport for students between football and baseball season (Swanson & Spears, 1995). Because of the game's simplistic set of rules, nominal equipment cost, and limited space requirements it was readily accepted at many levels of the social strata. As a matter of fact, basketball gained early international acceptance and appeal when YMCA missionaries took the sport to China during the mid–1890s (Cui, 2015; Mechikoff, 2010).

Semi-Professional Ethnic Cagers

It was also favorably received in the densely populated northeastern and mid–Atlantic metropolises: New York, Philadelphia, Baltimore, and Washington, D.C. The sport would eventually move toward the Midwest when its inventor relocated to Kansas. However, the growth of organized basketball was exponential in the urban areas along the northeast and mid–Atlantic corridor. Inner city settlement houses, schoolyards, recreation centers, and YMCAs became the major purveyors of the sport's talent pool, drawn mainly from the poorer ethnic groups. Basketball became indigenous to the inner city, and the style of those who played the game (Isaacs, 1984). The early athletes playing the sport were primarily German, Irish, Polish, and Jewish (Riess, 1990; Rosin, 2003). Eventually African Americans were introduced to the game through racially segregated YMCAs (Brooks & McKail, 2008). The 12th Street YMCA was the first and preeminent site for the development of basketball in the District of Columbia's African American community (Ashe, 1988; Kuska, 2004; Ungrady, 2013). During the late 19th and early 20th century professional basketball leagues formed. Also, touring semi-professional teams were established and began "barnstorming" throughout the northeast and select mid-western cities. Some of the more notable teams included the Celtics, South Philadelphia Hebrew Association, Harlem Rens, Buffalo Germans, and Savoy Big Five (aka Harlem Globetrotters). These early traveling teams competed in national tournaments in cities that permitted interracial sport competitions (Spencer, 2011).

The Burgeoning Collegiate Game

Basketball became a major sport in scholastic and collegiate programs nationally and was second only to football by the start of World War I (Mechikoff, 2010). Intra-city collegiate basketball rivalries with scheduled doubleheaders were common in large cities like New York and Philadelphia. The Palestra, built in 1926, was among the first facilities constructed in the United States specifically for basketball, and at one point was touted as having hosted more basketball games and NCAA playoff tournament contests than anywhere else in the world (Zingg, 1987). It currently stands as "the oldest major college arena still in use" (Zingg, 1987, p. 36). The increased interest in collegiate basketball and potential revenues facilitated organizations like the Amateur Athletic Union (AAU), National Association of Intercollegiate Athletics (NAIA), and the National Collegiate Athletic Association (NCAA) to sponsor postseason championship tournaments in the 1930s. These tournaments (i.e., NIT, NAIA, and NCAA) determined the nation's best collegiate basketball programs.

African American Involvement
and the Lack Thereof

However, like other collegiate sports basketball was devoid of black players in most of the major conferences. Racial segregation still inhibited the access of certain minority groups. Some blacks were afforded opportunities at "select" northern white institutions, but those that recruited African American basketball players were restricted in the competition they could schedule.

State laws and athletic conference rules limited interracial seasonal competitions and tournament play. For example, the Big Ten excluded black basketball players until after World War II (Ashe, 1988). Not surprising, the first Big Ten school to have an integrated team was the University of Iowa during the 1944–45 season (Martin, 2002); while its intrastate rival, Iowa State, was the first major Midwestern university to have a black football player in the 20th century (Lapchick, et al., 2008). Needless to say, the vast majority of black basketball players were relegated to small Historically Black Colleges and Universities (HBCUs) located primarily in the south (Ashe, 1988; Brooks & Althouse, 2013). The creation of Black athletic conferences like the Colored Intercollegiate Athletic Association (CIAA), Southern Intercollegiate Athletic Conference (SIAC), and Southwestern Athletic Conference (SWAC) fostered the development of basketball in the south, even though the vast majority of their experienced players were northerners. George (1992) stated:

> After World War I innumerable poor African-Americans from the North ventured South using their on-court prowess to attain an athletic scholarship and a college education. Because athletic facilities were available to Northern Blacks and basketball was already an established winter sport above the Mason-Dixon Line, the migration of these superior players to Black colleges inspired Southern youngsters to take up the game. The combination of up-North basketball know-how and Southern college exposure enabled superior teams and players to attain a national profile within Black America [p. 24].

The stellar talent pool of black basketball players, reared in northern urban environs, was due to the fact that football was the sport of choice in the southern states. Therefore, many of these transplants found viable sport and educational opportunities as a result of their migration south. The early success of celebrated HBCU basketball programs like Morgan State (1924–1927), which recorded an undefeated season in 1927 and "hailed as Black College basketball's de facto national champions" (George, 1992, p. 24); Xavier University's (1935–1939) 82–2 record with a starting five from one Chicago public high school; and Virginia Union (1939–1940), aka "the Dream Team" because of its two celebrated northern star players were never invited to participate in the aforementioned national basketball tournaments.

Crusaders for Social Justice and Game Changers

For more than 150 years institutionalized racism in American society has besieged and crippled various disenfranchised groups with minimal government intervention. In spite of a "so-called" democratic form of government, and a society supposedly based on meritocracy, basic civil rights were not afforded all Americans. This was particularly the plight of African Americans in such areas as education, employment, housing, armed forces, and sport for much of the first half of the 20th century. However, post–Civil War and Reconstruction Period social activism provided the impetus for the establishment of national organizations to combat racial discrimination and gross inequities within American society. Such groups included the National Association for the Advancement of Colored People (NAACP), National Urban League (NUL), Prince Hall Masons, and sundry social sorority/fraternity organizations. These African American groups, often led by college-educated individuals from HBCUs and "more liberal" northern white universities, sought social justice in all aspects of American life, including recreational pastimes and sport, oftentimes through the courts.

Social Activism On and Off the Court

Few individuals have impacted sport both on and off the court in so many different ways as have Edwin Bancroft Henderson, affectionately and deferentially referred to as the "Grandfather of Black Basketball" (Spencer, 2011); and John McLendon, a student of Dr. Naismith's at the University of Kansas and deemed "Father of Black Basketball" (Klores, 2008). These two legendary figures helped develop and "nurse" basketball in the African American community during its formative years. Yet Henderson and McLendon were much more than accomplished coaches. They were pioneers, civil rights activists, and social reformers prior to the celebrated Civil Rights Movement (1954–1968). Ironically, each was inextricably linked to James Naismith via basketball, but more importantly intertwined social justice with their sport "calling."

Edwin Bancroft Henderson
aka "Molder of Men"

Known as the architect of African American basketball in the Washington, D.C.–Baltimore metroplex (Henderson & Henderson, 1985) around the turn of the 19th century, E.B. Henderson spent the majority of his life in sport as an athlete, teacher/coach, administrator, and sport historian. He was educated at Howard University (B.A.), Columbia University (M.A.), and Central Chiropractic College (D.C.). However, his three-year summer program at the Sargent Normal School of Physical Training (Harvard University) not only equipped him with the requisite skills to teach physical education, it introduced him to the sport of basketball. Taylor (2013) noted that Henderson was the first black basketball player at Harvard University and first certified to teach physical education in the public schools of America, receiving the highest scores of those taking the examination in his class (Henderson & Henderson, 1985; Kuska, 2004; Ungrady, 2013). His physical training and basketball acumen were immediately implemented in his public school curriculum with unprecedented success in 1904. Eventually Henderson was appointed Director of Physical Education for the Colored Schools of Washington, D.C., and its local YMCAs, a position he held from 1925 to 1951.

Because opportunities to play basketball and hone his skills were not readily available in Washington, D.C., due to racial segregation, Henderson took it upon himself to create an environment that would teach the game and develop players. Unbeknownst to many, he created a "Basket Ball League" comprised of black teams as early as 1908 (Kuska, 2004; Ungrady, 2013), and championed the cause for building a YMCA for African Americans. His active lobbying and fundraising were instrumental in the establishment of the 12th Street YMCA. Henderson's vast basketball knowledge and skills enabled him to play and coach two back-to-back undefeated teams in 1909 and 1910. The former representing the 12th Street team, and unofficially crowned the Colored Basketball World Champions, and the latter team adopted by Howard University as its varsity squad (McKenna, 2008; Spencer, 2011). The 12th Street YMCA would become the "basketball mecca" for many of the elite African American players in the Washington, D.C.–Baltimore area and the impetus for the east coast inter-city competitions between New York and Philadelphia.

Noted widely for his contributions to D.C. basketball, Henderson was administratively involved in many aspects of African American amateur sports in the Mid-Atlantic States, and chronicled their achievements throughout the first half of the 20th century. He created and organized the Inter-Scholastic Athletic Association (ISAA) as well as the Public Schools Athletic League (PSAL) for black schools that were denied competition opportunities against white opponents. The goal was to promote competitive intercollegiate and interscholastic sporting events for African Americans. Ironically, it became the first such athletic conference for black and white teams in Washington, D.C. (McKenna, 2008). Henderson also established the Eastern Board of Officials (EBO), which facilitated the training and development of black athletic officials, while stressing the importance of African American involvement in administrative/leadership positions.

His sport involvement and prolific writing coincided with his social justice stance on racial segregation and discriminatory practices. As an outspoken civic leader and staunch advocate for fair housing, Henderson counseled with Harvard alumnus and friend W.E.B. Du Bois in the establishment of the Fairfax County NAACP in 1915. It was the first rural branch of the NAACP in the country. His lifetime involvement with the NAACP as a charter member of the Falls Church branch and sundry other administrative positions placed him at the forefront of the fight for civil rights. His biographers (Henderson & Henderson, 1985) contend that his most significant civil rights victory may very well have been the desegregation of the Uline Arena in the 1940s. Wiggins (1999) concurred with this assessment:

> The elimination of racially discriminatory practices at Uline Arena was a defining moment in Henderson's career and provides additional insight into the tactics he employed to combat racial discrimination, the tenor of the Civil Rights Movement during the middle decades of the twentieth century, and how the institution of sport made explicit white fears of black bodies [pp. 99–100].

Prior to Henderson's crusade, Uline Arena only allowed blacks to attend muscular combative events like boxing and wrestling but denied access to certain sports (e.g., basketball and ice hockey) and cultural events (e.g., Ice Capades, ballets, etc.) where scantily dressed white women performed in bathing attire (Coursey, 1971). Michael Uline's unwritten racial discrimination policy was based on the premise that "The white people who attend cultural shows are of a high type and do not wish to attend cultural programs with Negroes..." (Wiggins, 1999, p. 100). Dogged and resolute Henderson organized protests and sit-ins, wrote editorials, and urged blacks to boycott the arena. His intimate contact with other civil rights groups and sympathizers (e.g., Citizen's Committee Against Segregation in Recreation) paid huge dividends. With considerable public support for the protest and dwindling revenues Michael Uline eventually relented and opened the facility to all races in 1948 (Thomas, 2002). Henderson's efforts would also lead to the desegregation of other Washington, D.C. area arenas, theaters (e.g., National Theatre and Constitution Hall), parks, and recreational areas.

One would be remiss if E.B. Henderson's prolific writings were not mentioned. His voluminous letters to newspapers across the country ("Letters to the Editor"), journal articles, book chapters, and books chronicling African American and HBCU athletic achievements prior to the 1950s were indicting, informative, and engaging. It is estimated that he wrote more than 3000 articles and letters beginning as early as 1920 to newspapers including the *Washington Star, Washington Post, Norfolk Journal and Guide, The Baltimore Afro-American, Detroit Tribune, Pittsburgh Courier, Times Herald,* and the *Cleveland Call and Post,* to name a few (Coursey, 1971; Ungrady, 2013). In 1950 the *Washington Post* reported the following: "Dr. Henderson must have the record around here for making people angry. More than 1,000 letters have been printed over his name" (Henderson & Henderson, 1985, p. 19). Many of his letters decried the social injustices and "apartheid democratic" governance in America throughout much of the 20th century. For example, in a June 3, 1951, letter to the *Washington Post,* Henderson both bemoaned and chided the newspaper's tacit approval of a city college plan for two city colleges predicated on racial segregation. Henderson's letter addressed the pending court cases pertaining to segregation of public facilities, as well as the financial shortcomings of such a proposal. "Economically, two equal colleges would cost twice the cost of one, besides perpetuating the caste system. In the face of evident trend, an approach to dual city colleges is not realistic" (Henderson & Henderson, 1985, p. 60).

Henderson's voluminous Letters to the Editor were not always a haranguing discourse on the social injustices within sport and/or society of the day. Some were complimentary in nature with the intent of highlighting civic and community pride within various disenfranchised Baltimore neighborhoods. For instance, Dr. Henderson lauded the efforts of a Miss Frances Murphy and her community cleanup campaign in a 1939 column in *The Baltimore Afro-American* newspaper. He wrote:

> Last week, Miss Frances Murphy carried me on a tour of Clean Block streets in Baltimore, I was amazed. Could educators and civic workers and planners go through some of these 140 blocks, new ideas might seep in their minds for more effective urban programs. In street after street, there were beautiful flowers, clean streets, cleaner backyards, debris-free alleys, washed windows, freshly painted houses, group discussions among children for block beauty, and evidence of neighborly pride [Henderson, 1939, p. 20].

Such deeds did not escape the watchful eyes of Dr. Henderson, who extolled the many positive activities he witnessed in the black community, which was routinely omitted from mainstream media outlets. On other occasions he touted the early successes of African American athletes who competed in integrated national and international sport competitions like the Penn Relays (Henderson, 1951), the American Athletic Union (Henderson, 1946), and Olympic Games (Henderson, 1948).

His major journalistic works include *The Interscholastic Athletic Association Handbook,* which was first written in 1910. It was annually published each year through 1913, and was the first book specifically dealing with black athletics in black schools written by an African American (Coursey, 1971). *The Negro in Sports* (1939) was also the first book documenting the athletic achievements of black athletes written by an African American. This book is said to have had more influence than any other on subsequent research dealing with the history of black athletes in American sport (Wiggins, 1997). It detailed the triumphs and travails endured by black athletes in their quest to compete. A review of the 1949 revised edition in the Atlanta Daily World reads as follows: "No library of a sports lover can be called complete without a copy of the revised edition of 'They [*sic*] Negro in Sports' by Dr. E.B. Henderson..." (McClendon, 1950, p. 5). He further writes:

> Dr. Henderson's book does not deal alone in facts and figures, but also in philosophy and in argument for further integration of the colored athlete in all phases of American sports. He believes that another edition of "The Negro in Sports" will be

unnecessary "since integration and the growth of true democracy seems nearer." The contributions of the American Negro to the American Sports Scene is presented comprehensively and indisputably as one of the greatest of factors in the total development of this nation [1950, p. 5].

Lastly, *The Black Athlete: Emergence and Arrival* (1968) "is perhaps Henderson's most frequently cited work and certainly one of his more important" (Wiggins, 1999, p. 104). Other literary works were equally important in championing sport as a racial equalizer. He believed that interracial sport competitions were a means for bridging the racial divide during the early 20th century, a sentiment embraced by many black and integrationists of his generation. Examples include newspaper articles penned by Dr. Henderson in the Norfolk Journal and Guide titled *Sports Agencies Are a Cog in Race Relations* (1949) and *Athletes Become Chief Ambassadors of Good Will* (1951), as well as *Integrated Sports Programs in Army Camps Bearing Fruit* (1950) published in *The Baltimore Afro-American*.

Needless to say, few rival the immense impact and literary contributions of Henderson. As a matter of fact, due to his seminal works he has been dubbed the "Founder and Father of Black Sports History" (Taylor, 2013; Wiggins & Miller, 2003). His lasting legacy is probably best captured in the following quote: "Nearly every article, book chapter, and survey text written over the last half-century that includes information on the history of African American athletes has seemingly been influenced by Henderson's work in one way or another" (Wiggins, 1997, p. 222).

John McLendon: "An Agent for Change"

Equally noteworthy are the major accomplishments and contributions of John McLendon to the American sport landscape. Called the "Nobel Revolutionary of American Sport" (McLendon & Bryant, 2000, p. 720), McLendon was much like his turn of the century predecessor in using sport as a vehicle to impact change and facilitate racial inclusion. As a student and mentee of Dr. James Naismith, McLendon learned the game of basketball, even though he was prohibited from playing on the college team, and civil disobedience at the University of Kansas serendipitously through his major program of study. McLendon was the first African American to receive a B.A. degree in physical education from KU, and later a graduate degree (M.A.) from Iowa University.

Ironically it was the physical education swimming requirement at KU that led to McLendon's first major civil rights protest. Although required to pass a swimming course, as a core requirement for physical education, administrators waived the rule because the college pool was "off-limits" to blacks, as well as student teaching at white schools (Bryant, 2000). Not satisfied with the thought of receiving credits that he had not earned, McLendon refused the waiver and set out to fulfill his swimming course requirement. Banned from the swimming pool McLendon entered the pool regardless during class to practice the requisite skills to complete his requirement. Once leaving the area the pool was immediately drained. Katz (1990) aptly described the event: "After he got dressed and reentered the pool area he noticed the pool was drained. When he asked whether his actions were the reason for this, the pool attendant said curtly 'What do you think?' This made him even more determined and after organizing a 2 week black student protest, the university pool was officially integrated" (p. 35). Thus, McLendon became the first black student to swim in a University of Kansas swimming pool. With the aid of Dr. Naismith he was also able to complete his practice teaching requirement at Lincoln Elementary and Lawrence Memorial High School; thereby enabling him to become a member of the first class receiving a physical education degree from KU in 1936.

Unfazed by his inability to play basketball at KU, partly due to its discriminatory practices, McLendon learned the game's intricacies from Naismith and refined some of his mentor's tactics. Although not a particularly accomplished player on his junior college basketball team, McLendon understood the importance of physical conditioning and was able to quickly implement it into his unique "up-tempo" coaching strategy with immediate success. For example, as a first-year head basketball coach at Lincoln Memorial High School his team won the Kansas-Missouri Athletic Conference championship in 1936. This would be the start of a legendary coaching career in basketball, even though his early professional obligations included football and track.

After completing his graduate degree at the University of Iowa McLendon took an assistant coaching position at North Carolina College for Negroes (now North Carolina Central) where he coached multiple sports. Within three years he became the head basketball coach. His successful coaching career at NCC would lead to multiple conference titles including the Central Intercollegiate Athletic Association (CIAA) basketball championship tournament, which he and several HBCU colleagues established in 1946. During his 12-year tenure at NCC McLendon amassed a winning percentage of .812. Supremely confident of his HBCU success McLendon was eager to showcase the athletic prowess of his NCC basketball team and demonstrate that his program was on par with other national champions. As a result, McLendon scheduled games throughout the country with considerable success.

It was at NCC where McLendon defied state law and engaged in a clandestine activity that would become a guarded secret for many years. Known as the "Secret Game," this unconventional athletic contest pitted North Carolina College against Duke University's Medical team in a basketball game. Because it had not previously been attempted, for fear of public safety, there was no publicity nor spectators in attendance. Katz (2007) contends that it is uncertain how the game came about, but on Sunday, March 12, 1944, collegiate basketball became integrated. The NCC team won handily 88–44, but more importantly an amicable relationship emerged between teams that led to a second game. This time the two teams exchanged players. According to McLendon and Bryant (2000), "The Duke team suggested that half of their team play on the North Carolina College team and that half of the North Carolina College team play on the Duke team. We integrated the teams and had another great game" (p. 729). These private "experimental" contests eventually led to the first public integrated basketball game in North Carolina between McLendon's NCC basketball team and the Camp Lejeune Marines, which the Eagles also won. It must be noted that the stellar teams during the war years were those of the military (McLendon & Bryant, 2000). Decades later the first public intercollegiate basketball game in the state was played between Winston-Salem and High Point College in 1967.

Challenging the Collegiate Status Quo

An even-tempered coach and mild-mannered social activist, McLendon decried the inequitable treatment of HBCU basketball programs by collegiate tournament officials. For much of the 20th century HBCU basketball programs were denied the opportunity to participate in post-season collegiate tournaments that crowned the national champions. For years McLendon and other HBCU administrators lobbied for the opportunity to compete in the post-season national tournaments but were routinely denied access. It was quite evident that the omnipresent aura of Jim Crow law dictated the decision by tournament officials. Subsequently McLendon and his colleagues formed the National Athletic Steering Committee (NASC), an organization designed to study the problem of segregation and discrimination in intercollegiate athletics and make recommendations to bring about change.

Not only were HBCU teams barred from competition, certain annual championship tournaments (NAIA) prohibited black players. Uncharacteristic of his genteel and reserved demeanor, McLendon lashed out on the NCAA leadership. In a caustic diatribe he stated, "The NCAA may mean National Collegiate Athletic Association to some people, but to us it means No Colored Athletes Allowed" (Katz, 2007, p. 68). His admonishment of collegiate tournament officials did not necessarily fall on deaf ears as the NAIA tournament lifted its ban on black players in 1948. This was sweet news to the upstart coach of Indiana State University (John Wooden), whose black player Clarence Walker was permitted to play. As a result, he became the first African American to compete in the tournament. Wooden, later to be known as the "Wizard of Westwood" because of his unprecedented basketball success at UCLA, benefited from McLendon and his allies' crusade. He indicated that if Walker could not play he was not going to attend the tournament (Katz, 2007). After repeated attempts to gain entrance into post-season tournament play the NAIA finally relented and in 1952 created Division 29. This resolution led to the formation of a black college basketball tournament that sent the winning team to the NAIA National Championship Tournament (Pearson, 2013). Mack Greene, spokesperson for the NASC wrote, in a letter to *Athletic Directors and Administrators in Colleges for Negroes,* "The fact that a team was entered into the national tournament from a college for Negroes, located in a section of the United States where state laws prohibits inter-racial competition among colleges, is the salient and dramatic aspect" (Katz, 1990, pp. 36–37). In 1953 the HBCU champion became eligible to compete in the NAIA Championship Tournament. This was a victory of sorts, but McLendon saw the bigger picture and sought a more comprehensive victory.

Due to the strong showing of HBCU teams in the past NAIA Championship Tournaments, McLendon, now head coach at Tennessee A&I, (renamed Tennessee State University) conditionally accepted an invitation to play in the 1954 NAIA Christmas Tip-Off Tournament. He agreed to participate only if his team was afforded the same lodging accommodations as other competing white teams. This was not the norm in Kansas City, Missouri, where previous Tennessee A&I teams had competed and were housed in local homes, YMCAs, and hotels in depressed areas. McLendon's condition was approved and Tennessee A&I became the first black college team to stay and eat in the same hotel as other participating teams. Shortly thereafter other downtown businesses abandoned their discriminatory practices (e.g., restaurants, movie theaters, etc.). McLendon's social activism, along with the landmark 1954 Supreme Court decision (*Brown v. Board of Education*), and the burgeoning Civil Rights Movement were salient steps forward in the fight for equal access and treatment under the law for African Americans.

Part of McLendon's decision to push for equal tournament amenities were based on the premise that HBCUs were negatively impacted by their segregated treatment, as well as the basic pressures of competition. He believed that if the unfair accommodations were remedied his team only had to focus on their opponents. McLendon's amicable disposition and diplomacy aided in the NAIA Tournament's desegregation decision. A few years later the Tennessee A&I Tigers won the NAIA National Basketball Championship Tournament in 1957. It was the first time an African American college team had won a national title against a white opponent in any team sport. John McLendon's team would repeat as NAIA national champions for the next two seasons and become the first college team in history to "three peat" (1957–59). Their success brought national exposure to HBCU basketball programs: so much so that not to be out done by the NAIA, the NCAA opted to create a National College Division Championship. This decision would provide smaller colleges an opportunity to compete in post-season championship play.

Uncharted Territory

Well aware of the untapped black collegiate basketball talent pool, McLendon often urged National Basketball Association (NBA) officials to draft them. However, it wasn't until the 1950 CIAA Championship tournament, at the previously segregated Uline Arena, that the NBA took serious notice. McLendon's NCC team, with star point guard Harold Hunter, bested West Virginia State's two-time black college All-American Earl Lloyd in the championship game. Impressed by what they had witnessed, owners of the Washington Capitols basketball team contacted McLendon about a try-out for the two players. McLendon, serving as the players' contact and representative, escorted them to the try-out and ensuing contract signing. Historically, Hunter became the first black player to sign an NBA contract, but was released prior to the season. Lloyd would actually be the first African American to play in the NBA. Two other black players joined Lloyd in the 1950 NBA season: Chuck Cooper and Nate "Sweetwater" Clifton. Helping to sign the first African American players in the NBA was a milestone for McLendon, as well as his efforts to showcase HBCU basketball talent, but more importantly he opened the door for many black players to enter the league. By the mid–1960s half of the players selected in the first round of the NBA Draft were black. The number increased the following year when 8 of the 12 players selected in the first round were African American (Halberstam, 1996).

Because McLendon was a proponent of role modeling, when he was offered a semi-professional head coaching position with the Cleveland Pipers of the National Industrial Basketball League (NIBL), he accepted it. McLendon took the job because he was one of the individuals most critical of the paucity of black coaches (Thomas, 2002). He believed that this would be an opportunity to help address the problem. Shortly thereafter the Pipers became part of the American Basketball League (ABL) in 1961 making John McLendon the first African American head coach of a professional basketball franchise (Spencer, 2011). He experienced success as coach and vice-president in charge of player personnel for the team's short stint in the ABL. An ongoing feud with team owner George Steinbrenner, due to his constant meddling in team affairs, led to McLendon's departure.

Upon leaving the pro ranks he was immediately appointed American Basketball Specialist to Southeast Asia. In this position McLendon taught and coached basketball in Malaya and Indonesia while serving as a U.S. consultant at the 1962 Asian Games (Katz, 1990). His involvement in international basketball continued after short administrative and coaching stints at Tennessee State and Kentucky State when he became the first black coach to serve on the U.S. Olympic Committee in 1966, and subsequently basketball coaching staff at the 1968 Olympic games. During his U.S. Olympic involvement McLendon became the head coach of Cleveland State University, and the first African American hired to coach at a predominantly white university. However, while building the Cleveland State basketball program McLendon was once again courted by a professional team in an upstart league. Somewhat hesitant, but always willing to accept a challenge, McLendon signed on to become the head coach of the Denver Rockets of the American Basketball Association (ABA) in 1969. Much like his early decade signing with the Cleveland Pipers, McLendon became the first African American head coach in the ABA (Katz, 2007), a league that would rival the NBA and produce some of the game's most talented players.

Conclusion

Parallel Paths

The contributions of E.B. Henderson and John McLendon are immeasurable. They were consummate leaders as teachers, coaches, and administrators. Moreover, each was a social advocate and critic of an unjust system at a time when segregation and discriminatory practices were the norm in American society. Their unbridled passion for civil rights and equitable treatment in all aspects of life literally placed them in "harm's way." Celebrated role models within their respective communities, both Henderson and McLendon pursued various opportunities in an effort to challenge blacks to excel and create opportunities for others. As "legitimate" student-athletes, before the term was liberally applied to students who play sport for an education, Henderson and McLendon successfully navigated the educational labyrinth to become pioneers in their respective academic programs. These former athletes, and later coaches, were keenly aware of the importance of kinesiology principles and physical conditioning through their studies, which afforded them considerable success in sport. They were also scholars who chose to share their success and expertise over the years through various visual and print medias, as well as their dissatisfaction with societal injustices verbally.

Susan Rayl, in a *Washington Post* article (Ungrady, 2013), summarized the indelible impact that Henderson had on basketball in the black community:

Without E.B. Henderson you would have had a much slower introduction of basketball to African Americans.... He was the catalyst. He was a root, and the tree sprang from the root in D.C. for African Americans. His induction into the Hall of Fame is not just a good thing; it's absolutely necessary if you want to tell the true history of the game [para. 9].

With respect to John McLendon, biographers, sport historians, and "aged mentees" continue to laud his insight, wisdom, and social advocacy via sport. Needless to say, he was one of the most talented and influential basketball coaches of the 20th century (Grungy, 2001). "He cut the cords of racism within institutions while he wove the strength of character in individual lives" (Bryant, 2000, p. 720). "His most important contribution to American society is in the area of civil rights as a pioneer in the integration of intercollegiate and professional athletics" (Katz, 1990, p. 35).

Although not the panacea or elixir for a racist society, both Henderson and McLendon were firm believers that interracial conflict and strife could be alleviated to some extent through an integrated sport environment. And for much of their lifetime they tried to create such a space where mutual respect, equality, and opportunity were the norm.

Throughout their respective careers both men were showered with numerous accolades, honors, and awards not only because of their work ethic but roles as pioneers: the first in various pursuits. It was fitting for the Naismith Memorial Basketball Hall of Fame to recognize and induct each of these individuals: Henderson (2013) and McLendon (1978 & 2016). Their contributions to basketball, in particular, is evident through the vast number of African Americans playing the game competitively and recreationally. Recent data indicate that 77 percent of NBA and 58 percent of Division 1 male collegiate basketball players nationwide are African American (Lapchick & Guiao, 2015). There are also more African American head and assistant coaches at the professional and collegiate level than any other American sport.

REFERENCES

Ashe, A.R., Jr. (1988). *A hard road to glory: a history of the African-American athlete 1919–1945,* Vol. 2. New York: Amistad.

Brooks, D., & Althouse, R. (Eds.). (2013). *Racism in college athletics* (3d ed.). Morgantown, WV: Fitness Information Technology.

Brooks, S.N., & McKail, M.A. (2008). A theory of the preferred worker: A structural explanation for black male dominance in basketball. *Critical Sociology, 34*(3), 369–387.

Coakley, J.J. (2009). *Sports in society: Issues and controversies (10th ed.).* Boston, MA: McGraw-Hill.

Coakley, J.J. (2017). *Sports in society: Issues and controversies (12th ed.).* New York: NY: McGraw-Hill.

Coursey, L.N. (1971). *The life of Edwin Bancroft Henderson and his professional contributions to physical education.* (Doctoral dissertation). Available from ProQuest Dissertations and Theses database. (UMI No. 71–27, 453.)

Cui, J. (2015, June). American influence on Chinese basketball. *Insight: the Voice of the American Chamber of Commerce in Shanghai*. Retrieved from http://insight.amcham-shanghai.org/american-influence-on-chinese-basketball/.

Eisen, G., & Wiggins, D.K. (1994). *Ethnicity and sport in North American history and culture*. Westport, CT: Greenwood Press.

Gems, G.R., Borish, L.J., & Pfister, G. (2008). *Sports in American history: From colonization to globalization*. Champaign, IL: Human Kinetics.

George, N. (1992). *Elevating the game: Black men and basketball*. New York: HarperCollins.

Halberstam, D. (1996). Foreword. In M. Vancil (Ed.), *NBA at 50* (pp. 12–23), New York: Random House.

Henderson, E.B. (1939, August 19). Clean block drive seen as aid to race culture: Less abstract godliness, more cleanliness. *The Baltimore Afro-American*, p. 20.

Henderson, E.B. (1946, February 16). Negro tracksters top field in AAU. *Philadelphia Tribune*, p. 11.

Henderson, E.B. (1948, August 28). Olympics over, world sees again racial inferiority claim is no more than a myth. *The Baltimore Afro-American*, p. 8.

Henderson, E.B. (1949, April 2). Sports agencies are a cog in race relations. *Norfolk Journal and Guide*, p. B15.

Henderson, E.B. (1950, March 18). Integrated sports programs in army camps bearing fruit. *The Baltimore Afro-American*, p. 17.

Henderson, E.B. (1951, May 12). Henderson's comments. *The Baltimore Afro-American*, p. 16.

Henderson, E.B. (1951, July 21). Athletes become chief ambassadors of good will. *Norfolk Journal and Guide*, p. 20.

Henderson, J.H., & Henderson, B.F. (1985). *Molder of men: Portrait of a "grand old man"—Edwin Bancroft Henderson*. New York: Vantage.

Isaacs, N.D. (1984). *All the moves: A history of college basketball* (Rev. ed.). New York: Harper & Row.

Katz, M.S. (1990). Coach John B. McLendon Jr., and the integration of intercollegiate and professional athletics in post World War II America. *Journal of American Culture, 13*(4), 35–39.

Katz, M.S. (2007). *Breaking through*. Fayetteville: University of Arkansas Press.

Klores, D. (Producer & Director). (2008). *Black magic* [DVD]. Available from http://www.amazon.com/Black-Magic-Espn/dp/B001CDFY5K

Kuska, B. (2004). *Hot potato: How Washington and New York gave birth to Black basketball and changed America's game forever*. Charlottesville: University of Virginia Press.

Lapchick, R., Bartter, J., Brenden, J., Martin, S., Ruiz, H., & Sedberry, M. (2008). *100 pioneers: African-Americans who broke color barriers in sport*. Morgantown, WV: Fitness Information Technology.

Lapchick, R., & Guiao, A. (2015). *The 2015 racial and gender report card: National Basketball Association*. Retrieved from http://nebula.wsimg.com/6e1489cc3560e1e1a2fa88e3030 f5149?AccessKeyId=DAC3A56D8FB782449D2A&disposition=0&alloworigin=1.

Martin, C.H. (2002, June). The color line in Midwestern college sports, 1890–1960. *Indiana Magazine of History, 98*(2), 85–112.

McClendon, J. (1950, August 19). Sportsdust. *Atlanta Daily World*, p. 5.

McKenna, D. (2008, March 6). Hall pass: Basketball pioneer E.B. Henderson's ticket to hoops fame is yet to be punched. *Washington City Paper*. Retrieved from www.washingtoncitypaper.com/arts/theatre/article/13035086/hall-pass.

McLendon, J.B., & Bryant, J.I. (2000). Basketball coach John B. McLendon, the noble revolutionary of U.S. sport April 5, 1915–October 8, 1999. *Journal of Black Studies, 30*(5), 720–734.

McLendon, J.B., & Gundy, P. (2001). "A position of respect": A basketball coach who resisted segregation. *Southern Cultures, 7*(2), 84–91.

Mechikoff, R. (2010). *A history and philosophy of sport and physical education: From ancient civilizations to the modern world* (5th ed.). New York: McGraw-Hill.

Pearson, D.W. (2013). Basketball and ethnic diversity. In C.E. Cortes (Ed.), *Multicultural America: A multimedia encyclopedia*: (Vol. 1, pp. 321–325). Thousand Oaks, CA: Sage.

Rader, B.G. (2004). *American sports: From the age of folk games to the age of televised sports (5th ed.).* Upper saddle River, NJ: Prentice Hall.

Riess, S.A. (1990). Professional sports as an avenue of social mobility in America: Some myths and reality. In D.G. Kyle & G.D. Stark (Eds.). *Essays on sport history and sport mythology* (pp. 83–107). College Station: Texas A&M University Press.

Rosin, J. (2003). *Philly hoops: The SPHAS and Warriors.* Philadelphia, PA: Autumn Road.

Sage, G.H., & Eitzen, D.S. (2013). *Sociology of North American sport (9th ed.).* New York: Oxford University Press.

Spencer, A. (2011). Top 25: Black history's integration of pro basketball. *Yahoo! Contributor Network.* Retrieved from http://originalpeople.org/top-25-african-americans-who-pioneered-the-integration-of-pro-basketball/.

Swanson, R.A., & Spears, B. (1995). *History of sport and physical education in the United States (4th ed.).* Dubuque, IA: Brown & Benchmark.

Taylor, E. (2013, June 6). *Little known black history facts: E.B. Henderson.* Retrieved from http://blackamericweb.com/2013/06/13/little-known-black-history-fact-e-b-henderson/.

Thomas, R. (2002). *They cleared the lane: The NBA's black pioneers.* Lincoln: University of Nebraska Press.

Ungrady, D. (2013, September 6). E.B. Henderson brought basketball to the District. *The Washington Post.* Retrieved from https://www.washingtonpost.com/lifestyle/magazine/eb-henderson-brought-basketball-to-the-district/2013/09/06/5a09996c-05d9-11e3-9259-e2aafe5a5f84_story.html.

Wiggins, D.K. (1997). *Glory bound: Black athletes in a white America.* Syracuse, NY: Syracuse University Press.

Wiggins, D.K. (1999). Edwin Bancroft Henderson: Physical educator, civil rights activist, and chronicler of African American athletes. *Research Quarterly for Exercise and Sport, 70*(2), 91–112.

Wiggins, D.K., & Miller, P.B. (2003). *The unlevel playing field: A documentary history of the African American experience in sport.* Urbana: University of Illinois Press.

Zeigler, E.F. (Ed.). (1988). *History of physical education and sport (Rev. ed.).* Champaign, IL: Stipes.

Zingg, P.J. (1987). *Pride of the Palestra: Ninety years of Pennsylvania basketball.* Philadelphia: University of Pennsylvania Press.

Social Responsibility and Accountability

Dr. Harry Edwards and the Paradox
of the Black Male College Athlete

Fritz G. Polite *and*
Jeremai E. Santiago

"Believe in something, even if it means sacrificing everything."
—Colin Kaepernick, former NFL player
and social activist

This essay will attempt to examine constructs regarding social responsibility as it relates to black athletes, while expanding on the historical significance of Dr. Harry Edwards. The role of the black athlete within the black
community has taken a distinctive change of direction over the past several
decades. Black athletes historically have had highlighted presence within our
society. Dr. Edwards has always been interested in gaining a better under-
stating of the roles of the black athlete related to the role of social responsibility within institutions of higher learning. As the escalation and the
commercialization of college sports increases, the black athlete is being placed
in the center of the economic windfall, while not benefiting economically.
Many athletic departments are ill prepared to address many of the social and
economic issues that many of the recruited black athletes inhabit. Dr. Harry
Edwards and his historical impacts will also be addressed and expanded
upon. Dr. Edwards has been at the forefront of the black struggle in sport for
over 50 years. His work has been critical in the continued struggle and
informs us of current situations associated with social justice. This year
celebrates the 1968 classic "The Revolt of the Black Athlete." This was a

seminal piece that Edwards crafted in 1968 and it seems relevant in today's society.

With the rising emphasis in collegiate athletics, there is a need to investigate the attitudes of student athletes and administrators toward social responsibility and social accountability. College football (American) coaches make as much as nine million dollars a year in total salary and benefits (Atlantic, 2018). Coaches are many times the highest paid employee on campuses of institutions of higher learning. Although there has been a recent push for more civic involvement, service and student participation, it has been historically the responsibility of higher education to teach the principles of a democratic society (Boyer, 1990). There are several conceptual models within the business literature, the notion of strategic management, corporate responsibility, and stakeholder management have become critical links to business models (Katsoulakos & Katsoulakos, 2007). Corporate social responsibility (CSR) is an increasingly pervasive phenomenon on the European and North American economic and political landscape (Doh & Guay, 2006). CSR has been addressed from multiple angles (Babiak & Wolfe, 2006). Friedman (1962, 2002) offered the view that the main goal of corporations is profit and meeting the needs of shareholders. Others contend that organizations have to be more socially conscious to the impact of social contributions to general society in conjunction with profits (Lewis, 2003). The role of students and athletic administrators had been limited and research in this area is void of contributions within the field of sport management.

Theoretical Framework

The theoretical framework adopted for this essay will be based on Doh, Guay and Babiak & Wolfe's Corporate social responsibility framework. These frameworks addressed the importance of sport organizations utilizing their respective platforms for addressing social issues. Dr. Harry Edwards and his past and present work will also provide a platform for historical contexts.

It is important to examine paradigms regarding social responsibility and accountability as it relates to the constructs of race. It is imperative that the business literature aligned with social responsibility as well as accountability of student (athletes) and stakeholders be discussed as it relates to the role of the black athlete. The constructs of social responsibility and accountability are grounded within the corporate business literature. The formulation of this scholarship will assist in gaining a better understanding of the challenges of black students and the role that key stakeholders play, and their roles within institutions of higher learning. The number of hours required to compete at a high level, is in direct opposition with the rigors of academic success. This creates a paradox for many black athletes and their ability to receive a quality education.

Introduction

As the NCAA goes into its 109th year, the current model has been scrutinized via lawsuits, media, and by the academy. Policies, services, techniques, and programs of the NCAA have reached the point of questioning the true functions as it relates to academic missions of educational institutions. However, the current model is being challenged in terms of its ability to maintain legitimacy. Meyers and Rowan concluded that the organization must have social endorsement or, at minimum, acceptance from social actors that the organization is rational, reasonable, and valid. Organizations often strive to become institutionalized in order to cultivate or maintain legitimacy (DiMaggio & Powell, 1983; Zucker, 1987). Legitimacy allows for better access of resources necessary for the survival and growth of the company (Zimmerman & Zeitz, 2002). One initiative that firms are developing for organizational legitimacy is corporate social responsibility programs. In this context, this essay will probe the relationship that corporate social responsibility initiatives have with sport.

As the business of college sport continues to grow at an alarming rate, there is a need to remain concerned with Corporate Social Responsibility (CSR) in sport. In the United States, collegiate sport is a complex and thriving enterprise. This multi-billion-dollar enterprise has escalated itself as a major player within our educational systems. At the forefront of the business of college sports is the National Collegiate Athletic Association (NCAA) and its member colleges and universities. CSR has been reviewed extensively in the realm of professional sports, but scholarship related to CSR and its application in collegiate sports is lacking. For the plethora of good that the NCAA has done over the years, it is also an entity filled with negative paradoxes. Stakeholder theory serves as the foundation for discussing CSR. The purpose of expanding on these constructs is to discuss the concept of CSR and its relationship to college sports. This essay examines the organizational structure of the NCAA, its functionality, and the trappings of its fiscal operations. In addition, an analysis of the role CSR plays in the shaping of social responsibility and accountability as it relates to the CRT paradigm.

Collegiate sports are deeply engrained into the culture of our academic institutions. College sports are extremely popular on both regional and national scales, in many cases competing with professional organizations for prime broadcast and print coverage. The average university participates in approximately 20 different competitive sports. In total, during the 2015–16 academic year, nearly 460,000 student-athletes competed in the NCAA (Zgonc, 2014). The budgets of many National Collegiate Athletic Association (NCAA), Division 1 athletic departments, soar well beyond $100 million annually and some coaches are earning more than $7 million annually. College sports have grown from friendly competitions between rivals to a major conglomerate of major corporate sponsors, major media outlets and covering multiple modes of revenue streams.

One could make a strong case that sport in the United States has taken on a role deeply entrenched within the fiber of the society. The hiring of coaches in the National Football League (NFL) with salaries of multi million dollars per year as well as amateur coaches in the National Collegiate Athletics Association (NCAA) with salaries of 4–7 million dollars per year, speaks volumes to the value placed on the services of these coaches. From a professional perspective, these salaries are congruent with market value swings and demands. The challenges within the confines of the NCAA and its self-defined amateur status is that it operates within or in conjunction with academic institutions. With this rising emphasis in collegiate athletics, there is a need to investigate the constructs related to social responsibility and social accountability. Although there has been a recent push for more civic involvement, service and student participation, it has historically been the responsibility of higher education to teach the principles of a democratic society (Boyer, 1990).

The role of leadership, students, athletes and athletic administrators within the scope of CSR has been limited and research in this area is void of contributions within the field of sport business management, race and economic justice. The role of leadership in conjunction with the constructs of ethics and moral decision-making are crucial elements in addressing the quagmire of sport in our society. Many of the Greek Gods applied a descriptive approach to the examination of morals and the philosophical significance of studying it.

Over the years, the role of the black athlete within the realm of sport has taken on multiple discourses. More specifically, the role of the black athlete within the black community has taken a distinct change of direction over the past few decades. From the highlighted presence of Paul Robeson, Jim Brown, Muhammad Ali, and Jackie Robinson, the black athlete historically was an integral part of advancing the community, addressing political agendas, leading, mentoring, and outreach. Black athletes had a visible presence in, and were visibly highlighted by, leaders of the civil rights movement. This essay will explore the gamut of conflicts related to black athletes who grow up as prized members of predominantly black communities, and thus are recruited from these mostly black areas to play at and for predominantly white institutions. A review of the major areas of the works of Dr. Harry

Edwards will be analyzed and revisited by many of the leading scholars in the world in the areas of finance, law, social issues, human rights, race, and gender, to name a few. The reallocation of resources critical to the perseverance of black communities will be explored. Future implications and recommendations will be offered to offset the stated crisis.

Dr. Edwards is recognized as a pioneer in the study of the sociological implications of the black athlete. His organization of the Olympic Project for Human Rights (OPHR) in 1967 brought a major focus on the role sport played in American society. Dr. Edwards highlighted the unique duality of professional sport for black athletes: On the one hand, it served as a site for showcasing their athletic prowess; on the other hand, it served as a platform to vocalize and promote the political agenda of many black Americans during that time. The walls of higher learning did not shield the collegiate black athlete from the struggles and ramifications of the civil rights movement. Bringing public attention to this struggle was of grave importance to the research and scholarly activity of Edwards.

It is important to explore and analyze the historical impact of Edwards's research, as well as the implications for current black athletes in the continued quest for equality and the need for them to recognize the notion of social responsibility by using sport as a platform for social change. Several areas of his major works will be analyzed, and his experiences shared. He is a noted scholar, professor, athlete—and most important—one of the foremost leaders in the fight for equality and human rights.

Almost five decades ago, Edwards engaged in intense dialogue and discussion concerning the role of the black athlete. His objection to athletics being the major focus toward socioeconomic mobility for blacks created controversy and raised the ire of many, including local, state, and federal agencies. In *The Struggle, Must Continue* (1980), he wrote in the acknowledgments:

I must also acknowledge the aid of the Federal Bureau of Investigation, the Central Intelligence Agency, and the United States Military Intelligence for their partial compliance with the Freedom of Information Act in forwarding to my legal representative, Mr. Howard Moore, Jr., more than two thousand pages of highly censored documents, dispatches and other materials gathered by them while carrying out nearly ten years of surveillance of and sometimes participation in my personal, political and professional activities (ix acknowledgments).

This personifies the impact his work had at some of the highest levels of government. Many of the issues that were a part of his scholarly platform in the 1960s and 1970s are major current issues still being discussed today. Issues related to student athletes rights have surfaced at major institutions. From Temple, Missouri, Tennessee, The University of North Carolina (Chapel Hill), University of South Carolina, Ole Miss and UCLA. Ironically, some 50 years or more after the initial work of Edwards, discussions regarding human rights, graduation rates, participation rates, hiring practices, racism, and lack of mobility within the job market for blacks are all very evident, visible, and prevalent in our current society. Professor Edwards was the eminent scholar in the study of the black athlete and the impact of sport on and in society. Although he saw sport as a platform, he was clear that it was only that: a vehicle to place focus on other social, economic, and political issues. While black churches were being bombed, freedom riders were assaulted and murdered, and black males were drafted to fight in Vietnam, Edwards utilized sport as a vehicle to focus on and magnify many of the atrocities being raged against black people and other underrepresented peoples. He realized the impact and power of the media, and encouraged athletes to utilize it to gain exposure, and for highlighting important social and political issues. He also expounded on the stereotypes surrounding the notion of blacks being athletically superior and intellectually inferior to whites. He rationalizes this by conceptualizing: (1) long-standing, wildly held racism and ill-informed presumption of innate race linked black athletic superiority; (2) media propaganda portraying sports as a broadly accessible route to lack economic and social mobility; and (3) a lack of comparably visible high-prestige black role models beyond the sports arena (Miller and Wiggins, 2004). Edwards contended this psychosis was creating an intellectual deficit in other professional areas of society that are statistically more possible to attain than careers in sport.

Edwards further expanded on issues pertaining to education and its role in higher learning. He argued that education is paramount in changing social economic status and should play a primary role in defending and extending a democratic society. In most cases, education is not the main agenda being pursued by athletic departments as it relates to black athletes; however, the necessity for athletic departments (corporations) to recruit, train, and develop elite black athletes is crucial in continuing the major revenue-generating machines, most notably in football and basketball. Edwards further expands on the notion that many of these athletes came onto primarily white campuses ill prepared and lacking in academic skill levels. The lack of academic preparation along with the demands on students time away from the classrooms led to many of the current proposed athletic reforms.

Dr. Harry Edwards's contributions to the intellectual manipulation and stimulation of the focus of the role of the black athlete, human rights, the role of the media, and the commercialization of amateur sport, contributed significantly to the study of many areas of academia. Whether discussing law, economics, media, exploitation, commercialization, gender, or a multitude of other disciplines, his work touched on almost all areas. Never before—and possibly never again—will there be a time and place for a scholar to impact the infusion of the thought process related to the role of the black athlete. The time has come to stand up and recognize one of the most prolific scholars of our time.

Too often sport is taken for granted as being merely a source of entertainment. However, sport has been classified as a microcosm of the larger society and as a barometer for racial progress. Though these views illustrate the binary role sport can occupy in American culture, they also speak to the power of sport in either reflecting and reinforcing dominant ideologies, or serving as a form of resistance to these dominant ways of thinking. It is the latter purpose we seek to examine in this text.

The history of sport in the United States as a cultural practice and a corporate entity has documented occurrences of being a means of resisting dominant racial ideologies that have persisted in this country for centuries. From Jack Johnson's epic reign as the first black heavyweight boxing champion against the notions of white supremacy and black inferiority, to Jackie Robinson's re-integration of Major League Baseball (MLB), to Doug Williams's National Football League (NFL) Super Bowl XXII performance that tackled the stereotype of the intellectually inferior black athlete, we can see where sport has been a phenomenon that speaks to broader social issues.

Critical to the sport studies literature is a presentation of how sport has played a role in advancing social change in the United States, as well as globally. With this current volume, we seek to examine how sport has served as a platform for social activism in promoting racial progress. It was the civil rights movement and the construct of Black Power that birthed many foot soldiers who emerged as generals for social change and activism. Dr. Harry Edwards emerged as one of those generals in the fight for social justice. As the architect for the Olympic Project for Human Rights, Dr. Edwards's activism targeted racial apartheid in the United States and in South Africa, as well as the racial injustices occurring in the sport industry. His scholarship, *The Revolt of the Black Athlete, Black Student, The Struggle That Must Be, and Sociology of Sport,* were seminal pieces for scholars interested in race, sport, and the discipline of sport sociology. More than 40 years later, many of Dr. Edwards's past findings relating to his scholarship are current, pertinent, and relevant. The complicities of academic disenfranchisement, commercialization of athletics, racism, discrimination, and the dual system of business capitalism dominating the notion of education were rigorous aspects of his works.

Edwards has proven to be instrumental in providing a framework for examining the significance of sport in promoting social change. No one can question the mammoth contributions of Dr. Harry Edwards as a social activist, scholar, and public servant over the span of three decades. Prior to Dr. Edwards, minimal scholarly attention had been paid to the role of the black athlete on predominantly white campuses or universities. Furthermore, minimal perspectives had been investigated to attempt to understand the invisibility of blacks in power positions within sport. Patterns of exploitation, lack of positive assimilation, and the overvaluing of participation—while devaluing education—were critical points of Edwards's philosophy.

The notion of social responsibility and accountability in the face of a multi-billion-dollar enterprise is to be challenged. While representing 2.8 percent of the general student body, black men constitute 58 percent of football and basketball participants. Along with the extremely low graduation rates, low job placements and physical injuries, and the social responsibility of this platform, this should be grounds for Socratic questioning and confrontation.

Contemporary and Historical Examples of Social Activism

Historically, specifically, in the late 1960s there were numerous accounts of social activism from athletes. Displaying social activism in that time came from different races and genders. The athletes that were exhibiting acts of social activism had intentional objectives of triggering social change within their communities and society.

Examples of athletes involved social activism include, Katherine Switzer running in the Boston marathon in 1967, Muhammad Ali protesting and avoiding the American military draft in 1967, and the most famous social statement, Black athletes Tommie Smith and John Carlos demonstrating the Black Power salute. However, particularly, as it relates to Black male's athletes, Muhammad Ali was one of the most socially conscious athletes during his era. Ali was a great supporter and addressed issues of civil rights for Black Americans. Additionally, Ali was a staunch opponent against the Vietnam War. Ali's issues with the Vietnam War were directly related to killing brown people of Vietnam while black and brown people were being killed in United States. Ali stood firm in what he believed, and he was willing to be jailed for what he believed in.

At the end of the decade Olympic athletes Tommie Smith and John Carlos earned gold and bronze medals at the 1968 Olympic Games in the 200-meter race. While on the podium, both Smith and Carlos wore black gloves and raised their fists during the American National anthem. This act from Smith and Carlos has been coined the "black power salute." The gesture was in support for people fighting for human rights across the world. The athletes received a large amount of backlash because of their stance against unequal human rights across the global. After being expelled from the Mexico City

Olympics, Smith and Carlos including their families received death threats for the actions displayed at Olympic games.

In the late 1960s a group of nine black athletes' at Syracuse University were experiencing the hatred of racism. They were segregated from their team when traveling by being forced to stay in separate hotels and were specifically told that they were not to date white students. Several schools refused to play Syracuse because they had black players. They were also not allowed to take certain course as well as major in certain fields of study. These nine students were labeled the Syracuse 8 and demanded that the university start a black studies program as well as hire a black assistant coach. The players boycotted practice and were eventually kicked off of the team. Several of the students were NFL prospects but were never selected by NFL teams. In 2006 Syracuse University issued an apology and received the Chancellors Medal (Universities highest honor) and their letterman's jackets.

Fast-forward to the 1990s you will discover that Colin Kaepernick was not the first Black athlete to refuse to stand during the American national anthem. In 1996, NBA player Mahmoud Abdul-Rauf member of the Denver Nuggets exercised his constitutional right and decided not to stand for the national anthem. In an interview by Ed Moore of the *Daily Press* quoted Abdul-Rauf saying Islam taught him that he could not stand or respect the American flag because it represents oppression and tyranny.

Now in most recent history in America where there is frequent slaughtering of Black males across the United States of America. In 2012, the then 17-year-old Trayvon Martin was killed by George Zimmerman. Current, NBA superstar LeBron James tweeted a picture of himself and Miami Heat teammates wearing hoodies to bring awareness to Black males being stereotyped for what they wear but most importantly to fight for justice for the spilling of innocent Black blood.

Derrick Rose of the New York Knicks brought light to the killing of Eric Garner. Rose wore a shirt during warm-ups that stated, "I can't breathe." Those words are the some of the last words that Eric Garner said has he was being chocked by a police officer in Staten Island, New York. Rose expressed in an interview that he does not want he son growing up being afraid of police and that this unfortunate killing could have been him or anyone from his family. In August of 2014 in Ferguson, Missouri, Michael Brown was shot and killed by a local law enforcement officer. Protesting ensued in Ferguson and all throughout the country. Players from the St. Louis Rams organization decided to participate in the protesting as well. They demonstrated their solidarity with the community while entering a game with their hand raised. This act represented the "hands up, don't shoot."

Colin Kaepernick has started a major debate with his social protest against the United States national anthem. At the genesis of his protest Kapernick sat during the playing of *The Star-Spangled Banner* and after the game Kaepernick gave a rationale of why he decided to sit during the national anthem. Kaepernick explained that he could not express pride in a flag that have oppressed black and other peoples of color. After major backlash Colin Kaepernick did decide to switch from sitting to kneeling to show respect for United Stated military veterans and also current military members serving. Regardless if Colin Kaepernick was right or wrong in his actions to sit/kneel during the national anthem, however, I contend that Kaepernick accomplished his goal of using his sport platform to bring awareness to the oppression and more specifically the senseless killings of Black Americans and other peoples of color. Furthermore, Kapernick is advocating for and fighting against the injustices that are committed against communities of color. Colin Kapernick social activism work has had an impact on his career has a professional athlete and he also has received death threats.

In college athletics, there have also been athletes involved in social activism. More recently, demonstrations have occurred at the University of Missouri with Black male athletes uniting with other black students to address issues of marginalization toward students of color. Black male athletes who were members of the University of Missouri football team decided not to participate in any football related activities until University system president resigned or relived of duties. This was in response to the inactions of the administration to address and acknowledge the breadth of racial issues that occurred on campus. White students scattered white cotton balls outside the Black Culture Center, along with the police shooting of an unarmed black teenager sparked multiple protests across the campus. This particular case has been interesting because these Black athletes understood the power they held. First, they understood if they did not play Missouri did not have the best chance to win but most importantly these players not playing would harm the financial structure of the team, athletic department, the university, and university system. Players boycotting ultimately would mean the team would have to forfeit and that would have cost the university a significant amount of money. It is not surprising that Tim Wolfe stepped down a few days after the players mentioned they would boycott football related activities. It appeared the players understood the power that they wielded, and the player also understood how to leverage that power to force a decision (resignation of Wolfe) that they strongly believed should have happened because of Wolfe's disregard to address issues of campus racism. Many have supported the students and this display of social activism has impacted many from the university, to the university system, athletic department, to local and state government. However, there was a counterattack on players. Some Black male athletes were threatened with scholarships being revoked for participating in the protest. This that type of behavior further shows a level of racism that the players had to endure. The rhetoric of pulling scholarships showed that some people actually believed that these Black males should not participate in protest, because they were not brought to University of Missouri to protest; they were brought to play football. Now since they are not entertaining on the football field, their scholarships should be rescinded. That type of behavior is dangerous and that is why this social activism was important.

Additionally, at the University of Wisconsin Nigel Hayes a basketball player attended ESPN's College GameDay with a sign that read "broke college athlete, anything helps." The sign also indicated an account of where people could send money. This case was a classic case of a college athlete bringing awareness of the unethical nature of the collegiate athletic system. Nigel Hayes protest showed how he cannot profit from his athletic skills, but he has to spend a significant amount of time preparing for the sport while hundreds of thousands or people come to see him and his teammates play. While others make millions upon billions of dollars off of his work. Dr. Billy Hawkins' addressed this paradigm in his seminal work *The New Plantation: Black Athletes, College Sport, and Predominately White NCAA Institutions.* In the book Hawkins provides a through description of capital that predominately white institutions build off the athletic work of Black male athletes. The illustration of Hawkins' work is exactly what Nigel Hayes was protesting his struggles of being a broke college student while the institution he played for and the NCAA makes money off his body of work on the basketball court. Like many other cases of Black athlete involved in social activism Hayes did receive backlash.

Each of these social activism moments, in both professional sports and collegiate athletics, there were significant contributions and examples of athletes using their platforms to speak out about and against social injustices that were happening in the United States but, also around the world. Many of these cases has not seen social change overtime the impact has caused awareness, discussions, and some social change. Most importantly these athletes were conscious of their platforms and use those platforms to address issues of injustices that they experience but of the injustices that others experienced equally. As new and upcoming athletes are entering professional athletics and high-level college programs, social activism remains an imperative for these athletes. From the work that they do in social activism to ensure justice, liberty, and domestic tranquility will be the only way that the United States and the world as a whole will witness positive social change.

In January 2017, Jim Brown, Kareem Abdul Jabbar, Takeo Spikes, Chris Webber, Anquan Boldin and Tommy Smith gathered to launch the Institute for the Study of Sport, Society and Social Change at San Jose State University. Although some conditions have improved for black athletes, racial tensions and pleas for equality prompt many still unanswered questions. The power and influence athletes possess should be utilized to raise the consciousness of those that populate the stadiums, arenas, tracks and other popular sporting events. Bill Russell, Jim Brown and Jackie Robinson all used the platform of sports to address racial issues in sport. This may not be the case for all black athletes, but the role of activism is ripe for drawing attention to many of the social ills plaguing our country.

> "Perhaps the most critically important lesson that I have learned over my half century of political struggle is that activism divorced from strategic intellectual analysis is conducive to nothing so much as contradiction and chaos."
> —Harry Edwards, Ph.D.

REFERENCES

Babiak, K & Wolfe, R. (2006). More than just a game? Corporate Social Responsibility and Super Bowl XL. *Sport Marketing Quarterly*, 15–4, 214–222.

Boyer, E.L. (1990). *Scholarship reconsidered: Priorities of the professorate.* Princeton, NJ: Carnegie Foundation for the Advancement of Teaching.

Doh, J.P., & Guay, T.R. (2006) Corporate Social Responsibility, Public Policy, and NGO Activism in Europe and the United States: An Institutional-Stakeholder Perspective. *Journal of Management Studies* 43:1, 47–71. January 2006.

Friedman, M. (1962). *Capitalism and Freedom*. Chicago: University of Chicago Press.

_____. (2002). *Capitalism and Freedom* (40th Anniversary ed). Chicago: University of Chicago Press.

Katsoulakos, T., Katsoulacos, Y. (2007). Strategic management, corporate responsibility and stakeholder management. *Corporate Governance*. 7–4, 355–369.

Lewis, S. (2003). Reputation and corporate responsibility. *Journal of Communications Management*, 7(4), 356–365.

African American Sport Activism and Broader Social Movements

JOSEPH N. COOPER, MICHAEL MALLERY, JR.,
and CHARLES D.T. MACAULAY

Introduction

African Americans[1] fulfill a distinct place within the history of sports in the United States (U.S.). Their athletic success at the local, state, regional, national, and international levels have been well documented (Wiggins & Miller, 2003). When names such as Jack Johnson, Jesse Owens, Bo Jackson, Orenthal James (O.J.) Simpson, Michael Jordan, Tiger Woods, Alice Coachman, Venus Williams, and Serena Williams are referenced, commonplace stereotypes purport that these gifted athletes were born with unique abilities that enabled them to excel in their respective sports. The normalization of these stereotypes reflect both the public's amazement with African American prowess in sport as well as deeply entrenched racist beliefs regarding human capabilities (Hoberman, 1997). Despite facing widespread discrimination and marginalization, African American athletes have excelled at unprecedented heights in nearly every sport, which coincided with Black progress in U.S. society beyond sport in areas such as education, law, business, science, politics, music, and art (Harris, 2000; Stewart, 1996). Consequently, a majority of research and popular discourse on African American athletes has focused on their sport-related accolades.

Beyond medals, championships, and records within sporting spaces, African American athletes have also served as pivotal agents of activism, advocacy, and social change (Cooper, Macaulay, & Rodriguez, 2017; Edwards, 2016). Despite their engagement in social justice efforts since the mid–1800s, scholarly contributions related to African American athlete activism has focused on the Civil Rights era and notable athlete activists such as Muhammad Ali, Tommie Smith, John Carlos, Jim Brown, Kareem Abdul-Jabbar (formerly Lew Alcindor), and Bill Russell to name a few. However, Colin Kaepernick's activist act of taking a knee during the 2016–2017 National Football League (NFL) season has reignited a public conversation and shifted attention towards the historic role African American athletes have fulfilled in the broader Black struggle in the U.S. for human rights and justice.

The purpose and meaning associated with African American participation in sport has historically been different based along racial lines. For White organizers and spectators, the exclusion and limited participation of African Americans in sport was intended to serve as reinforcement of the dominant ideology that Whites were innately superior to Blacks mentally, physically, intellectually, and morally (Wiggins & Miller, 2003). In contrast for Blacks, sports served as an opportunity to demonstrate their humanity, a signifier of racial uplift, cultural empowerment, and upward mobility (Cooper, Cavil, & Cheeks, 2014; Wiggins, 2000). From Tom Molineaux versus Tom Cribb in 1810 to Jack Johnson versus Jim "The Great White Hope" Jeffries in 1910 to Joe "The Brown Bomber" Louis versus Max "The Aryan" Schmeling in 1936 and 1938 to Jesse Owens versus athletes of European descent (namely German athletes from Adolf Hitler's Nazi Germany regime) in the 1936 Olympics in Berlin, Germany, popular sporting events from early 19th century through the modern day 21st century have been touted as sites to prove racial superiority (Rhoden, 2006; Stewart, 1996; Wiggins & Miller, 2003). When Black athletes emerged victorious over their opponents much to the chagrin of the predominantly White audiences, the prevailing racial order was disrupted. Black communities throughout the U.S. celebrated as the victories symbolized collective hope for freedom and equality in a society that had created conditions that suppressed their human dignity and progress as a race.

As such, sport as a social institution has been and remains intertwined with societal occurrences and arrangements related to power and privilege (Sage, 1998). Similar to the plight of African Americans in the U.S. society more broadly, Edwards (2016) posited that African Americans involved in sport utilized this distinct platform to gain legitimacy, acquire political access and positional diversity, demand dignity and respect, and secure and transfer power via economic and technological capital. In other words, the meaning and power of sport for African Americans transcended the wins and losses within the sport and connected to broader social aims of the race (Cooper et al., 2017; Wiggins & Miller, 2003). The purpose of this essay is provide a socio-historical analysis of the parallels between broader Black social movements in the U.S. and African American sport activism.

African American Sport Activism

Traditionally activism has been viewed within a limited scope focusing on individual athletes and their respective protests. Acknowledging the problematic nature of viewing activism within a myopic lens, Cooper et al. (2017) proposed a typology of African American sport activism. African American sport activism differs from previous conceptions of athlete activism in that the former "encompasses a broader range of actions, individuals, and groups, including sport scholar activists, sport organizations/institutions, and entrepreneurs" (Cooper et al., 2017, p. 16). The African American sport activism typology includes five categories: (a) *symbolic*, (b) *scholarly*, (c) *grassroots*, (d) *sports-based*, and (e) *economic*. According to the authors, activism is defined as

> engagement in intentional actions that challenge a clearly defined opposition and disrupt hegemonic systems perpetuating oppression, injustice, and inequity while simultaneously promoting empowerment among those historically oppressed, fairness/equity, human dignity, and demands for a shift in power relations in concert with broader social justice movements [Cooper et al., 2017, p. 4–5].

Key components of activism include clear oppositionist(s), concrete disruption and challenging (as opposed to reinforcing) of hegemonic structures, norms, and mental processes, specific goals and objectives (often times in the form of demands) to assess progress, and connection to broader social justice movements. All of African American sport activism incorporates a cultural theory approach whereby characteristics such as emotions, collective identities, and subcultures are integral in guiding social movements and often leaders use framing techniques to construct schemata of understanding to garner support from individuals who may not have a personal attachment to the movement (Davis-Delano & Crosset, 2008).

Symbolic activism involves "deliberate actions exhibited by athletes designed to draw attention to social injustices and inspire positive change in political, educational, economic, and social sectors" (Cooper et al., 2017, p. 16). An example of symbolic activism is the famous Black power salutes by Tommie Smith and John Carlos at the 1968 Olympics in Mexico City, Mexico to draw international attention to the injustices against African Americans and all poor people in the U.S. *Scholarly activism* refers to "the transmission of ideas by individuals and groups that enhance a person's understanding of oppressive systems such as sport and mechanisms through which they can be deconstructed" (Cooper et al., 2017, p. 18–19). The foremost scholar-activist of the 20th century is Dr. Harry Edwards who published texts such as *The Revolt of the Black Athlete* (1969), *Sociology of Sport* (1973), *The Struggle That Must Be: An Autobiography* (1980), which challenged dominant ideologies embedded with sporting structures and disrupted educational norms related to critical scholarship.

Grassroots activism is defined as "counter-hegemonic actions performed at the meso- and micro-level by activists, including individual relationships, community engagement, and statewide and association-wide efforts both within and beyond sport" (Cooper et al., 2017, p. 20). An example of grassroots activism is Colin Kaepernick's *Know Your Rights Camp*, which focuses on educating and empowering youth in disadvantaged neighborhoods regarding their legal rights and strategies they can activate to protect themselves from police brutality and other forms of abuse. *Sport-based activism* refers to "specific actions taken by athletes to alter and mitigate the hegemonic nature of structural arrangements, rules/policies/bylaws, and practices through sport organizations that serve to reinforce subordination, marginalization, and exploitation of certain groups" (Cooper et al., 2017, p. 22). Venus Williams's successful lobbying of the Wimbledon Tennis Association (WTA) for equal prize money for women (compared to their men counterparts) in 2007 is an example of *sports-based activism*. Related to sports-based activism, *mobilization/organizational activism* is reflected with the Olympic Project for Human Rights (OPHR) created in 1967 by Dr. Harry Edwards and the more recent College Athletes Players Association (CAPA) founded in 2014 by Ramogi Huma (Cooper et al., 2017).

Moreover, *economic activism* involves "actions by individuals and/or groups connected to sport who intentionally create businesses in historically disadvantaged communities with a keen focus on stimulating economic and social empowerment, stability, and mobility" (Cooper et al., 2017, p. 24). The Negro baseball leagues of the 1920s-1960s were examples of *economic activism* whereby Black consumption and financial resources were invested into Black owned, managed, and operated businesses as well as the African American community at large (Lomax, 2003, 2011). In 1960, Jim Brown's New Industrial Economic Union (NIEU) is another example of *economic activism* where the collective fiscal resources of African American professional athletes was channeled towards same race owned businesses (Brown & Delsohn, 1989). Economic activism connects with what Davis-Delano and Crosset (2008) describe as resource mobilization theory, which includes the utilization of resources possessed or acquired by groups such as money, solidarity, leadership, labor, time, knowledge, skills, and established organizations. In addition to the aforementioned, forms of activism, the authors noted how pioneering, advocacy, and agency can constitute activist acts under certain conditions, but not inherently. Examples of each type of activism include: (a) Jack Johnson becoming the first Black heavyweight boxing champion in 1908 (*pioneering activism*), (b) the famous "Ali Summit" on June 13, 1967, in Cleveland, Ohio, with Muhammad Ali, Jim Brown, Bill Russell, Kareem Abdul-Jabbar (formerly Lew Alcindor), John Wooten, Jim Shorter, Willie Davis, Curtis McClinton, Sid Williams, Bobby Mitchell, Walter Beach, and Carl Stokes to express support for Ali's decision to refuse his draft request to fight in the Vietnam War (*advocacy activism*), and (c) the hairstyle of large afros donned by African Americans including activists during the 1960s and 1970s to embrace Afrocentric features in a society that privileged White Anglo Saxon phenotypical traits (*agentic and cultural activism*) (Cooper et al., 2017; George, 1992; Wiggins & Miller, 2003; Wiggins, 2000).

Building on this framework, additional categories of African American sport activism are presented: (f) *media*, (g) *political*, (h) *legal*, (i) *music and art*, and (j) *military*. The expansion of the typology facilitates as more nuanced understanding of distinct ways (albeit often overlapping) by which individuals and groups leverage their activist agendas to cultivate positive social change. *Media activism* refers to the use of newspapers, journals, television, radio, and/or Internet (i.e., social media) to generate awareness and action related to social justice aims. During the early 1900s, leading Black sport historians such as E.B. Henderson and Sol White documented the historic accomplishments of African American athletes and sport organizations in an effort challenge the dominant ideology that position them as inferior to Whites. Frank "Fay" Young, a renowned journalist, wrote for *The Chicago Defender* and stimulated national awareness about and interest in the prowess of Black sports including the Negro Leagues and historically Black colleges and universities (HBCU) athletics (Corbett & Stills, 2007)). *Social media activism* refers to the use of the Internet to galvanize support for and involvement in human and civil rights efforts. In 2012, LeBron James and his Miami Heat teammates initiated the #WeAreTrayvonMartin campaign to express their support for stronger protections under the law for Blacks in the U.S., which reached a global audience of followers that exceeded 38 million. In 2016, following Colin Kaepernick's symbolic activism against injustice in the U.S., the #TakeAKnee campaign was created (Cooper et al., 2017).

Political activism involves the direct challenging of oppressive ideologies, structures, and systems connected to controlling governments and related entities. This form of activism is related to political process theory, which involves the leveraging of social structures to create opportunities and remove constraints for social movements (Sage, 1999). This tenet focuses on the larger political environment a social movement is operating and recognizes the influence of other political actors, public opinion, media, and government (Davis-Delano & Crosset, 2008). Examples of political activism exhibited by African American athletes include Paul Robeson in the 1920s, Muhammad Ali in the 1960s, and Mahmoud Abdul-Rauf (formerly Chris Jackson) in the 1990s with their explicit resistance against the U.S. government's adoption of policies rooted in White systemic racism, militarism, and exploitative capitalism, which significantly impacts Blacks, economically disadvantaged, and religious groups deemed threats to the hegemonic social order (i.e., Muslims). *Legal activism* refers to the use of the judicial and legal systems to challenge unjust laws, policies, and/or practices (i.e., enforcements) in the pursuit of justice and equitable treatment. In 1969, Curt Flood's lawsuit against MLB reflected an example of sports-based legal activism in an effort to challenge and abolish the reserve clause, which restricted players' rights (*Flood v. Kuhn, 407 U.S. 258* [1972]). In 1971, Muhammad Ali challenged the U.S. government by appealing his 1967 draft evasion conviction when he declined to join the military for the Vietnam War (*Clay v. United States, 403 U.S. 698*) (Zirin, 2009). In 2009, former college basketball player star Ed O'Bannon spearheaded a class action lawsuit against the National Collegiate Athletic Association (NCAA) and Electronic Arts Sports (EA Sports) in an effort to secure rights for current and former college athletes regarding their images and likeness and challenge anti-trust law protections for the NCAA (*O'Bannon v. Nat. Collegiate Athletic Association, 7 F. Supp. 3d 955* [N.D. Cal. 2014]). More recently, standout athletes such as Anquan Boldin and Malcolm Jenkins of the NFL and Maya Moore of the Women's National Basketball Association (WNBA) have leveraged their respective platforms to advocate for criminal justice reform on behalf of Blacks who have experienced unjust sentencing and penalization under current laws (Dodson, 2017; Moore, Dupree, & Krinsky, 2017).

Music and art activism refers to music and arts being used as tools of disruption to heightened consciousness, critical thought, and action towards social justice issues. Paul Robeson utilized his acting and musical skills during the early 20th century to drawn attention to widespread injustices in the U.S. (Robeson, 1998). Ernie Barnes, a renowned painter and former professional football player, used his artistry to depict compelling stories related to race relations in and around sport during the Civil Rights era (i.e., The Beauty of the Ghetto Exhibition) (Barnes, 2017). *Military activism* refers to the use of arm forces and related strategies to challenge oppressive systems within and across specific societies. Although, this form of activism is less common among African American athletes, Muhammad Ali's explicit support of the Black Power movement and the Nation of Islam (which included militaristic aims), is an example of military activism (Edwards, 1969).

Convergent Activism Within and Beyond Sport

The strength and effectiveness of any social movement is rooted in its collectivism. Throughout history, African Americans within and beyond sport have exercised their agencies to achieve positive gains for the race. Each era since African Americans have been inhabiting U.S. soil has required specific strategies and tactics in order to redress the prevailing challenges of systemic racism. Within this section, the authors will outline convergent activist actions demonstrated by both African Americans within and associated with sport and in the broader U.S. to underscore the interconnectedness of each respective social movement.

Ante-Bellum Period (Early 1800s–1860s)

During the Ante-Bellum period (early 1800s–1860s), convergent activist actions that contributed to racial uplift within and beyond sport included mobilization/organizational (both grassroots and sports-based) and pioneering activism. Mobilization/organizational activism was exhibited in the broader African American social movement. Despite being confronted with inhumane circumstances, Blacks in the U.S. engaged in a myriad of resistance acts in order to persevere their humanity and secure freedom for their race. Throughout the 19th century, several Blacks who were enslaved organized and carried out revolts against oppressive Whites. Building on the momentum gained from the successful Haitian revolution led by Toussaint l'Ouverture from 1791 to 1804, African Americans in the U.S. from Florida to New York utilized their collective resources to challenge their oppressors via strategic revolts. The most notable revolt on U.S. soil was initiated in 1831 in Southampton, Virginia, by Nat Turner where he and his troops engaged in force to threaten the stronghold of White supremacy and chattel slavery (Stewart, 1996). Later in 1849, Harriet Tubman utilized the famous Underground Railroad to lead over 300 Blacks who were enslaved into freedom (Smith, 1994). From 1830 to 1855, Black abolitionists organized various resistance efforts such as the National Negro Conventions to discuss and strategize over political issues of the day affecting African Americans throughout Northern abolitionist and Southern slave states (Stewart, 1996). Segregated living conditions and collective goals for racial progress were integral leverage points for organizing group resistance and empowerment efforts. In sports, Black baseball was established in 1867 with the Championship of the Colored Clubs (Brooklyn Uniques versus Excelsiors of Philadelphia) (Lomax, 2003). The success of barnstorming Black baseball teams such as the Philadelphia Pythons in the late 1800s served as activism against the dominant racial order that deemed Blacks inferior physically and intellectually, which were both aspects valued in America's pastime (Lomax, 2003). The aforementioned success of these teams would later lead to the creation of the Negro Leagues in the early 1900s and eventually the success of future baseball pioneers such as Jackie Robinson and Frank Robinson.

Regarding pioneering activism, in 1827, John Russworm and Samuel Cornish launched the first African American newspaper, *Freedom's Journal*, to provide a platform to document first-hand narratives of injustices against the race (Fortenberry 1974). Although this journal only lasted for two years, it was the first African American medium created to combat the prevailing negative stereotypes of free and enslaved African people. Both mobilization/ organizational activism and pioneering activism was reflected in the establishment of HBCUs (e.g., The African Institute [now Cheyney University] in 1852, Ashmun Institute [now Lincoln University in 1854], and Wilberforce University in 1856), which benefited the broader Black community (Smith, 1994). Similarly in the sporting realm, pioneers such as Tom Molineaux who defeated Tom Cribb the first time (after forty-four rounds) in 1810 in Sussex, England disrupted the notion of White physical superiority (Stewart, 1996; Wiggins & Miller, 2003). Collectively, the resistance efforts of Blacks during this era combined with growing support for the abolishment movement led to the eventual passage of the *Emancipation Proclamation in 1865* and passage of the Thirteenth Amendment (abolition of legalized enslavement of African Americans), *Civil Rights Act of 1866* (citizenship rights for African Americans with the exception of voting), the *Reconstruction Act of 1867* (stricter requirements on Confederate states for reentry into the Union related to Black voting rights), Fourteenth Amendment (equal protection under the law for African Americans), and Fifteenth Amendment (limited voting rights act due to previously established states' rights over suffrage) (Hine et al., 2006; Stewart, 1996). Thus, the Ante-Bellum era in terms of Black resistance was marked by organized revolts and strategic partnerships to procure safety, freedom, and upward mobility from chattel slavery conditions.

Black Liberation Through Reconstruction (1860s–1920s)

Following the Ante-Bellum period, the Black Liberation movement through Reconstruction reflected a progressive agenda whereby Blacks born post–1865 were living in a U.S. society where landmark legislations afforded them more rights than their predecessors, albeit still largely limited due to Black Codes and Jim Crow practices. During this era, political, mobilization/ organizational, economic, educational, and pioneering activism manifested within and beyond sport were among the most salient forms of disruption. The creation of the National Association of Colored Women (NACW) in 1896, National Association for the Advancement of Colored People (NAACP) in 1909, National Urban League (NUL) in 1910, Universal Negro Improvement Association and African Communities League (UNIA-ACL) in 1914, and the Association for the Study of Negro Life and History along with the increased representation of Blacks in political offices throughout the South during the Reconstruction era signified political activism confronting Jim Crow realities (Smith, 1994). Related to sport, political and mobilization/organizational activism were reflected in the creation of numerous HBCU athletic conferences starting in 1906 with the Interscholastic Athletic Association of the Middle Atlantic State (ISSA) and four additional conferences established between 1910 and 1920 (Cooper et al., 2014). Despite being exiled from the mainstream White-controlled NCAA formed in 1906, HBCUs created their own athletic spaces and served as a political and mobilized resistance against White racist sporting structures.

In addition to political mobilization, African Americans were also coalescing to form economic enclaves (read: economic activism) under the auspices of Jim Crow segregation. Throughout the U.S. in urban metropolises as well as other areas where there was a concentration of employed and mobilized Blacks, cooperative economics was practiced (i.e., The Great Migration) (Hine et al., 2006). For example, during the early 1900s, Black Wall Street in Tulsa, Oklahoma, was thriving prior to a domestic terrorist attack from White supremacists in 1921 (Smith, 1994). In 1886, the National Colored Farmers' Alliance was formed in Houston County, Texas, in response to being excluded from the White Farmers alliance. The organization represented an important phase of agrarian protest and in its height of existence in 1891 boasted membership of 1.2 million Black farmers (Holmes, 1975). Similarly, Black baseball teams were thriving in northern and Midwestern urban spaces in Philadelphia, New York, New Jersey, Chicago, Detroit, and St. Louis prior to the formal creation of the Negro Leagues in the 1920s as documented in Sol White's seminal text, *The History of Colored Baseball*, published in 1907 (Lomax, 2003). Moreover, pioneering activism was also disrupting the social order of the time. Edwards (2016) surmised the first wave of Black athlete activism occurred during the turn of the 20th century and focused on gaining legitimacy. The success of pioneers such as John "Bud" Fowler in 1878 (first African American to participate in White professional baseball), Moses Fleetwood Walker (first African American to participate in college baseball at a historically White institution [HWI]), and Marshall "Major" Taylor excelled internationally in the cycling field between 1896 and 1901 served as indicators of Black athlete activism in an era where the notion of White physical superiority supported by pseudoscientific assertions associated with Social Darwinism was ubiquitous (Hoberman, 1997; Edwards, 2016; Rhoden, 2006; Stewart, 1994).

Harlem Renaissance (1920s–1930s)

In the Harlem Renaissance era, music and art activism, scholarly activism, media activism, and economic activism were primary tools of disruption and empowerment. The Harlem Renaissance within itself was a cultural awakening in which black intellectuals, artists, musicians, and writers became unapologetic about expressing their cultural identity in a myriad of ways. In a society where racist practices were continuing to lead to a lack of economic opportunities for blacks, the Harlem Renaissance provided economic uplift and new jobs for African Americans through art, music and poetry. This era was indeed the "Syncronization of the literary and social revolt in the United States" which brought about the mood necessary for the cultural Renaissance (Hudlin, 2004, p. 8). These forms of expression also demonstrated racial and political pride to the White majority power structure. These talented artists showcased their skills in Harlem, New York, which was recognized as the epicenter of Black progressiveness. Legendary musicians such as Billie Holiday, Louis Armstrong, Duke Ellington, and Ella Fitzgerald to name a few all performed at the famous Apollo Theatre in Harlem, New York. In the arts, riveting authors and poets such as Zora Neale Hurston, Lois Mailou Jones, Langston Hughes, Aaron Douglas, and Jacob Lawrence captivated readers with their evocative texts that carried moral and racially empowering undertones. Eager to gain a political voice in the 1920s due to widespread racial hatred, sparked people like Alain Locke, an African American writer, to coin the term "New Negro," which highlighted a spur of young black artists (Hudlin, 2004). In concert with these efforts, Black athletes such as Paul Robeson utilized his platform as an international theater star to draw attention to the plight of African Americans. In several of his performances, he would sing African American spirituals and subsequently express his critical political views of U.S. capitalism and racism (Robeson, 1998; Stewart, 1996).

Moreover, the intellectual contributions of Marcus Mosiah Garvey, William Edward Burghardt (W.E.B.) DuBois, Booker Taliaferro (T.) Washington, James Weldon Johnson, Carter Godwin (G.) Woodson, and Ida B. Wells-Barnett among many others coincided with the growth of African American sports history archived by individuals such as E.B. Henderson, Sol White, and Frank "Fay" Young (Wiggins & Miller, 2003). In 1939, E.B. Henderson published *The Negro Sports*, which was a historic comprehensive archive of African American sport participation (Wiggins & Miller, 2003). Popular media outlets such as *The Crisis*, *The Guardian*, *The Chicago Defender*, and *The Messenger* were filled with contributions from intellectuals such as within and beyond sport (Lomax, 2003, 2014). Related to economic activism, A. Phillip Randolph formed the Brotherhood of Sleeping Car Porters in 1925 to unionize for improved labor conditions for Black railroad employees (Stewart, 1996). Within sports, in 1920, the National Negro League (NNL) was formed by Andrew "Rube" Foster and its first world series, coined as the "Colored World Series," with the Eastern Colored League (ECL) was held in 1924 (Kansas City Monarchs defeated the Hilldale Athletic Club [AC]) (Lomax, 2003). Collectively, the Harlem Renaissance represented a period of Black progressiveness and respectability in the face of separate and unjust conditions. These Black organizations and individuals sought to use their respective platforms (music, art, education, social, and political) to exemplify excellence and resistance against prevailing White norms that continually suppressed their humanity.

Black Integration (1930s–1960s)

Throughout the Black Integration movement, mobilization activism, political activism, and sports-based activism were common within the broader Black social movement and Black resistance efforts in sport. The formation of National Negro Congress in 1935, NAACP Legal Defense and Educational Fund (LDF) in 1939 (incorporated in 1940), Congress of Racial Equality (CORE) in 1942, United Negro College Fund (UNCF) in 1944, and Southern Christian Leadership Conference (SCLC) in 1957 underscored the progressive aims of the time focused on racial equality through integration. Edwards (2016) outlined how the second wave of Black athlete activism focused on acquiring political access and positional diversity. Within sport, Jesse Owens earned four gold medals at the 1936 Olympics in Berlin, Germany, which demystified the idea of White Aryan superiority (Harris, 2000; Rhoden, 2006; Wiggins, 2000). In another international sporting event with significant racial, sociocultural, political, and nationalistic implications, Joe Louis defeated Max Schmeling of Germany in 1938, which further added credence the prowess of African Americans when provided an equal opportunity to excel (Wiggins & Miller, 2003).

Given the backdrop of World War II (1941–1945), the U.S. was under increased pressure to provide better treatment of Blacks domestically in order to fulfill their international military and political aims (Stewart, 1996). Thus, gradual integration began to occur in spaces such as Major League Baseball (MLB) in 1947 when Jackie Robinson broke the color barrier (Edwards, 2016). In 1953, the National Association of Intercollegiate Athletics (NAIA) began accepting HBCUs as members and in 1965 the NCAA followed suit (Cooper et al., 2014). The landmark Supreme Court case *Brown v. Board of Education of Topeka, Kansas* (1954), which unanimously overturned *Plessy v. Ferguson* (1896), deemed racial segregation in public schools unconstitutional (Hine et al., 2006). This decision was emblematic of the popular Black freedom struggle at a time that sought to redress inequalities via racial segregation through integration policies. Through the 1950s and 1960s, the Tennessee State Tiger Belles' women's track and field program led by legendary coach Ed Temple earned international recognition for their success with standout athletes including Audrey Patterson, Wilma Rudolph, Lucinda Williams, Barbara Jones, Martha Hudson, and Wyomia Tyus. In 1956 and 1957, Althea Gibson engaged in pioneering activism by becoming the first African American woman to win the French and Wimbledon tennis tournaments (Wiggins, 2000; Wiggins & Miller, 2003). Throughout this era, Black efforts to demonstrate their self-worth through assimilationist efforts were prevalent across numerous societal spaces.

Civil Rights Movement (1960s)

The Civil Rights Movement (CRM) was comprised of extension grassroots and broader mobilization, political, legal, sports-based, and media activism. The Civil Rights Movement (CRM) of the 1960s is among the most celebrated periods in U.S. and world history due to the high visibility of public demonstrations, the extent of societal shifts that occurred via federal and state legislations, and cultural changes regarding racial integration. A major force undergirding this movement included Black college students. In 1960, four Black students (Ezzell Blair, Jr. [now Jibreel Khazan], Franklin McCain, Joseph McNeil, and David Richmond) from North Carolina Agricultural and Technical State University (NC A&T), spearheaded a nationwide boycott movement in Greensboro, North Carolina, when they engaged in a sit-in at an all–White Woolworth's restaurant (Hine et al., 2006). Similar to their predecessor Rosa Parks, these Black activists utilized boycott and subsequent media coverage as a means to generate widespread awareness of the injustices facing Blacks in the South. In 1960, the Student Non-Violent Coordinating Committee (SNCC) was founded in Raleigh, North Carolina, and served as a pivotal mobilization unit within the CRM (Smith, 1994). The sit-ins sparked another wave of resistance to the majority power structure which was a called Freedom Rides. On May 4, 1961, the first contingent of Freedom Riders departed Washington, District of Columbia (D.C.) via bus for the Deep South to outwardly challenge Jim Crow ordinances, customs, and practices that enforced racial segregation in Alabama and Mississippi (Hine et al., 2006).

The March on Washington occurred on August 28, 1963, and it was the largest public demonstration against injustices in U.S. history including over 250,000 attendees (Smith, 1994). This event gained international attention to express their grievances towards the U.S. government's apathy towards the plight of African Americans. In 1964, the SNCC called on young volunteers both black and white and from across the U.S. to commit to the using their summer holidays to support the end of segregation in Mississippi (e.g., 1,000 volunteers assisted with the Freedom Schools, teaching typing and reading, and providing general information about U.S. laws and African Americans history) (Hine et al., 2006). The cumulative efforts of Black organizations, communities, and political leaders including SCLC, SNCC, and CORE led to the passage of milestone legislations such as the 24th Amendment in 1964 (prohibited the use of poll tax to prevent voting among eligible citizens) *Civil Rights Acts of 1964* (outlawed labor discrimination based on race, color, religion, sex, or national origin), *Voting Rights Act of 1965* (banned racial discrimination with voting), and *Civil Rights of 1968* (prohibited housing discrimination). These victories were not attained without sacrifice. The infamous "Red Summer" of 1967 resulted in over 40 riots and 100 other disturbances (Hine et al., 2006; Smith, 1994; Stewart, 1996).

Several of the protests at postsecondary institutions included the participation of African American athletes across the country at institutions such as the University of California, Berkeley, Texas Western University (now University of Texas El Paso), Syracuse University, Michigan State University, and several others (Wiggins, 2000). The famous 1967 Ali Summit and 1968 Olympic protests spearheaded by Tommie Smith and John Carlos epitomized the use of symbolic activism through sport during this era (Cooper et al., 2017; Edwards, 2016). Within the broader CRM, organizational activism was performed by SNCC, SCLC, and CORE among other grassroots groups. Within sport, several standout athletes including Muhammad Ali, Jim Brown, Kareem Abdul-Jabbar, and Bill Russell were using their respective platforms to express their discontent with racism throughout the country. Legal and sports-based activism was demonstrated in 1969 when Curt Flood sued the MLB to challenge the longstanding exploitative reserve clause (Cooper et al., 2017). Even though, he was not successful in terms of having the clause revoked at the conclusion of his case, his activism led to subsequent efforts which resulted in the eventual adoption of free agency in professional sports. This challenge of the legal system was also indicative with activist efforts that resulted in the passage of the Civil Rights Acts of 1964 and 1968 (Stewart, 1996). From educational activism standpoint, African American intellectuals such as Dr. Martin Luther King, Jr., and Malcolm × were producing insightful and evocative texts while within sports the critical research on race and sport was beginning to emerge from scholars such as Dr. Harry Edwards and Arthur Ashe (Brooks & Althouse, 2000; Edwards, 2016).

Black Power and Feminism Movements (1960s–1980s)

The Black Power and Black Feminism movements involved political, educational, symbolic, advocacy, and military activism. In terms of political activism, the Black Power movement led by the Black Panther Party shifted the activist discourse from interracial unity towards a more Black Nationalist racial solidarity. The foundation of the BPM was the creation of the Black

Panther Party (BPP) in 1966 by Huey P. Newton and Bobby Seale in Oakland, California (Smith, 1994). During the same year, CORE adopted "Black Power" as their mantra. Connecting to Pan-Africanist tenets, the BPM focused on empowerment across the African diaspora and challenging all forms of knowledge and authority under Eurocentric beliefs that reinforced the White supremacy ideology. Instrumental in promoting the agenda were Black Power leaders such as Eldridge Cleaver, Fred Hamilton, Stokely Carmichael (Kwame Ture), Amil Jamil Abullah Al-Amin (Hubert [H.] Rap Brown), Bobby Hutton, George Jackson, Martin Clark, Assata Shakur, Angela Davis, and Malcolm X (formerly Malcolm Little) of the Nation of Islam (Hine et al., 2006; Stewart, 1996). In 1967, Stokely Carmichael and Charles V. Hamilton published the critically acclaimed book, *Black Power: The Politics of Liberation*, which served as a foundational text for the movement (Hine et al., 2006). Connecting to the Ante-Bellum movement tactics and in contrast to the CRM approach, the BPM was rooted in political and military strategies. Within sport, Dr. Harry Edwards organized the OPHR in 1967, which successfully boycotted the New York Athletic Club's (NYAC) 100th anniversary track meet resulting in racial desegregation and effectively orchestrated the 1968 Olympic protests in Mexico City, Mexico headlined by Tommie Smith and John Carlos' Black Power salute demonstrations (Cooper et al., 2017). Concurrently, Muhammad Ali was challenging the U.S. social order via political and legal means. In 1967, he was charged with draft evasion for declining to participate in the U.S. military during the Vietnam War. Subsequently, he co-organized the famous Ali Summit in 1967 and filed an appeal against the U.S. government in 1969 (Cooper et al., 2017; Zirin, 2009). Foundational texts such as *Black Power: The Politics of Liberation* (Carmichael & Hamilton, 1967) coincided with disruptive sport-centric texts such as *The Revolt of the Black Athlete* (Edwards, 1969), which reflected both political and scholarly activism.

The BFM centered the voices, experiences, and prowess of Black women who had experienced marginalization within predominantly White women-led Feminist movements of the 20th century. Historically, Black women have played a pivotal role in broader Black struggles dating back to Harriet Tubman, Ida B. Wells-Barnett, and many more who lived and fought throughout the 17th through 20th centuries (Hine et al., 2006). Out of response to biased and sexist news media coverage of black women, the National Black Feminist Organization is established by Eleanor Holmes Norton and other black women in 1973 (Rojas, 2007). Activists such as Angela Davis were among the most outspoken and visible leaders who embodied both the BPM and BFM. In 1970, Angela Davis was indicted for owning guns used in a Marin County courtroom shootout in California (Barnett, 2003). After going underground for a while, she was caught by the FBI and jailed for two years. She became known as a political prisoner, which sparked national protests for her freedom, in route to her being acquitted in 1972 of all charges (Barnett, 2003).

In the political sector, Shirley Chisholm became the first Black woman elected to U.S. Congress in 1968 and later in 1972 she became the first Black candidate for a major political party in the U.S. Chisholm was also the first woman to run for the Democratic Party presidential nomination (Smith, 1994). In 1969, Mary Ann Weathers published the critically acclaimed article titled, *An Argument for Black Women's Liberation*. In 1989, Kimberle Crenshaw coined the phrase "intersectionality" to highlight the unique plight of Black women whereby they experience intersecting oppressions related to racism, sexism, and additional identities (Crenshaw, 1989). Similar to the *Black Power: The Politics of Liberation* book for the BPM (Carmichael & Hamilton, 1967), both texts served as important foundational documents for the BFM. The BPM and BFM redefined African Americans' identity and aided in furthering their racial consciousness in the 1960s. As an influential political force, this movement in turn became the precursor to the academic discipline known as Black Studies (Rojas, 2007). In sport, African American female athletes and coaches such as Tina Sloan Green, Lucia Harris, Wyomia Tyus, and Marian E. Washington were engaging in pioneering activism within their respective sports, which disrupted racist and sexist ideologies regarding the athletic abilities of Black women (Corbett & Johnson, 2000).

Black Lives Matter (2010s)

The BLM movement has been comprised of media, political, symbolic, legal, grassroots, and sport-based activism. In 2013, three Black women (Alicia Garza, Patrisse Cullors, and Opal Tometi) created a social media movement titled, #BlackLivesMatter, in wake of the acquittal of Trayvon Martin's murderer, George Zimmerman. In addition to Trayvon Martin, the heightened awareness of numerous unjust killings of Black Americans such as Jordan Davis (2012), Renisha McBride (2013), Michael Brown (2014), Eric Garner (2014), Tamir Rice (2014), Sandra Bland (2015), Freddie Gray (2015), Alton Sterling (2016), Philando Castille (2016), and sadly too many more were highlighted via social media campaigns (Black Lives Matter, 2017). This prompted the arrangement of activists to shift the BLM movement to Ferguson, Missouri, to support protests by the community activists in August 2014. However, Ferguson protests were just the beginning for activists, which since then have gone on to inspire over 900 additional #BlackLivesMatter marches, protests, and demonstrations worldwide between July 2014 and June 2015 (Langford & Speight, 2015). The BLM hashtag also fueled multiple additional grassroots movements such as local chapters of BLM, Black Youth Project

100, and protests across the country including in Baltimore, Maryland, and Sanford, Florida.

Moreover, subsequent social media activism would end up being birthed and garnering massive attention due to the efforts and successes of these women. Hashtags such as #IfTheyGunnedMeDown, #HandsUpDontShoot, #MikeBrown, #Ferguson, #SayHerName went viral (Langford & Speight, 2015). The use of the Internet as a modern technological tool enabled the BLM movement to generate international visibility, support, and organization. Consistent with previous movements, communication was pivotal for mobilization efforts (e.g., word of mouth with the Underground Railroad, Black operated radio and magazine outlets in the Black Liberation Movement through Reconstruction, churches and television during the CRM, etc.). #BlackLivesMatter has surpassed just the black celebrity, athlete, entertainer, and political figure, all of whom are deemed tokens of Black identity, to something that has become truly inclusive of the entire race which experiences institutional, social, and legal discrimination on a daily basis. A common thread across each of the Black social justice movements involve the use of different resources to generate awareness, action, and change in the face of oppressive conditions.

The use of social media as a mobilizing activist tool is a unique feature of 21st century activism. Along the same lines, African American athletes began using their social media platforms to advocate for social justice (e.g., #WeAreTrayonMartin, #TakeAKnee, etc.) (Cooper et al., 2017). Symbolic activism was also prevalent within the BLM movement via staged protests nationwide from Ferguson, Missouri, to Baltimore, Maryland, to Charlottesville, Virginia, to name a few. Symbolic activism within sport included Colin Kaepernick taking a knee to protest oppression and racial injustice in society during the 2016–2017 NFL season, National Basketball Association (NBA) players wearing "I Can't Breathe" t-shirts in warms up during the 2016–2017 season to show solidarity the family of Eric Garner, WNBA players' protests pre and post games in support of the BLM movement, and the University of Missouri football team protests in 2015 of the racist campus climate at the university. Regarding legal activism, the NAACP and several race-based organizations were influential in the high-profile cases of African Americans who were unjustly killed (e.g., Trayvon Martin, Michael Brown, etc.). Related to sport, legal and sports-based activism was exhibited in the Ed O'Bannon's class action lawsuit against the NCAA and EA Sports in 2009, the Martin Jenkins versus NCAA class action lawsuit in 2014, and the Northwestern football team's filing for employee status with the Chicago Regional Director of the National Labor Relations Board (NLRB) in 2015 all disrupted the social order associated with exploitative arrangements within current big-time college sports (Cooper et al., 2017). In concert with Edwards' (2016) fourth wave of Black athlete activism, resistance efforts both within and beyond sport in the 21st century have focused on securing and transferring power via economic and technological capital.

Conclusion

African American sport activism has historically and contemporarily served as vital tool for disruption, awareness, and empowerment for social change in the U.S. African American sport activism reflect the strategies employed by broader social movements that manifested during the same eras (Cooper et al., 2017; Edwards, 2016). These actions included, but were not limited to, disruptive protests, organized collective action, creation of counter/empowerment associations/businesses/organizations/institutions, symbolic athletic accomplishments, scholarly research, legal cases and judicial decisions, federal and state legislations, organizational rule changes, empowering media coverage and contributions, political engagement, cultural expressiveness, and critical social discourse. Renowned sport sociologist, Edwards (1969) challenged the notion that sport was a utopic space separate from society, but rather deeply interconnected with its structures, systems, and manifestations. African American sport activism cannot be analyzed or understood in isolation, but rather it must be contextualized in connection with broader social movements and societal conditions. As outlined in this essay, African Americans within and beyond sport have utilized a range of activist tactics to pursue their social justice aims. These activist actions include *symbolic, scholarly, grassroots, sports-based, economic, media, political, legal, music and art*, and *military*. These actions are intertwined and work towards the common goal of disrupting and eliminating oppressive hegemonic forces embedded within a society rooted in White racism, neoliberalism, and capitalism. African American athletes have long been recognized for their athletic accomplishments. It is also important they also be celebrated and remembered for their activist actions within and beyond sport.

NOTE

1. The terms "African American" and "Black" will be used interchangeably to refer to the racial distinction associated with people of African descent within the United States.

REFERENCES

Barnes, E. (2017). Ernie Barnes website. Biography page. Retrieved from http://www.erniebarnes.com/official-biography.html.
Barnett, B.M. (2003). Angela Davis and women, race, & class: A pioneer in integrative RGC studies. *Race, Gender & Class, 10*(3), 9–22.
Black Lives Matter. (2017). *Homepage.* Retrieved from http://www.blacklivesmatter.com.

Brooks, D., & Althouse, R. (2000). *Racism in college athletics: the African American athlete's experience* (2d ed.). Morgantown, WV: Fitness Information Technology.

Brown, J., & Delsohn, S. (1989). *Jim Brown: Out of bounds*. New York: Zebra Books Kensington Publishing Corp.

Carmichael, S., & Hamilton, C.V. (1967). *Black power: the Politics of liberation in America*. New York: Vintage.

Carty, V. (2002). Technology and counter-hegemonic movements: The case of Nike Corporation. *Social Movement Studies, 1*(2), 129–146.

Clay v. United States, 403 U.S. 698 (1971.)

Cooper, J.N., Cavil, J.K., & Cheeks, G. (2014). The state of intercollegiate athletics at historically Black colleges and universities (HBCUs): Past, present, & persistence. *Journal of Issues in Intercollegiate Athletics, 7*, 307–332.

Cooper, J.N., Macaulay, C., & Rodriguez, S.H. (2017). Race and resistance: A typology of African American sport activism. *International Review for the Sociology of Sport*, 1–31. DOI: 10.1177/1012690217718170.

Corbett, D., & Johnson, W. (2000). The African American female in collegiate sport: Sexism and racism. In D. Brooks and R. Althouse (Eds.), *Racism in college athletics: The African American athlete's experience* (2d ed.) (pp. 199–226). Morgantown, WV: Fitness Information Technology.

Corbett, D.R., & Stills, A.B. (2007). African Americans and the media: Roles and opportunities to be broadcasters, journalists, reporters, and announcers. In D.D. Brooks and R.C. Althouse (Eds.), *Diversity and social justice in college sports: Sport management and the student athlete* (pp. 179–200). Morgantown, WV: Fitness Information Technology.

Crenshaw, K. (1989). Demarginalizing the intersection of race and sex: A Black feminist critique of antidiscrimination doctrine, feminist theory, and antiracist politics. *University of Chicago Legal Forum*, 1989, 139–67.

Davis-Delano, L.R., & Crosset, T. (2008). Using social movement theory to study outcomes in sport-related social movements. *International Review for the Sociology of Sport, 43*(2), 115–134.

Dodson, A. (2017). Anquan Boldin and Malcolm Jenkins speak at congressional forum on community-police relations. *ESPN the Undefeated*. Retrieved from https://theundefeated.com/features/anquan-boldin-and-malcolm-jenkins-speak-at-congressional-forum-on-community-police-relations/.

Edwards, H. (1969). *The revolt of the Black athlete*. New York: The Free Press.

Edwards, H. (2016). *The fourth wave: Black athlete protests in the second decade of the 21st century*. Keynote address at the North American Society for the Sociology of Sport (NASSS) conference in Tampa Bay, Florida.

Flood v. Kuhn, 407 U.S. 258 (1972.)

Fortenberry, L. (1974). Freedom's journal: The first Black medium. *The Black Scholar, 6*(3), 33–37.

George, N (1992). *Elevating the game: Black men and basketball*. Omaha: University of Nebraska Press.

Harris, O. (2000). African American predominance in sport. In D. Brooks and R.. Althouse (Eds.) *Racism in college athletics: The African American athlete's experience* (2d ed.) (pp. 37–52). Morgantown, WV: Fitness Information Technology.

Hine, D.C., Hine, W.C., & Harrold, S. (2006). *The African-American odyssey: Since 1965* (3d ed. Vol. Two). Upper Saddle River, NJ: Pearson Prentice Hall.

Hoberman, J.M. (1997). *Darwin's athletes: How sport has damaged Black America and preserved the myth of race*. Boston: Houghton Mifflin Company.

Hudlin, W. (2004). Harlem Renaissance Re-examined. In H. Bloom (Ed.) *The Harlem Renaissance* (p. 5–12). Philadelphia, PA: Chelsea House Publishers.

Langford, C.L., & Speight, M. (2015). #BlackLivesMatter: Epistemic positioning, challenges, and possibilities. *Journal of Contemporary Rhetoric, 5*(3/4), 78–89.

Lomax, M.E. (2003) *Black baseball entrepreneurs, 1860–1901: Operating by any means necessary*. Syracuse, NY: Syracuse University Press.

Lomax, M.E. (2014). *Black baseball entrepreneurs, 1902–1931: The Negro National and Eastern Colored Leagues.* Syracuse, NY: Syracuse University Press.

Moore, M., Dupree, M., & Krinsky, M. (2017). Op-ed: WNBA star Maya Moore pushing for change to criminal justice system. *USA Today.* Retrieved from https://www.usatoday.com/story/sports/2017/11/22/op-ed-wnba-star-maya-moore-pushing-change-criminal-justice-system/887868001/.

O'Bannon v. Nat. Collegiate Athletic Association, 7 F. Supp. 3d 955 (N.D. Cal. 2014).

Rhoden, W.C. (2006). *40 million dollar slaves: The rise, fall, and redemption of the Black athlete.* New York: Crown Publishing Group.

Robeson, P. (1998). *Here I Stand.* Boston: Beacon Press.

Rojas, F. (2007). *From Black power to Black studies: How a radical social movement became an academic discipline.* Baltimore: Johns Hopkins University Press.

Sage, G.H. (1998). *Power and ideology in American sport* (2d ed.). Champaign, IL: Human Kinetics.

Sage, G.H. (1999). Justice do it! The Nike transnational advocacy network: Organization, collective actions, and outcomes. *Sociology of Sport Journal, 16*(3), 206–235.

Smith, J.C. (1994). *Black firsts: 2,000 years of extraordinary achievement.* Detroit, MI: Visible Ink Press.

Smith, M.P., Clark, L.D., Harrison, L., Jr. (2014). The historical hypocrisy of the Black student-athlete. *Race, Gender & Class, 21*(1–2), 220–235.

Stewart, J.C. (1996). *1001 things everyone should know about African American history.* New York: Doubleday.

Wiggins, D. (2000). Critical events affecting racism in athletics. In D. Brooks and R. Althouse (Eds.), *Racism in college athletics: The African American athlete's experience* (2d ed.) (pp. 199–226). Morgantown, WV: Fitness Information Technology.

Wiggins D.K., & Miller, P. (2003). *The unlevel playing field: A documentary history of the African American experience in sport.* Urbana: University of Illinois Press.

Zirin, D. (2009). *People's history of Sports in the United States: 250 years of politics, protest, people, and play.* New York: The New Press.

Refusing to Play Their Games!

A Fanonian Analysis and Robesonian Proposition on Sports, Race and Divestment

Miciah Z. Yehudah

Introduction

Many scholars have attempted to establish the United States' sports industry as a more recent arm of the colonial enterprise tradition.[1] They have identified the purpose of the industry in modernity as not only an attempt at the commercialization of competitive physical activities within its national jurisdiction, but also as a means of promoting nationalistic ideals for its citizenry. But if such political aims (commercialization and indoctrination) were imperative, how would the said objectives coincide with the country's avowed norm of an assumed White superiority and Black inferiority? And, equally of note, how might the racialized Black group ward off and effectively respond to such attempts at dehumanization and exploitation?

Frantz Fanon, in his classic text, *The Wretched of the Earth*, described colonialism (via the French attempt at the colonization of Algeria) as a violent endeavor that creates more long-lasting psychological damage than the physical causalities it brings forth in its immediate aftermath.[2] Such an invasive program requires a response that psychologically stabilizes and propels the colonized group. Furthermore, the colonized group must also use nonconventional destructive means, since, according to Fanon, decolonization is an inherently violent phenomena. Violence is not solely used here to pinpoint a mere physical force, but rather, it is being used to symbolize and represent ideological constructs so sudden, bombarding, and forceful that their ability to influence and manipulate psyches are more effective than the physical act itself. The two, in fact, work hand in hand. Once one sees an entity perpetuating physical acts of violence it becomes ever so difficult to differentiate even its words and ideas from such actions.

What is proposed in this essay is a new endeavor controlled and ethically guided by people of African descent that shatters externally imposed/internally assumed psychological shackles, and equally disrupts the colonial moneymaker that is the sports industry. What is offered is a strategy of divestment. The premise is that struggling to voice one's thoughts within the industry, although honorable in the current dispensation, is the least revolutionary act an athlete of African descent can take within professional sports. While the possibility for creating more breathing space within the U.S. sports world exists, it ultimately does nothing to reform the cultural assumptions undergirding or the White supremacist ideologies guiding the industry. As such, the most revolutionary act a Black athlete in modernity can take would be to completely divest from the industry and create her own institution that allows for maximum cultural respite. Many talking heads questioning such a program argue that 21st century United States is not a colonial state, and, certainly if it was, could not be equated to the condition of 19th Century Africa.[3] In anticipation of possible rebuttals to such assertions a brief comparison and synthesis is offered.

Fanon and Colonialism

"America is a melting pot, not a colonial state," is how most naysayers would begin their rebuttal.[4] But if a simple definition of colonialism is utilized, it is difficult to dismiss the argument that the United States is a colonizing entity. In *The Wretched of the Earth* Fanon identifies colonialism as the financial exploitation, political dominance, and cultural decapitation of the indigenous (colonial subjects) by an invading entity (colonialists).[5] The lifeblood of the colonizing entity is fueled equally by its citizenry's and subjects' acceptance of the easily rebuttable but hegemonic assumptions that the colonized are less than human, and the colonizers ultimately represent the epitome of humanity. But what of the "outpost" designation? What of the notion that a country must invade in order to be considered a colonial entity? What of the notions that "America" stopped colonizing once it declared its own independence from Britain?

Firstly, an outpost is imagined as something being located in a remote place. And typically the colonizer is the invading force acting out its desires on the population already settled in the land.[6] The problem with such frameworks of analyses is that they rely on an unreasonable and archaic "second-first" argument. In other words, the group that was there first are the colonized, while the group that were there second are the colonizers. It overlooks the sole intent of colonialism, which is to clone its system while recreating actors out of its subjects and settlers that will further the exploitation. The subjects are forced violently into submission against their will. They must play the game by the colonial state's pre-determined rules. The settlers are encouraged by the thought of spreading the greatly lauded qualities of its homeland civilization abroad to the infidels. They too play the game by the rules, but they are able to secure enough victories to be content about the system despite its contant exploitation of the colonized. Hence, the location of the dominance is not as important, since all space is situated along the settler-indigenous dichotomy and the boundaries are always manipulated to empower the colonizing entity.

In the United States of America these boundaries are enforced. Zoning laws and gentrification policies keep each group at bay. But metaphysical boundaries are more important and enforced stringently in areas of employment (including meaningful and leadership positions), health care, financial supplementation, and home ownership, to name a few. If Black people work with the White world, they are rarely if ever in positions of influence. If they live in the same city, the White neighborhoods are typically the more kept and protected. If they play the same sports, Blacks are assumed to be the most athletic, but the less pensive and intelligent.[7] So although Africans had been brought from their continental homeland into North America, the environment they find themselves in is one in which they are othered,[8] or as W.E.B. Du Bois suggested, made to exist on one side of the veil.[9]

The colonial world is a Manichean world. The colonizer not only exploits the subject and unleashes its settlers to enclose the subjects, but also labels the subject as the very personification of evil. No different than the relegation to Blacks being the cursed seed of Ham without the awareness of righteousness, the colonial state makes it normal and almost prerequisite for African pessimism to exist. The customs and culture of the dominated group are made to be the very sign of that "poverty of spirit." It is folklore, not history, and it cannot ever be made to be acceptable unless White folks recreate it in their own image (i.e., Blues music, Rap music, corn rows, old Michelle Obama speeches, etc.). The subject is perceived physically and intellectually as an animal. As an animal he is extremely athletic and untamed. As an intellectual he has no capacity to think or to reason. The settler population knows of the farce but refuses to speak out on it for fear of losing the privilege associated with going along with it. The racial contract[10] is in full effect. Deny that the privilege exists, never point out the farce, and you shall reap the harvest.

Since the colonized space is Manichean there are dichotomies. On one side of the spectrum is the colonialist space. On the other end of the spectrum is the colonized space. As stated previously these spaces could be physical communities or ideological frameworks and structures, whereas the righteous intelligent do-no-wrong colonials are extreme polar opposite of the wicked emotional do-no-right colonized. Anything good going for the colonized is certainly a result of some intervention by the colonials, while on the other hand, all evil that befalls the colonials can be blamed somewhat on the colonial subjects.

Fanon speaks also of the colonized bourgeoisie who serve as exemplars for the other colonized people of what to attain towards.[11] Since they are able to speak with the bourgeoisie of the colonizing state the illusion is promoted that they are on equal terms and footing, but they are used by the colonialists to re-enforce the group's submission into the alien culture. This group is the exception. They may be extremely talented, and for that, wheeled into the sphere of influence. While in this sphere of influence, they believe that they are the "Chosen Few," and point down at the others that don't fall in line, blaming their shortcomings on their lack of worth ethic or criminal, inhumane nature. For the colonized bourgeoisie the only way out of the colonized group is to play the game (later we'll see this literally) of the colonial group. Some choose to disown their culture completely and adopt the culture of the alien culture wholesale. Others choose to take pieces and try their luck in academic, medical, political, or athletic spaces, never knowing that for the colonial "once a Nigger always a Nigger!"

The bourgeoisie amongst the colonized group are made to be extremely individualistic. She never returns to her community, except to tell them to be more like her and like the dominant culture. Her family is moved out of the original setting and moved to an area closer to the dominant group. They are made to be the mouthpiece for the colonized group. They decry tradition, and in fact, argue that their backward tradition is what has led them into the downtrodden state that their people are constantly in. The dominant group is never blamed for its invasiveness or impositions. The dominant group is never the subject of historical analyses or identified as causing the conditions that brought about the helplessness of the colonized. Unless the colonized individual is himself made an example of, he will keep his mouth shut. The colonial subject begins to fight for integration, forgetting that the basis of the fight is the defeat of colonialism. To save face he fights for one cause only, refusing to aim towards the complete overthrow of the system, but rather piecemeal feel good reform.

If the education of the colonial state was effective the masses of the colonized are in agreement with piecemeal reform. They too want to be like the colonized bourgeoisie since it appears as if they are now in close communication with the dominant group. They too become individualistic and tend to be hostile towards their own traditions and cultural heritage. Since the objective is to be in the same spaces as the colonialist everything that is not of the colonialists is hostile towards that goal, even the nonexistence of his own people.

Mainstream culture (referred to as pop culture nowadays), replays through its imagery and activities, the values and traditions created, reworked, and promoted by the dominant group or colonial state. At times, the bourgeoisie of the colonized are held up as examples for their own group, for they best exemplify what a colonized person should be, the values they should keep, and the goals they should aspire to. The objective is keeping the system intact at all times. But even embedded in the culture are messages intended for the colonized which remind him to always know his place and not to even appear as to go beyond the unwritten limits. The educational system is always in constant communication with the messages of mainstream culture for they are one and the same. Mainstream culture enforces the values of the colonizing entity. The Manichean boundaries are reinforced through imagery. People in the society without a critical eye would not think twice of it, but those resisting against colonization, and not yet colonized see the imagery for what it is, an overload, an annoying excess, a constant imposition, and an unrelenting psychological barrage. Colonialism, according to Fanon, distorts, disfigures, and destroys the pre-colonial culture of the people and places the colonial state as its subjects' new nurturer and protector.

As Pavlov conditioned canines with the bell, the threat of violence is intended to sound within th psyche of the oppressed before he is able to even naturally conceptualize his own independent response to the subjugation. In this way violence militates against critical thinking. But before violence is utilized other methods are used to keep the minds of the oppressed too busy to rationalize their experiences. One such method is athletic competition. Ever ready to outgrow the confines of the colonial boundaries, sports provide a venue for the colonized to blur the lines and live in their oppressors' world for a little bit.

Sports and Colonialism

The exceptional athletes among the colonized group are able to garner recognition, not only in their world, but also the outside world. Since they tend to be more talented than the colonial populace, their physical exploits make them the subject of colonial admiration and resentment. Admiration, because in colonial spaces, their talent is unheard of and rarely witnessed. Resentment, because they look so much at ease in their talent, that the colonial fears that this natural talent may be used to overthrow his rule. How the colonial group manages such trepidations is through its sports industry, which funnels the energy of the colonized youth into pointless activity, while also filling its coffers. Through the use of a few athletic exemplars (or All Stars), it runs a sort of lottery system that gives hope to the youth that they can find a way out of their lowly status by simply achieving athletically. At a young age anyone has an opportunity to make it, but as the years pile on, the opportunity to strike out at the lottery diminishes with each passing day.

Although the financial stakes are high, the Black athlete is always reminded that at the end of the day, he is still Black. What he accomplishes is not due to any intelligence, but to his being closer to his animal nature than human tendencies. So when a White athlete is able to defeat the Black athlete or a team spearheaded by a Black athlete, that White athlete is to be celebrated because has fought with a beast and fought the good fight. This works hand in hand with the propaganda. Everyone is accepted of all races and creeds, unless they break the unwritten rule. "Don't use our platform to criticize our empire"!

The sports industry is just as political as the other industries in the country. The myth of entertainment for entertainment's sake is laughable. Sports are an additional form of cultural education. Whereas the policemen and soldiers teach by "rifle butts & napalm" in order to force the undesirables into submission a la Fanon,[12] sports craftily bewilders the exploited. It creates an illusion that all is well and that the boundary can be overcome while it continually maintains that stringent border. Military members are continuously honored during athletic events and the two seem to go hand in hand.[13] In fact, the athletic enthusiast will learn about the goodness of the nation's military through his participation or viewership of athletic events. He need not go to a local military center. He will get his first education at local and national sporting events. National holidays that coincide with sporting events are used as opportunities to teach about the national culture.

The myth of entertainment for entertainment's sake is accepted as fact because the sport industry promotes it as fun, games, and devoid of politics. However, any protests against the politics of the empire (such as Colin Kaepernick refusing to stand for the national anthem) are viewed as sacrilegious. "That doesn't have a place in sports" is what most colonial sympathizers would say. However, no one is ever up in arms when players run onto the field with flags or the President (or his Vice President) shows up at "important" sporting events.

Harrell correctly posits that in a Manichean world media is one of the mechanisms used by the system to reinforce its culture and mores.[14] But when an athlete uses the media platform for political critique it is not received well. Colonial sympathizers paint the protester as someone ungrateful for the privilege of playing professional sports, and demonize them at any chance. Although the right to free speech is guaranteed in the United States Constitution it tends to be disregarded when the voice is used to speak about some of the inhumane treatments against colonized subjects. Sports are sacred to the colonials. It is a space that should be free of critique of its politics, because after all, in the tradition, it is the elite that are gracious enough to allow the non-elite to play this game professionally in their dominion.[15]

The colonial system and its sympathizers are so passionate about keeping politics out of sports because they are aware of the platform provided for its subjects to exercise speech. Whereas in the normal colonial environment their voices are drowned out, in the sports industry, they continuously have the country's ears. When he speaks for the Empire, and ultimately renders his voice as a non-voice because he chooses to be silent on issues affecting his people, he is lauded and held up as an example of an American athlete.[16] When he chooses the side of "evil," and uses his voice to be critical and non-submissive he is demonized and painted as being emotional and irrational. He has now displayed his Blackness. No matter the greatness of his talents, his time in the industry is now short lived.

So given the assumptions of the system and the purpose of the colonial system how has the Black athlete responded? How might she respond in the future to maintain dignity and uplift her community? Listed below are possibilities, including an option that may at this point be unimaginable, even inconsiderable, but nonetheless an approach Black athletes in the United States of America may consider and implement in order to uplift their community and breed further ideas of self-determination.

Actions of the Colonized

Ultimately the goal is to find one's voice and to simultaneously have others in the colonized community recognize and acknowledge it when it speaks. How one chooses to use his/her voice is contingent upon what long-term goals one aims for. How one determines their long-term goal is itself contingent upon what possibilities they believe to exist. The danger with being colonized educationally is that subjects can only conceptualize possibilities from options that the colonial system dictates. In other words, the colonial world teaches its subjects to only think of possibilities within the colonial world. With the colonized mind no other world exists. No other world is possible. This is how in modernity, people, even African descendants, can boldly promote the false claim that Africans had no educational systems or infrastructure before Europeans came. Such outlandish statements are only proof of the success of the colonial education. So essentially, can people of African descent overcome the constant attempts at dehumanization while simultaneously participating in the United States of America's sports industry? Ultimately, the question this essay poses is, would anyone with any sense of self worth not be enraged at being constantly put down, diminished, or reduced?

The Jordan Tradition

The Jordan Tradition speaks to the athletes personifying ideals of self-withdrawal and visual apathy. The athlete in this zone is apathetic and extremely individualistic. He is not using the platform for his community, because, he has no community that he must tend to. He has no alliance to the Black world because he rarely identifies with the political circumstances of Blackness in the United States of America. He is simply an American athlete. Although he may be talented, and even the most talented, his true greatness is questioned, mainly because his character is always brought into question.

The tradition is named after the basketball player Michael Jordan who was known for his tenacity and his athletic grace. His moves were mimicked but never actually replicated because his demeanor remained calm and steady while he performed the unimaginable. He made it appear as if he could do it in his sleep. His style of play stemmed predominantly from an inherently African/African American tradition. But what made him a beloved National superstar was his way of approaching politics in the country. His approach was in fact not to make any positive or negative comments about politics. If he was pressed, and that was rare, he would always side with the hegemon. For the colonial side, he was the prototype of the Black athlete. He was the "best" in the game for them, not only for his immense talents and statistical achievements and hardware to support such notions of greatness, but truly because he promoted the sentiment that he did not have time to focus on anything but basketball and basketball related activities.[17] Had he spoken out about the crack epidemic or the war on Black neighborhoods caused by Reagan's economic system, his greatness would have been questioned and his unquestionable stats would have been subjected to reservations or asterisks.

The type of athletes in the Jordanian model are likened to the colonized bourgeoisie in the Fanonian model that dream of possessing the settlers' town, bed, and wife if possible. In *Black Skin White Masks* Fanon devotes an entire chapter to the subject "The Man of Color and the White Woman." Ridiculing the Black man that goes after women to legitimize his humanity he asks "Who better than a white woman to bring about the becoming of a Black man?"[18] Fanon is not against interracial relationships but rather against going about such relationships to fill a cultural void or to legitimize one's humanity. He is unsympathetic to the idea that "having White women is like having White civilization." He labels such behaviors as that of the abandonment neurotic who lacks confidence and needs constant reassurance.

These abandonment neurotics believe that they have not achieved any real measure of success unless they are living far away from their communities, ideologically and physically. If they are successful they are held up as examples. They're supplied with contracts and endorsement deals. They flood the television with multiple appearances. They have become de-facto cultural ambassadors. They are paraded around the world to show the international community that America is a multicultural post-racial country. More importantly, they are not the least bit aggressive in their critique of the system. If they say something that can be misconstrued they quickly recant their statements.

Their actions off the playing field largely echo their apolitical stance. They donate to charities that address mainstream issues. If they seek to address irregularities through their charities and causes they choose to take on are those stereotyped as commonly accepted (popularly projected) Black issues. This approach is the least revolutionary approach. In fact, athletes that fit the mold are comfortable with playing the role of the stereotype[19] while they are paid for their political silence.

The Ali Tradition

The Ali tradition takes its name from legendary boxer Muhammad Ali. It is named as such for the athletes that utilize the platform provided to speak to issues dear to their communities. For such critique against the colonial system the athletes in this category are subject to ridicule and threatened with expulsion from their teams or the industry itself. It is a noble, honorable, and difficult approach to take, for one sacrifices their very livelihood to publicly voice concerns. But even in its radical nature it is not completely revolutionary, for it does not seek to overthrow the basic assumptions underlying the system, it just seeks to carve out a space for all athletes to be treated equally.

With this said, Muhammad Ali, is not only the exemplar for this category but the radical in this group. He was at peace with having his championship belt stripped as a consequence for refusing to enlist in the military draft. He did not see the consequence as just, but one he was wiling to endure in order to prove a point that fighting in the war for a country that oppressed his people daily is tantamount to suicide. His assertion that "no Vietcong ever called me nigger" spoke to the depths of his critique.

Despite the poignancy of this approach, its constituents tend to overlook the power of the industry itself in reinforcing colonial subjugation. If it was hypocritical to fight for a system that oppresses the people you love, then would it not be equally hypocritical to put your body at risk in order to fill the coffers of that same country that is exploiting you? Boxing is a bit different than the other contact sports because it is an individual sport and it does not rely on the on-the-field play of teammates. In boxing Ali felt as if he was in control of not only the outcome of the match but also his health. One begs to wonder what form his activism would have taken had he been a football or basketball player.

Alternatively, this type of activism displays the polarity that exists in American Sports. For one the Constitution supports freedom of speech. But on the other hand a Black athlete that uses her right to free speech is threatened with expulsion. The problem is not only in the protest but in the venue that she is choosing to do so in. The sports arena is a sacred arena. It is not supposed to be political. Actually, it is not supposed to be a space where political statements against the status quo are made. It is a space where boat rocking is not allowed. Every sports contest begins with flag bearing or the national anthem. It is supposed to be a space where the two zones are blurred so much, that in order to keep the two sides from clashing, no athletes, especially the Black ones should point out the elephant (of racialized segregation) in the room.

One fact that cannot be overlooked is the background that helped to transform Cassius Clay into Muhammad Ali. The Nation of Islam, since the 1930s has been a staunch advocate of separation from the mechanisms of the "devils." Guided by an ideology that equated "devils" with the creators of the colonial system, and the sports industry with one of her minions, it is easy to understand why Ali felt so supported in his decision to turn his back on the demands of the boxing and government authorities. His rise to stardom coincided with his membership in the Nation of Islam under the leadership of Elijah Muhammad. Although he would eventually leave the Nation, his philosophy on human rights and Black self-determination were forever impacted by the Nation of Islam ideology. The importance of ideology in transforming the athlete into a dignified Black man/woman first and entertainer second is imperative for creating community-centered athletes.

The exemplars of the approach, like Ali, are consistent in their activism. This is what separates them from the other athletes that may occasionally voice displeasure once their individual opportunities are immediately affected. Also, the activism of this group is larger than just themselves, and speaks to a larger group that they associate with.

Other athletes associated with the Ali tradition include the likes of Colin Kaepernick and Mahmoud Abdul Rauf. Kaepernick had always been a tremendous athlete and star quarterback for the San Francisco 49ers of the National Football League, but it has been his activism that has thrust him into the news cycle.[20] His refusal to stand for the national anthem until police brutality and mass incarceration were addressed, caught on like wildfire across the country. Hundreds, from elementary school students, to high school, college, and other professional athletes joined in with similar protests.[21] Behinds the scenes Kaepernick has been very active. As recent as January 2017 he donated $100,000 to Standing Rock Sioux Tribe members in North Dakota fighting to restrict the building of the pipeline. In addition to his on the field activities he donated $1 million to causes of social justice before the start of the 2017 NFL season.[22] His efforts have attracted the hostility of everyone from political pundits and the general public to retired and current NFL players. During the offseason and current NFL season many await word for what will happen with his contract and whether his playing days in the NFL will continue. Many expect the "privilege" of being in the NFL to be pulled from him.

Mahmoud Abdul-Rauf, a retired NBA star from the 1990s with the Denver Nuggets of the National Basketball Association also refused to stand for the National Anthem. He did receive media coverage for his actions but word did not spread as fast as Kaepernick's. He felt the anthem was a reminder of the country's infatuation with tyranny and oppression.[23] He too like Ali was inspired by the Muslim ideology of self-determination and dignity. He was suspended a game for his protest, had his minutes reduced, and was eventually left without an NBA job. Yet, Kaepernick's activism is thought to be a reverberation from Abdul-Rauf's earlier efforts.

The Ali method is a necessary approach for Black athletes to take until the collective arrives at an understanding that even the radical approach will not completely revolutionize the sports industry, since the industry will remain tied into the economy and function as a tool for culturally socializing the citizens of the hegemon.

The Robeson Tradition

Paul Robeson is known not only for his acting prowess but his strong unflinching devotion to human rights. A little-known fact about this legendary figure is that he actually was an All-American football player at Rutgers University (Rutgers College at his time of attendance) in 1918 and by 1922 a professional football star for the Akron Pros. After an additional season with the Milwaukee Badgers of the NFL he retired in order to devote his energy to human rights. He could have continued playing but felt that his energy would be better served by joining the world struggle for human rights. While playing collegiate football (and three other intercollegiate sports) he earned the status of valedictorian. During his professional sports career he earned a law degree. After suffering discrimination in the field of law he turned to acing and singing and gave noteworthy performances in the theater and film.[24]

His activism was inspired by his circumstances. His acceptance and enrollment at Rutgers College made him just the third student of African descent to ever attend the institution. His tryout for the football team was successful, but was met with the most violent treatment by his future teammates, suffering injuries during practices with the team.[25] Once he actually made the team the disruptions continued. One opponent refused to play against his team because of what his presence meant for race relations of the time. Rather than throwing their support behind him, his team ousted him, benching him in order to acquiesce to the other teams' demands. The disrespect continued long after his career ended, when it took nearly eighty years for Rutgers to induct him into their sports Hall of Fame despite his making All-American status for his final two years on its football team, and his being called the greatest athlete to ever participate for the University. His acting career, although successful, was also filled with multiple incidents in which he was racially othered.[26]

On August 29, 1949, Robeson attempted to perform at the Peekskill New York's Lakeland Picnic grounds. However, the city's White locals decided that they would attack others peacefully assembled at the event. The proceeds of the concert were dedicated to the Civil Rights Congress but the White mob, upset at his support of Russia, and his stance against World War II and White imperialism in Africa, determined that they would not support his performance. In turn, they erected a dummy, attached it to a cross and burned it, along with the promotion material for the event.[27] He had suddenly become more polarizing off the field than he had ever been on it, but his efforts on the field helped to propel him into the national spotlight. He would go on to form the Council on African Affairs and become a consistent pacifist and human rights activist.

The athletes fitting in the Robeson category see something larger than just becoming popular through entertainment. They actually take an anti-sports industry approach at best, and a user of the industry approach (rather than a being abused by it approach) at worst. Robeson utilized the money he earned from sports to pay for his schooling. He saw his athletic abilities as means to help raise funds in order to advocate for his people, and nothing more. The Robesonian athlete of today will be aware of how the sports industry is another arm of the empire and will be clear on their place in it if participating in it. They then will use whatever they earn to fund independent institutions that fuel their own community's cultural resurgence and sustainability, following the example set by Robeson's founding of the Council on African Affairs. The individualism present in pop culture today is not a characteristic of athletes of this category. The athletes fitting in the Robeson category will be the complete opposite. They will be ones that carry out their initiatives for the good of the collective, even forfeiting their participation in the sports industry, if necessary.

One thing is also for certain; the athletes of the Ali and Robeson traditions, because of their using their platform as professional athletes to speak out politically, could expect to be faced with socio-political and economic retaliation. Paul Robeson's ability to book shows as a performer and be paid accordingly for his services was seriously hindered due to his anti-war stance. His passport was revoked which impacted his earning potential abroad and his concerts in the United States. Eighty-five in total (1949) were cancelled. Ironically, Jackie Robinson, an athlete Robeson once supported, testified against Robeson before the House Un-American Activities Committee, labeling Robeson as a heretic that does not represent the views of all African Americans.[28] Robinson was unafraid of speaking out about the contradictions of racism in the United States, but borrowed a page from the Jordan tradition (although he pre-dated it) by allowing himself to be used as the voice of the empire. He would later come to regret this decision.[29] Although Robeson had his detractors (none more popular than Robinson) he had others come to his defense. Malcolm X, once admittedly a self-proclaimed Jackie Robinson fan as young Malcolm Little, stated in a op-ed letter addressed to Jackie Robinson in New York's Amsterdam News, that through such efforts to isolate Robeson by testifying against him, Robeson was "still trying to win 'The Big Game'" for his "White Boss."[30] For Malcolm X, freedom meant sacrificing one's loyalty to the country's institutions. For Robinson, freedom was contingent upon peaceful integration between all American citizens. The two (Malcolm and Jackie) would continue in their debate about what roads would best lead to Black freedom, but it took the boldness of Robeson and his sacrifice to bring such discussions to the surface. The nature of the industry, factored with the need for continuous media sound bytes forced lines of demarcation to be drawn in the sand—specifically over who should have the platform and what they were allowed to speak into the ears of the country. Years later Muhammad Ali would face similar challenges.

Main Bout Inc., a company that Ali created in 1966 to manage and navigate the multi-million dollar industry of fight promotions on his behalf, was the subject of retaliation once politicians and investors in the boxing industry learned that the Nation of Islam controlled 50 percent of the company's stock, although the organization was not its only stockholder. The others were Mike Malitz, a closed-circuit television operator (20 percent), Bob Arum, Malcolm's attorney (20 percent), and Jim Brown, the hall of fame Cleveland Browns running back (10 percent). Other promoters, once willing to pay top money for Ali to fight in their jurisdiction, were suddenly no longer willing to welcome him. One sportswriter voice argued that Black Muslims would take over the heavyweight title. A newspaper suggested that people should reconsider their purchasing tickets for Ali's fights as any profits would benefit the Nation of Islam. Richard Daley, the Mayor of Chicago, and the Illinois Attorney General William Clark, both refused to allow Ali to fight in their jurisdictions—declaring the fight illegal. States across the United States and even locales across Canada followed suit until it was finally allowed to be hosted in Toronto. The revenue it generated was forty times less than what Ali had earned from his three previous championship fights. After a little over a year and a half Main Bout Inc. folded, and all other investors in the company, with the exception of the Nation of Islam, formed other companies not associated with Ali. The Nation of Islam, and Muhammad Ali, the greatest fighter in the world, had effectively been isolated from the multimillion-dollar industry. One can argue that it was not simply Ali's refusal to join the United States armed forces in their fight in Vietnam that brought on industry's boycott of his fights, but his alliance with the Nation of Islam. As such, the hope that Main Bout Inc. would serve as the predominant entity that would finance an independent autonomous African American economic network quickly faded.[31]

A New Community Oriented Sport Tradition in the Colonized Zone

If the actualization of an athlete in the Robeson tradition is to come to pass, then a continuous bombardment on the tentacles of the colonial society is a necessary imperative. The sports industry is just one of the tentacles, but it is an important tentacle, in that it plays a major role in informing citizens of how to fall in line with the values and principles of the dominating society. If Black athletes do decide to participate in the sports industry, it is imperative that athletes enter into it with a Robesonian mind. But equally as important as using the industry is creating a sports culture in alignment with the imperatives of the once-colonized culture. As mentioned earlier, what is proposed may, at this nescient stage seem unimaginable and even inconsiderable, but whatever the approach, the task will be daunting, and a belief of victory is necessary for the achievement of that result. Imagining a new reality will equally require a reimagining of what is or is not practical.

Firstly, sports heroes should be created and promoted, not just for their amazing skills, but their character and their emulation of the values and principles of the new society. They should not be paid to rupture the developing economy but compensated fairly and practically for their efforts. An athlete should neither earn nor be glorified more than an educator or physician. They should be honored for representing the national culture, but never elevated above tradesmen/tradeswomen.

Secondly, sports should be practical. They should involve movements, maneuvers, and practices, that mirror the professions and values intended for the new society. Swimming, fishing, the martial arts & fighting, hunting, track and field, etc.... all find their origins in traditional African culture. They were practical in that the society would benefit from the general public practicing these skills in their regular lives. A look at the pyramid walls of ancient Kemet (Egypt) display that such sports as archery, horse riding, martial arts fighting, foot races, long/high jump, shooting, fishing, and acrobats were practiced during leisure times.[32] In addition, fighting traditions that have emerged in the Atlantic in modernity are continuities from pre-colonial African traditions.[33] Certainly, a sport tradition was present in African societies prior to European imperialism, but the orientation to the athletic contests and its practitioners were not intended to camouflage an exploitative racialized tradition.

Fanon warned against using old colonial methods in the creation of a new society. He cautioned against creating new sports leagues and having those leagues exist as mirror opposites to the White colonial leagues that once assisted in their oppression. He argues that such sports only breed values that are antagonistic to the new system one hopes to create. He says:

> If games are not integrated into the national life, that is to say in the building of the nation, and if you turn out national sportsmen and not fully conscious men, you will very quickly see sport rotted by professionalism and commercialism. Sport should not be a pastime or a distraction for the bourgeoisie of the towns.[34]

Such an approach, given the overwhelming popularity of modern sports, seems lofty and naïve at first glance, but ideas that once seemed impossible are now manifested in contemporary reality. In the United States, African American athletes have continued to carry forward the spark levied by Kaepernick, despite threats by team owners and the President of the United States that taking a knee for injustice would no longer be tolerated. These initial steps of protest and subsequent Black outrage at the liberal and conservative attacks on peaceful Black protest for legitimate concerns are sparks that have already lead to the creation of alternative institutions such as Ice Cube's BIG3 professional basketball league, very much intended to counter the media monopoly the NBA holds on professional basketball. The emergence of new sports leagues such as The BIG3 are natural progressions when a raise in consciousness, awareness, and Black rage coincide. Although the league is commercially driven and intertwined it does promote an alternative to the NBA, which has been vested with carrying on the national colonial message. In fact, Mahmoud Abdul-Raub, mentioned previously as one of the athletes in the Ali tradition, actually played a primary role as a starting point guard on a team that made it to the first championship game. He continued his anthem protest in the BIG3 league, but because it was not done on the state supported NBA, neither the owners nor the fans viewed it as newsworthy. Leagues such as the BIG3, and even murmurings from rapper Master P about forming an alternative to the NFL,[35] are an initial step, but in order to up the ante, leagues must be created that do not seek as their primary aim to rival the major professional leagues, but rather to provide an outlet for athletes and the general public that is aligned with the moral and practical imperatives of the culture.

The youth, and some adults look up to sports figures. Ideas of masculinity and femininity are embedded in the American sports tradition. We are under no illusions that it would take a complete cultural shift to make a completely separate, and culturally driven sports league to exist that is successful amongst people of African descent. But with psychological fortitude, a strong sense of self-determination, and an understanding of what it means for overcoming oppression and constant exploitation it is not a long reach. Overcoming certain impediments will make the effort worthwhile and efficient.

Impediments to an African-Centered, No-Longer-Exploitative Sports Tradition

Relying solely on the masters' tools will lead to an eventual dead end![36] If the famous quote by Audre Lord may be applied to the Sports Industry, it becomes clear that partial protests within a respective sports game will only create temporary change, and after while, the system will find another Black body to replace the one that is sending messages hostile to their purpose. A wholesale pulling out from the sports industry, on all levels is imperative. If the divestment happens from athletes and fans or supporters, it is that much easier to dismantle the masters' house. Voicing displeasure while still playing the game may make the space more comfortable, but at the end of the day, the house of oppression and exploitation is still kept in tact. The goal in overturning White supremacy should never be to become Black supremacists.

Distrust of other Black athletes will divert attention of community-centered Athletes away from the work that needs to be done irrespective of individualistic athletes' participation or not. Some will go with the money out of love for the systems accouterments. That is to be expected. But when they are ridiculed and shamed by their own community their actions and orientations will change. An athlete of the Robeson tradition should not be moved by the threat of another Black athlete replacing him/her. These are fear tactics fueled by the lure of personal wealth and individualistic leanings. Black athletes must resist the urge to be the stereotype, or one that knows what's at stake, yet continues to follow the colonial prototype in order to achieve colonial standards of success and excellence. As Fanon states, the man that decides that he wants to be a Black Man (in the way that the colonial state defines it) is no man at all.

The lack of knowledge about previous practices in African culture can make a person of African descent feel as if the only options available are those that they've been exposed to. In other words, if it is not on television or in pop culture, it not only is nonexistent, but any mention of it is to be doubted. The link to the past is an opportunity to see other possibilities. Fanon famously asserted "a national culture under colonial domination is a contested culture whose destruction is sought in systematic fashion." Athletes that believe what the mainstream culture teaches about the dominated culture that they belong to will second-guess themselves often when it comes to assisting their community first. The team-owners and supporters of the economic structure see attachment to traditions as refusal to be "coached" or "marketed."

The terminology and rhetoric used to discourage the development of new African-centered cultural activities must be expected and rendered as indicative of the fear of their demise. Fears that we are "returning to segregation," "fighting racists by being racist," or being "so un–American" are commonly used phrases to discourage anyone that publicly questions their oppression. Segregation was and is the separation of people for a specific reason or set of reasons. The people that attempt to intimidate those self-determining individuals always use the argument that the group is all about segregation or reverse racists, but never actually discuss the defacto segregation and racism that already exists in society. Because such acts have been deemed illegal in the books neither means that such practices have ended nor that the general public or the judicial system actually enforces such policies. Colin Kaepernick has been called un–American or anti–American because of his protests, but no actions have been more American than his in the past twelve months. He loves democracy and the country so much that he is willing to use his constitutional rights to challenge a disruption of the basic tenet that all men are created equal.

Humans created the world they lived in. We cannot ever forget that when the time comes to reconstruct the world that we want to see. Until ideologies of White Supremacy run rampant we should see a wholesale divestment from its institutions. Although this essay calls for people of African descent in the USA sports industry to chart new directions and alternatives, the call also goes out to the general public, irrespective of race, to divest from systems that rely on unfounded othering of people for exploitative reasons.

"De Colonization," Fanon says, is "the replacing of a certain 'species' of men by another 'species' of men." He argues that De Colonization is "always violent" asserting that all traces of the old colonizer must be removed if the space is contested. But before the physical colonizer can be removed (or the colonized can create their own space) the ideas, ethos, goals, and influence of the colonizer must be made to be naught. In this case the decolonization is vicious. It is critical but does not throw the proverbial baby out with the bathwater. Since people are so emotionally invested in the sports industry, any resistance against its decolonization must be relentless, since the removal of an entire social structure from the mind would be a necessary prerequisite before a new liberated conceptualization could emerge.

NOTES

1. Jared Ball. *I Mix What I Like!: A Mixtape Manifesto*. (Oakland,Edinburgh: AK Press, 2011). Drew Brown, "*Drafting Into Manhood: Black NFL Draft Prospects Conceptions of Manhood and Ideas of Playing in the NFL*" (PhD diss., Temple University, 2015). C.L.R. James, *Cricket* (London/New York: Allison & Busby, 1986.)

2. Frantz Fanon. *The Wretched of the Earth. the Handbook for the Black Revolution That Is Changing the Shape of the World* (New York, Grove Press, 1963), 36.

3. Khalid Itum, "*America's Goals Are Not Imperialistic*" foxnews.com April 20, 2003. Accessed January 15, 2017, http://www.foxnews.com/story/2003/04/30/america-goals-are-not-imperialistic.html

Shikha Dalmia. "*America's Foreign Policy Problem Is Fumbled Humanitarianism, Not Imperialism*" reason.com September 3, 2013. Accessed January 15, 2017, http://reason.com/archives/2013/09/03/americas-real-foreign-policy-problem-is

4. "*The Melting Pot Works*." *The Economist*. Feb 5, 2015. Accessed January 15, 2017. http://www.economist.com/blogs/democracyinamerica/2015/02/immigration-america

5. Fanon, *Wretched of the Earth*, 38.

6. "*Outpost*." Merriam-Webster.com. Accessed January 15, 2017. https://www.merriam-webster.com/dictionary/outpost.

7. Casey Gane-McCalla, "*Athletic Blacks vs. Smart Whites: Why Sports Stereotypes Are Wrong*." *The Huffington Post*. May 20, 2009. Accessed January 15, 2017. http://www.huffing tonpost.com/casey-ganemccalla/athletic-blacks-vs-smart_b_187386.html Michael Powell "*Warren Moon, Who Helped Clear Way for Black Quarterbacks, Recalls His Struggles*." *The New York Times*. February 5, 2016. Accessed January 15, 2017 https://www.nytimes.com/2016/02/06/sports/football/warren-moon-clearing-way-for-black-quarterbacks-recalls-his-struggles.html. Lindsay Gibbs, "*Then and Now: Cam Newton and the Ongoing Plight of the Black Quarterback*." *Think Progress* February 3, 2016. Accessed January 15, 2017. https://think progress.org/then-and-now-cam-newton-and-the-ongoing-plight-of-the-black-quarterback-c04802c34c1b#.juimrosmi

8. Stuart Hall. "Cultural Identity and Diaspora." In Jonathan Rutherford, *Identity, Community, Culture, Differences* (London: Lawrence and Wishart, 1990) 226–228. Edward W. Said. *Orientalism* (London: Routledge & Kegan Paul Ltd. 1978), 26.

bell hooks. "Eating the Other: Desire and Resistance" chapter in bell hooks, *Black Looks: Race and Representation* (Boston: South End Press, 1992), 21–40.

9. W.E.B. Du Bois. *Darkwater: Voices from Within the Veil* (New York, Dover Thrift, 1999), viii.

10. Charles W. Mills. *The Racial Contract* (Ithaca NY, Cornell University Press: 1997).

11. Fanon, *The Wretched of the Earth*, 148–205. In this section of his analysis Fanon actually refers to this group as the native or national bourgeoisie.

12. Fanon, *The Wretched of the Earth*, 36.

13. William Astore, "The Militarizaiton of Sports—and the Sportiness of Military Service." *The Huffington Post*. September 28, 2011. Accessed January 15, 2017. http://www.huffingtonpost.com/william-astore/the-militarization-of-sports_b_912004.html Tim Baysinger "Here's How Much the Pentagon Paid Sports Teams for Military Tributes." *Adweek* November 4, 2015. Accessed January 15, 2017. http://www.adweek.com/news/advertising-branding/here-s-how-much-pentagon-paid-sports-teams-military-tributes-167939. Bill Theobald, "Pentagon Paid Sports Teams Millions for Patriotic Events" November 4, 2015. Accessed January 15, 2017. http://www.usatoday.com/story/news/2015/11/04/millions-paid-pro-teams-patriotic-events-sens-flake-mccain-say/75141688/

14. Camara Jules P. Harrell, *Manichean Psychology Racism and the Minds of People of African Descent* (Washington D.C.: Howard University Press, 1999).

15. Des Bieler. "*Adam Jones: No Anthem Protests in Baseball Because It's 'a White Man's Sport*.'" *The Washington Post*. September 12, 2016. Accessed January 15, 2017. https://www.washingtonpost.com/news/dc-sports-bog/wp/2016/09/12/adam-jones-no-anthem-protests-in-baseball-because-its-a-white-mans-sport/?utm_term=.8469be6dd81c

16. Frantz Fanon, *Black Skin White Masks* (New York: Grove Press, 1952), 7. Fanon speaks of the colonial subject that has visited colonial territory as no longer speaking or understanding his native language and chooses to only speaks the colonial language in order to assert that now he is no longer a peasant. He also assumes a critical attitude toward his fellow subjects. If he speaks well they would know that he was there. If he criticizes he is made to be a fool that cannot recognize a good thing if it hit him in the mouth.

17. Michael Crowley "Muhammad Ali Was a Rebel. Michael Jordan Is a Brand Name. in Celebrating Jordan as a Hero, Are We Merely Worshipping Capitalism?" *Nieman Reports*. Fall 1999. Accessed online January 15, 2017 http://niemanreports.org/articles/muhammad-ali-was-a-rebel-michael-jordan-is-a-brand-name/

18. Fanon. *Black Skin White Masks*. 45.

19. This role, typically known in spaces as that of the "jigga-boo," "uncle Tom," "coon," is displayed by people of African descent that are not true to their historical selves and almost out of touch with their existential realities. In a sense, when one acts in a manner contradictory to their true selves they are in fact acting inhuman.

20. Marissa Payne, "Colin Kaepernick Refuses to Stand for National Anthem to Protest Police Killings" *The Washington Post*. August 28, 2016. Accessed January 15, 2017, https://www.washingtonpost.com/news/early-lead/wp/2016/08/27/colin-kaepernick-refuses-to-stand-for-national-anthem-to-protest-police-killings/?utm_term=.811cb9c17e69

Nick Wagoner, "Colin Kaepernick Continues Anthem Protest; Other 49ers, Rams Join." ESPN, September 13, 2016. Accessed January 15, 2017. http://www.espn.com/nfl/story/_/id/17534211/colin-kaepernick-san-francisco-49ers-again-kneels-national-anthem

21. John Breech, "*Here Are the 11 Players Who Joined Colin Kaepernick's Protest in Week 1*" cbssports.com September 12, 2016. Accessed January 15, 2017. http://www.cbssports.com/nfl/news/here-are-the-11-players-who-joined-colin-kaepernicks-protest-in-week-1/AP. "Many Young Athletes Joining Colin Kaepernick's National Anthem Protest." CBS News, September 14, 2016. Accessed January 15, 2017. http://www.cbsnews.com/news/many-young-athletes-joining-colin-kaepernicks-national-anthem-protest/

22. "Kaepernick Donates Another $100K, Spends Time at Homeless Shelter." *The Sacramento Bee*. Last Accessed 8 January 2017 http://www.sacbee.com/sports/nfl/san-francisco-49ers/article124969084.html

23. Khalid Salaam "Colin Kaepernick's Legacy Might Look a Lot Like Mahmoud Abdul-Rauf's" bleacherreport.com September 9. 2016. Accessed January 15, 2017. http://bleacherreport.com/articles/2662443-colin-kaepernicks-legacy-might-look-a-lot-like-mahmoud-abdul-raufs Patrick Ochs "Mahmoud Abdul-Rauf: 'My Career Was Never the Same.'" *Sun-Herald*, August 30, 2016. Accessed January 15, 2017. http://www.sunherald.com/sports/spt-columns-blogs/patrick-ochs/article98847212.html

24. Paul Robeson. *Here I Stand* (Boston: Beacon Press, 1998). Paul Robeson. *Paul Robeson Speaks: Writings, Speeches, and Interviews, a Centennial Celebration*. (New York: Citadel, 2002.)

25. Robert Van Gelder. "*Robeson Remembers: An Interview with the Star of Othello, Partly About His Past*" *The New York Times*. January 16, 1944, pp, X1.

26. Muhammad Ahmad. *African American History Since 1900. Third Edition* (New York: Custom Publishing 2008), 89–91.

27. Robeson, *Paul Robeson Speaks*, 91.

28. "Text of Jackie Robinson's Testimony in DC: Famed Ballplayer Hits Discrimination in U.S." *New York Amsterdam News*, City Edition; New York, NY July 23, 1949; p.8.

29. Robinson, Jackie. *I Never Had It Made: An Autobiography of Jackie Robinson*, Hopewel NY: Ecco Press 1995.

30. "Malcolm X's Letter" *New York Amsterdam News*. November 30, 1963; p.1.

31. Ezra, Michael. "Main Bout, Inc., Black Economic Power, and Professional Boxing: The Cancelled Muhammad Ali/Ernie Terrell Fight." *Journal of Sport History*. Vol. 29, No. 3 (Fall 2002) pp.413–437.

32. Wolfgang Decker. *Sports and Games of Ancient Egypt*. (Connecticut: Yale University Press, 1992) Joyce A. Tyldesley. *Egyptian Games and Sports*. (Bloomsbury: Shire Publications, 2008.)

33. T.J. Desch Obi. *Fighting for Honor. The History of African Martial Art Traditions in the Atlantic World* (Columbia: The University of South Carolina Press. 2008).

34. Fanon, *The Wretched of the Earth*, 196.

35. Chiari, Mike. "Master P Says He May Try to Start New Football League with Colin Kaepernick," October 18 2017. bleacherreport.com Accessed October 29, 2017. http://bleacherreport.com/articles/2739408-master-p-says-he-may-try-to-start-new-football-league-with-colin-kaepernick.

36. Audre Lourde and Cheryl Clarke. "The Master's Tools Will Never Dismantle the Master's House" chapter in Audre Lorde's *Sister Outsider: Essays and Speeches* (New York: Crossing Press, 2007), 110–114. The quote speaks to Lourde's famous quote "The Master's Tools Will Never Dismantle the Master's House" which was her critique of homophobic and patriarchal Black liberation ideologies.

References

Ahmad, Muhammad. *African American History Since 1900*. 3d ed. New York: Custom Publishing 2008.

Associated Press. "Many Young Athletes Joining Colin Kaepernick's National Anthem Protest." CBS News September 14, 2016. Accessed January 15, 2017. http://www.cbsnews.com/news/many-young-athletes-joining-colin-kaepernicks-national-anthem-protest/.

Astore, William. "The Militarization of Sports—and the Sportiness of Military Service." *The Huffington Post*. September 28, 2011. Accessed January 15, 2017. http://www.huffingtonpost.com/william-astore/the-militarization-of-sports_b_912004.html.

Ball, Jared. *I Mix What I Like! A Mixtape Manifesto*. Oakland, Edinburgh: AK Press, 2011.

Baysinger, Tim. "Here's How Much the Pentagon Paid Sports Teams for Military Tributes" Adweek. November 4, 2015. Accessed January 15, 2017. http://www.adweek.com/news/advertising-branding/here-s-how-much-pentagon-paid-sports-teams-military-tributes-167939.

Bieler, Des. "Adam Jones: No Anthem Protests in Baseball Because It's 'a White Man's Sport.'" *The Washington Post*. September 12, 2016. Accessed January 15, 2017. https://www.washingtonpost.com/news/dc-sports-bog/wp/2016/09/12/adam-jones-no-anthem-protests-in-baseball-because-its-a-white-mans-sport/?utm_term=.8469be6dd81c.

Breech, John. "Here Are the 11 Players Who Joined Colin Kaepernick's Protest in Week 1." cbssports.com. September 12, 2016. Accessed January 15, 2017. http://www.cbssports.com/nfl/news/here-are-the-11-players-who-joined-colin-kaepernicks-protest-in-week-1/.

Brown, Drew. "Drafting Into Manhood: Black NFL Draft Prospects Conceptions of Manhood and Ideas of Playing in the NFL." Ph.D. diss., Temple University, 2015.

Chiari, Mike. "Master P Says He May Try to Start New Football League with Colin Kaepernick." BleacherReport.com. October 18, 2017. Accessed October 29, 2017. http://bleacherreport.com/articles/2739408-master-p-says-he-may-try-to-start-new-football-league-with-colin-kaepernick.

Clarke, Cheryl, and Lourde, Audre. *Sister Outsider: Essays and Speeches*. New York: Crossing Press, 2007.

Crowley, Michael. "Muhammad Ali Was a Rebel. Michael Jordan Is a Brand Name. In Celebrating Jordan as a Hero, Are We Merely Worshipping Capitalism?" *Nieman Reports*. Fall 1999. Accessed January 15, 2017. http://niemanreports.org/articles/muhammad-ali-was-a-rebel-michael-jordan-is-a-brand-name/.

Dalmia, Shikha. "America's Foreign Policy Problem Is Fumbled Humanitarianism, Not Imperialism." reason.com. September 3, 2013. Accessed January 15, 2017. http://reason.com/archives/2013/09/03/americas-real-foreign-policy-problem-is.

Decker, Wolfgang. *Sports and Games of Ancient Egypt*. New Haven, CT: Yale University Press, 1992).

DuBois, W.E.B. *Darkwater: Voices from Within the Veil*. New York: Dover Thrift, 1999.

Ezra, Michael. "Main Bout, Inc., Black Economic Power, and Professional Boxing: The Cancelled Muhammad Ali/Ernie Terrell Fight." *Journal of Sport History* vol. 29, no. 3 (Fall 2002): 413–437.

Fanon, Frantz. *Black Skin White Masks.* New York: Grove Press, 1952.

Fanon, Frantz. *The Wretched of the Earth. the Handbook for the Black Revolution That Is Changing the Shape of the World.* New York: Grove Press, 1963.

Gane-McCalla, Casey. "Athletic Blacks Vs Smart Whites: Why Sports Stereotypes Are Wrong." *The Huffington Post.* May 20, 2009. Accessed January 15, 2017. http://www.huffington post.com/casey-ganemccalla/athletic-blacks-vs-smart_b_187386.html.

Gibbs, Lindsay. "Then and Now: Cam Newton and the Ongoing Plight of the Black Quarterback." *Think Progress.* February 3, 2016. Accessed January 15, 2017. https://think progress.org/then-and-now-cam-newton-and-the-ongoing-plight-of-the-black-quarter back-c04802c34c1b#.juimrosmi.

Hall, Stuart. "Cultural Identity and Diaspora." In Jonathan Rutherford, *Identity, Community, Culture, Differences.* London: Lawrence and Wishart, 1990.

Harrell, Camara Jules P. *Manichean Psychology Racism and the Minds of People of African Descent.* Washington, D.C.: Howard University Press, 1999.

hooks, bell. "Eating the Other: Desire and Resistance." *Black Looks: Race and Representation.* Boston: South End Press, 1992, 21–40.

Itum, Khalid. "America's Goals Are Not Imperialistic." foxnews.com. April 20, 2003. Accessed January 15, 2017. http://www.foxnews.com/story/2003/04/30/america-goals-are-not-imperialistic.html.

James, C.R.L. *Cricket.* London: Allison & Busby, 1986.

"Kaepernick Donates Another $100K, Spends Time at Homeless Shelter." *The Sacramento Bee.* Accessed 8 January 2017. http://www.sacbee.com/sports/nfl/san-francisco-49ers/article124969084.html.

"Malcolm X's Letter." *New York Amsterdam News.* November 30, 1963; p.1.

"The Melting Pot Works." *The Economist.* Feb 5, 2015. Accessed January 15, 2017. http://www.economist.com/blogs/democracyinamerica/2015/02/immigration-america.

Mills, Charles W. *The Racial Contract.* Ithaca, NY: Cornell University Press: 1997.

Obi, T.J. Desch. "Fighting for Honor." *The History of African Martial Art Traditions in the Atlantic World.* Columbia: University of South Carolina Press. 2008.

Ochs, Patrick. "Mahmoud Abdul-Rauf: 'My career was never the same.'" *Sun Herald.* August 30, 2016. Accessed January 15, 2017. http://www.sunherald.com/sports/spt-columns-blogs/patrick-ochs/article98847212.html.

"Outpost." Merriam-Webster.com. https://www.merriam-webster.com/dictionary/outpost.

Payne, Marissa. "Colin Kaepernick Refuses to Stand for National Anthem to Protest Police Killings." *The Washington Post.* August 28, 2016. Accessed January 15, 2017. https://www.washingtonpost.com/news/early-lead/wp/2016/08/27/colin-kaepernick-refuses-to-stand-for-national-anthem-to-protest-police-killings/?utm_term=.811cb9c17e69.

Powell, Michael. "Warren Moon, Who Helped Clear Way for Black Quarterbacks, Recalls His Struggles." *New York Times.* February 5, 2016. Accessed January 15, 2017 https://www.nytimes.com/2016/02/06/sports/football/warren-moon-clearing-way-for-black-quarterbacks-recalls-his-struggles.html.

Robeson, Paul. *Here I Stand.* Boston: Beacon Press, 1998.

Robeson, Paul. *Paul Robeson Speaks: Writings, Speeches, and Interviews, a Centennial Celebration.* New York: Citadel, 2002.

Robinson, Jackie. *I Never Had It Made: An Autobiography of Jackie Robinson.* New York: Ecco Press, 1995.

Rutherford, Jonathan. *Identity, Community, Culture, Differences.* London: Lawrence and Wishart, 1990.

Said, Edward W. *Orientalism.* London: Routledge & Kegan Paul, 1978.

Salaam, Khalid. "Colin Kaepernick's Legacy Might Look a Lot Like Mahmoud Abdul-Rauf's." bleacherreport.com. September 9. 2016. Accessed January 15, 2017. http://bleacherreport.com/articles/2662443-colin-kaepernicks-legacy-might-look-a-lot-like-mahmoud-abdul-raufs.

"Text of Jackie Robinson's Testimony in DC: Famed Ballplayer Hits Discrimination in US." *New York Amsterdam News*, City Edition. July 23, 1949; p.8.

Theobald, Bill. "Pentagon Paid Sports Teams Millions for Patriotic Events." *USA Today*. November 4, 2015. Accessed January 15, 2017. http://www.usatoday.com/story/news/2015/11/04/millions-paid-pro-teams-patriotic-events-sens-flake-mccain-say/75141688/.

Tyldesley, Joyce A. *Egyptian Games and Sports*. Bloomsbury: Shire Publications, 2008.

Van Gelder, Robert. "Robeson Remembers: An Interview with the Star of Othello, Partly About His Past." *New York Times*. January 16, 1944, x1.

Wagoner, Nick. "Colin Kaepernick Continues Anthem Protest; Other 49ers, Rams Join." ESPN. September 13, 2016. Accessed January 15, 2017. http://www.espn.com/nfl/story/_/id/17534211/colin-kaepernick-san-francisco-49ers-again-kneels-national-anthem.

PART III

Gender and Identity

Black Women's Sports Experiences Beyond the Game

F. Michelle Richardson *and*
Akilah R. Carter-Francique

> I am where I am because of the bridges I have crossed.
> Sojourner Truth was a bridge. Harriet Tubman was a bridge.
> Ida B. Wells was a bridge. Madame C.J. Walker was a bridge.
> Fannie Lou Hamer was a bridge.
> —Oprah Winfrey (Newman, 2000, p. 36)

Introduction

In 2016 the Games of the XXXI Olympiad were held in Rio de Janeiro, Brazil (Olympic Games, 2017); and for Black women in the United States (U.S.), the Games served as a social media host of #BlackGirlMagic (Reid, 2016). The Twitter handle boast of numerous podium-filled performances of Black women in basketball, track and field, tennis, gymnastics, swimming, and fencing. For instance, in basketball and track and field, sports historically participated and often overrepresented by Black women (Smith, 1992; 2000; The Institute for Diversity and Ethics in Sport [TIDES]—The Racial and Gender Report Card: College Sports, [2017]; Vertinsky & Captain, 1998), Black women earned gold, silver, and bronze medals. Sportswomen like Tianna Bartoletta (long jump), Michelle Carter (shot put), Brianna Rollins (100-meter hurdles), Dalilah Muhammad (400-meter hurdles), and the all Black 4x400-meter relay team of Allyson Felix, Phyllis Francis, Natasha Hastings, Courtney Okolo with alternate members Taylor Ellis-Watson and Francena McCorory earned gold medals. Similarly, Simone Biles, Ibtihaj

Muhammad, and Simone Manuel also earned gold medals in gymnastics, fencing, and swimming respectively, sports with historically low participation rates by Black women.

The listing of the Black sportswomen and their corresponding achievements may read as incessant; however, according to personal interviews and newspaper and social media coverage, some of the talented and phenomenal women also deemed their achievements a burden (Reid, 2016). The paradoxical feelings may best be attributed to the resultant effects of "white supremace capitalistic patriarchy" (hooks, n.d.). This characterization, a conception professed by bell hooks (n.d.), encompasses the hegemonic undertone of the U.S. and scores of felt racist, sexist, and classist marginalizations to include negative characterizations experienced by Black women in society and in sport (Bruening, 2005; Collins, 2000, 2004; hooks, 1984; Giddings, 1984; Smith 1992).

The paradoxical feeling that some of the Black sportswomen felt at the Rio Games can be understood when juxtaposed and contextualized within the historical treatment of Black female Olympians. For example, consider the experiences of Black women 84 years prior in the 1932 Los Angeles Olympics, when Theodora "Tidye" Pickett and Louise Stokes earned membership on the U.S. track and field team. Documented as the first two Black women to make an Olympic team, 17-year-old Pickett and 18-year-old Stokes experience was demarked by sexism and racism (Osgood, 2016). The X Olympiad marked the second games with the return of women's track and field as it is documented that Games officials, and others, felt that women would damage their reproductive organs through strenuous athletic participation in such events. Therefore, the presence of women in the strenuous sport of track and field posed challenges for all women, but the presence as Black women posed experiences of racial discrimination, segregation, abuses, and "shut out of the hero's treatment given to other athletes" (Osgood, 2016) for Pickett and Stokes. Hence, with heart filled pride these two women finished sixth and fourth respectively in the 100-meter, earning Stokes membership on the 4x100-meter relay and Pickett as a relay alternate.

Shortly after their selection discriminatory treatments ensued. For example, separate room and board accommodations while traveling by train with the U.S. team, famed member and teammate Mildred "Babe" Didrikson threw a pitcher of ice water on Pickett and Stokes while sleeping, and the women were isolated and alienated from the team in the evenings due to racially segregated dorms and dining facilities. The crowning discriminatory treatment was the removal of Pickett and Stokes from the 4x100-meter relay at the Los Angeles Games; their replacement by two slower White women that was enforced by coaches and societal prejudice; and, the inability to be a part of the gold medal winning team.

Pickett and Stokes returned four years later to participate in the 1936 Berlin Games. Stokes, once again, sat in the stands and would not compete in the Games. But Pickett did, in the 80-meter hurdles this time. Unfortunately, in the second round of the event she hit a hurdle breaking her foot, leaving her unable to finish the race and compete in any other races. The women would leave another Games with no medals. Moreover, the cancellation of the 1940 and 1944 Games, due to World War II, did not afford them the opportunity to try to make another team. But their hearts, representation, and survival efforts would inspire other Black women as reflected in the increased representation of Black women in the Olympic Games to follow and attainment of their medals (e.g., Alice Coachman, gold medal in the high jump—1948; Wilma Rudolph, gold medal in the 100-meter, 200-meter, 4 × 100-meter relay—1960, Wyomia Tyus, gold medal in the 100-meter—1964 and 1968; see Davis, 1992).

Hence, the representation and achievements of Black women at the Rio Games is significant and indeed a reflection of #BlackGirlMagic. Winfrey indicates in the quotation introducing this essay, a listing of the brave Black women whom life experiences and perseverance despite their racial, gender, and class status made them pioneers, leaders, and "bridges" for other Black women. Similarly, Pickett and Stokes should also serve as representative bridges, or as we will present "community othermothers," within the Black female collective and among Black sportswomen. In this essay, we aim to explicate their significance through (a) discussing the underrepresentation of Black sportswomen as participants, coaches, and administrators; (b) presenting the concept of community othermothering; (c) contextualizing the barriers Black sportswomen endure as participants, coaches, and administrators; (d) historical efforts of activism to overcome barriers; and (e) contemporary strategies that promote participation and representation at the intersection of race, gender, and social class.

Persevering Despite Underrepresentation

It is a blessed feat to train and make an Olympic team as only a selected few can do, but to then have this feat ruined by acts of racism, sexism, and classism—some may find unfathomable. Black women experience numerous acts rooted in racism, sexism, and classism, or multiple jeopardies, resulting in barriers as (a) participants in sport and (b) aspiring coaches and administrators in sport. Moreover, the barriers are rooted in Black women's social location as a marginalized body, or "Other," within the U.S. (Collins, 2000; hooks, 1981, 2000; Giddings, 1984). This historic and contemporary positionality as the "Other" have resulted in many negative and unintended consequences that have reduced the beneficial intentions of institutional policies (e.g., Affirmative Action) and legislation (e.g., Title IX of the Educational Amendments of 1972 [Title IX]). For example, in 2012 a group of Black sportswomen (i.e., coaches, athletes) and stakeholders (i.e., lawyers, professors) met to address the Title IX and the comparative state of progress the amendment has provided for Black women and White women. On the 40th anniversary, the women discerned that for all intents and purposes Title IX did address gender equity, but failed to adequately and equally address racial equity. Therefore, the disproportionality of access and opportunity between Black and White girls as youth is exposed when they reach institutions of higher education and intercollegiate play indicating that opportunities have increased for both racial groups, but not at the same rate, not across ALL sports and in ALL aspects of sport (e.g., participants, coaches, administrators). Black female athletes remain concentrated in the sports of basketball and track and field, yielding low participation rates in "…lacrosse (2.2 percent), swimming, (2.0), soccer (5.3), and softball (8.2)" (Rhoden, 2012). The Black sportswomen presented that the limited accesses and opportunities and low participation rates in the listed sports has a trickle up effect for Black women's representation as coaches and administrators.

Black women have worked diligently to close the gaps in sports participation, coaching, and administration; however, there is a need to recognize that there are still issues that need addressing. Thus, advocating for accessing and increasing wider participation opportunities to Black girls and women. Matthewson (1996) explains that training and development in other sports are dependent upon youth and interscholastic level access to sports *other than* basketball and track and field. Therefore, to see more #BlackGirlMagic in sports participation, it must be reflected in every aspect of sports to include participation, coaching, and administration.

According to Dr. Richard Lapchick and colleagues (2016), of the 110 Football Bowl Subdivision (FBS) institutions no Black women that hold the position of Athletic Director (AD). Comparatively, at the time of their study, nine White women (7 percent), 110 White men (85.9 percent), and 13 Black men (10.2 percent) were employed as Division I FBS ADs. Mathewson's (1996) notion to aspire to higher heights, one must see a reflection of themselves to know that such aspirations are possible. Therefore, Black girls and women should not have to look back a half a century to find role models.

The significance of this essay resides in the historical and ongoing social inequalities within sport. Thus, in addition to the underrepresentation as participants, management (e.g., coaches, academic advisors, Faculty Athletic Representative), and administrators (e.g., athletic directors, commissioners, directors); there are a host of issues that stifle Black girls and women's sporting experiences that include: education, health and wellness, financial freedom, work-life balance, and media representation. Scholars contend the contributing factors to these issues reside at the intersections of Black women's social location based on their race, gender, and social class as well as the unintended consequences of legislation to include Title VII of the Civil Rights Act of 1964, Title IX, and Affirmative Action (Abney, 2007; Bruening, 2005; Carter-Francique & Flowers, 2013; Carter-Francique & Richardson, 2015; Mathewson, 1996; McDowell & Carter-Francique, 2016; Smith, 1992, 2000). (The identified legislative acts are discussed in greater detail in section Activist Efforts of Black Sportswomen).

The Importance of Black Feminism

Throughout this essay, we employ the standpoint of Black Feminist Thought for three reasons. First, this standpoint allows Black women to be the center of analysis and situate her historical treatment within the hegemonic and institutionalized structures of "White supremacist capitalist patriarchy" (hooks, n.d.). Second, this standpoint acknowledges that Black women have a unique perspective and while not a monolithic group, we share a common experience. Third, and last, this standpoint acknowledges that not every Black woman is conscious of her unique perspective and the sisterhood of shared experiential commonalities. And so we, embrace Collins (1986) charge to "produce facts and theories about the Black ... [sportswoman's] ... experience that will clarify a Black woman's standpoint for the Black woman" (p. S16). We aim to do so understanding: (a) the meaning of self-definition and self-valuation, (b) the interlocking nature of oppression, and (c) the importance of Black women's culture.

Black Women, Othermothering and Community Othermothering

The notion of community othermothering is rooted in the conceptualization of othermothering (Collins, 2000). According to Collins (2000), othermothering, or othermothers, is when women, who are kin (e.g., grandmothers, aunts, sisters, and/or cousins) and fictive kin (e.g., community friends and neighbors), help biological mothers in the raising of their children. This woman-centered network of "community-based child care" provides an essential purpose for the African American community in which othermothers nurture, educate, and instill the cultural traditions of the community. Hence, Black females are nurtured at a young age to become othermothers; and, as Collins (2000) explicates, "experiences both of being nurtured as children and being held responsible for siblings and fictive kin within kin networks can stimulate a more generalized ethic of caring and personal accountability among African American women" (p. 189).

Activism Through Community Othermothering

The ethic of caring[1] and personal accountability serve as essential components for Black women's adoption of community othermothering. But, the title of community othermother is granted to Black women often over the age of 40 (James, 1993), because they have endured a significant number of lived experiences and challenges and consequently developed great wisdom. This wisdom coupled with an understanding of the traditions and cultural nuances of the Black community cultivate a positionality of their analyses and criticisms (James, 1993). Thus, community othermothers are aware of the needs, inequities, and injustices of the "children" stimulating their efforts to address and redress issues through community organization and social activism. Accordingly, Black women's familia and community relationship and an "ethic of socially responsible individualism" influenced their decisions to accept the assignment and embrace social activism.

There are a host of Black women, known and unknown, that accepted the assignment of community othermother. The most notable names include Ida B. Wells, Mary McCleod Bethune, and Fannie Lou Hamer that provoked social change on a national level. While Daisy Bates and Ella Baker are less recognized, they were just as impactful with their social justice efforts for racial integration in public schools and mobilization of the Southern Christian Leadership Conference (SCLC) and the Student Nonviolent Coordinating Committee (SNCC), respectively (James, 1993). Based on the efforts and movements these women lead, they arguably could be situated as activist mothering (Naples, 1991, 1992).

ACTIVIST MOTHERING

The role of the community othermother and her involvement in political activism is also termed activist mothering (Naples, 1991, 1992, 1996). In 1992, Nancy Naples discussed the term in *Activist Mothering: Cross-generational Continuity in the Community Work of Women from Low-Income Urban Neighborhoods*. In this article, Naples argues that activist mothering is a more comprehensive articulation of the activities in which Black women, and Latina women, engage. More plainly, Naples states that this term "…provides a new conceptualization of the interacting nature of labor, politics, and mothering—three aspects of social life usually analyzed separately—from the point of view of women whose motherwork has often been ignored or pathologized

(Moynihan, 1967) in sociological analysis" (Naples, 1992, p. 446). She then iterates that activist mothering reflects the "…power of knowledge generated from 'self-defined, subjugated standpoints' to decenter dominant frameworks" (Naples, 1992, p. 446).

Situating Black women's ability to decenter dominant frameworks is steeped in their "Otherness" which undergird a collectivist framework that aims to challenge notions (a) of subjugated knowledge and that (b) marginalized persons cannot interpret their own experiential knowledges. Reflecting the Black Feminist Thought standpoint, community othermothering illuminates how interlocking marginalizations of race, gender, and class foster a need for an activist response in social and cultural institutions like sport. Therefore, whether recognized as "community othermothers" or "activist mothering," the conceptualization of the "othermother" serves as the foundation for Black women's social justice concerns and, ultimately, their political activism.

Barriers for Black Sportswomen

The conception of community othermothering, as explicated, is to serve as an advocate for the community; hence, the need to be abreast of the struggles of the community. Acknowledging the purpose of this essay, Black girls and women face a number of systemic and career specific barriers due to "the interlocking nature of oppression" as participants and professionals in sport.

Participants

In 2011, the Women's Sports Foundation (WSF) released a report highlighting four barriers women of color, to include Black women, face when accessing and participating in sport to include (a) baseline data, (b) economic challenges, (c) gender stereotyping, and (d) cultural barriers. First, the report explicated that lack of baseline statistical data about the actual numbers of Black women participating in sporting activities locally and nationally can affect a woman and/or her parents' willingness to participate in said sport. Second, a woman and her family's economic status may hinder her ability to participate in certain sports, particularly if not offered within K-12 institutions, due to the cost of play which may include entry fees, uniforms, shoes and equipment, and varying travel fees (e.g., gasoline, hotel and food during stay) (e.g., lacrosse, golf, gymnastics, tennis). Third, systemic sexism in the U.S. undergirds notions of gender stereotyping that assumes a woman's sexuality based on engaged sport (e.g., participation in softball or basketball deemed a lesbian; participation in track and field deemed sexually promiscuous); and limited media visibility which is noted to limit the number of Black female role models as well as influence participation rates. Fourth, and last, cultural barriers found at the intersection of gender, race, and ethnicity may collide with sport engagement (e.g., Muslim women must manage religious obligations with uniform sporting requirements such as clothing coverage from head [Hijab], arms, and legs; Black women's sport engagement in certain sports over others like track and field over swimming due to cultural experiences with water and its effect on hair texture).

Understanding the four barriers is important, but knowing how to overcome them is essential. For example, in 2016, Carter-Francique identified strategies for Black girls in K–12 institutions and educators that work with them, to overcome the four barriers. (See Carter-Francique, 2016.) As presented, Black women also engage in sport as coaches, administrators, and other leaders (i.e., agents, managers, and lawyers, reporters and journalists, facility managers). Understanding the barriers they face is necessary to address the range of Black girls and women's challenges.

Coaches and Administrators

In 1991, Abney and Richey illuminated and detailed the *Barriers Encountered by Black Female Athletic Administrators and Coaches* for access and treatment when serving in these positions. The authors conveyed that "…racial discrimination, 'womanism' (the act of women hindering the success of other women), class oppression, inadequate or biased counseling at the precollegiate and collegiate levels, and a lack of minority women as role models as mentors" limit the initial visibility of African American [Black] women in coaching and administrative positions" (Abney & Richey, 1991, p. 19). These initial barriers then contributed to and further hindered their ability to the developmental advancement of their careers in historically White institutions of higher education (HWIHE) and historically Black colleges and universities (HBCUs). (See table 1.)

Table 1. The Five Highest Ranking Barriers During the Career Development of Black Women

Black Women at HBCUs	Black Women at HWIHE
Inadequate salary	Inadequate salary
Lack of support groups	Lack of support groups
Being a woman	Being Black
Employer discrimination (sexism)	Being a woman
Low expectations by administrators and others	Lack of cultural and social outlets in the community

*Note: This table is adapted from Abney and Richey (1991, p. 20).

Activist Efforts of Black Sportswomen

The social construction of community othermothering and the ideals of activist mothering for Black women is significant. As stated, Black women utilized a range of platforms from which to engage in social justice efforts (Barnett, 1993; Collins, 2000; Naples, 1992); however, Black sportswomen's community othermothering engagement is virtually unknown and has received limited examination (Carter, 2012; Davis, 1992; Staurowsky, 2012). Therefore, before examining the role of community othermothering for Black sportswomen, it is necessary to explore the experiences of Black sportswomen and how their various occupations and participation efforts could embrace the aspects and/or viability of community othermothering.

Federal legislation such as Brown v. Board of Education of Topeka, the Civil Rights Act of 1964, and the Title IX have all played a vital role in increasing access, participation, and pay equity. Moreover, *Brown v. Board of Education* of Topeka, Title II of the Civil Rights Act of 1964, and Title IX were the catalyst change in sports. *Brown v. Board of Education* dispelled the notion of separate but equal, and the Supreme Court found it to be unconstitutional (The National Center for Public Policy Research, n.d.). Title II of the Civil Rights Act of 1964 did away with discrimination based on race, color, religion, sex, and national origin, and thereby allowing Black men, women, and children to gain access to educational and sports participation opportunities at institutions that prohibited their attendance (The United States Department of Justice, 2016). While Title IX increased the sporting opportunities for women broadly, it did not increase opportunities for Black women specifically.

Consequently, for Black women to reap the benefits of Title IX, gender equity and racial equity must be on par with one another (Carter-Francique & Richardson, 2015; Hattery, 2012; Mathewson, 1996). For instance, in 1993 Sanya Tyler was awarded $2.4 million dollars (later reduced to $1.1 million) in a sex discrimination lawsuit filed against her employer, Howard University. Tyler's victory was the first time money was awarded under Title IX law (Orem, 2012). Similarly, the day before Venus Williams was to play Lindsay Davenport for the Women's Singles she appealed to Wimbledon's governing body to make the women's prize money equal to the men's (The Reliable Source, 2013). Then, in 2006, Williams very publicly called out Wimbledon and the All England Lawn Tennis Club on the issue of pay equity via an Op-Ed piece titled *Wimbledon Has Sent Me a Message: I Am Only a Second-Class Champion*. Williams spoke of how Wimbledon treated men and women the same in all aspects except pay, and how men and women who compete in the U.S. Open and Australian Open have enjoyed equal pay for over thirty years.

I feel so strongly that Wimbledon's stance devalues the principle of meritocracy and diminishes the years of hard work that women on the tour have put into becoming professional tennis players. I believe that athletes—especially female athletes in the world's leading sport for women—should serve as role models. The message I like to convey to women and girls across the globe is that there is no glass ceiling. My fear is that Wimbledon is loudly and clearly sending the opposite message. I intend to keep doing everything I can until Billie Jean's original dream of equality is made real. It's a shame that the name of the greatest tournament in tennis, an event that should be a positive symbol for the sport, is tarnished [Williams, 2006, p. 21].

As a result of Williams' outspoken activism, in 2007 she became the first Wimbledon Women's Singles Champion to win prize money equal to the Men's Singles Champion (The Reliable Source, 2013).

The experiences and consequential actions of Tyler and Williams are significant. Each attained a level of respect in their sporting communities as a collegiate coach and elite athlete respectively. This respect, coupled with wisdom of the "community's traditions and culture" (James, 1993, p. 47) made them able to "provide analyses and/or critiques of conditions or situations that may affect the well-being of her community" (James, 1993, p. 48). Thus, their ability to understand the historical plight of women in sport and the broader implications for girls and women as sportswomen speak to the very characteristics of community othermothers. The value of their efforts resides in the strategic processes to uplift not only Black women but to uplift the broader community by challenging the oppressive power structures that limit marginalized person's access and opportunity. Moreover, in these instances, equal pay for women is an issue that affects women across racial groups and social class categories (Carter-Francique & Flowers, 2014; Osborne & Yarborough, 2000; U.S. Equal Employment Opportunity Commission, n.d.).

Tyler and Williams are not the only Black sportswomen to perform acts of community othermothering. Black sportswomen before and after Pickett and Stokes 1932 and 1936 historical entrance into international competition have the residue of community othermothering. However, due to the Black women's "Othered" status, many of their actions remain hidden under the blanket of racism, sexism, classism, heterosexism, and religious dominance that diminishes the importance of their sporting achievements and existence.

Who Will Speak for the Black Sportswoman?

Oglesby (1981) indicated that nobody knows the Black sportswoman, and contended that only a few elite sportswomen (e.g., Althea Gibson, Wilma Rudolph, Wyomia Tyus) were visible and conscious to the American sports public. Despite that reality, scholars contend that the Black sportswoman's visibility is necessary to inspire the next generation (Boreland & Bruening, 2010; Carter-Francique & Richardson, 2016; Houzer, 1974; Staurowsky, 2012). The nature of Black sportswoman necessary visibility derives, in part, from a need for organizations and associations diversity agendas that have acknowledged the need for safe spaces. Moreover, to serve as host to support groups that provide safe places where Black women can speak freely and find support amongst other Black sportswomen that are enduring or have endured challenges and barriers. In the vast landscape of specialized groups, organizations, and associations devoted to the needs of Black women; one can find an array of professional and civic organizations that fit their various representational needs. However, finding organizations and associations that benefit the unique intersecting needs of Black sportswomen specifically, is a more daunting task. Nevertheless, the following race-based and gender-based organizations and associations have demonstrated efforts of inclusion and concerns for the Black sportswoman's needs.

Race-Based Organizations

Organizations such as the *Minority Opportunities Athletics Association* (MOAA) and *Advocates for Athletic Equity* (AAE) (formerly known as the Black Coaches Association) are inclusive of Black women, but their collective focuses on Black sportspeople. The goals and mission of MOAA "provide opportunities to exchange ideas, advocate increased participation and administrative opportunities for minorities in athletics. MOAA also promotes generating a sports culture that supports the values necessary to teach and learn respect for self and others" (National Association of Collegiate Directors of Athletics [NACDA], 2017). Advocates for Athletic Equity (AAE) (2017) mission is "to advocate and promote ethnic minority coaches for positions of leadership at all levels of sport." Black sportswomen are inclusive in AAE through their membership and the Achieving Coaching Excellence (ACE) Program for Women. The goal of this program is to provide education, professional development, and networking opportunities for women basketball coaches aspiring to be head coaches. This program is to be commended but has a limited reach of support to Black sportswomen. That said, the benefit of having such organizations and associations allows Black women to build an alliance that she can call upon for support, inspiration, and reassurance as well as inspire and encourage other groups (Boreland & Bruening, 2010; Pastore, 2003; Weaver & Chelladuri, 1999). To date, MOAA is still in operation; however, in 2016 the AAE, the second manifestation of the Black Coaches Association, ceased operations due to a shortfall of financial support.

Gender-Based Organizations

Similar to the race-based organizations and association, gender-based organizations such as the *Women's Sports Foundation* and the *Women Leaders in College Sports* are two of primary fixtures espousing for women. Founded in 1974, the *Women's Sports Foundation* (WSF) has long been a collective voice for the female athlete and administrator. The WSF has been at the forefront of the issues of pay inequity, equality, and the rights of girls and women to participate in sports on every level; as well as funding scholarly research on the issues of women's equity and inclusion in sports (Women's Sports Foundation, n.d.). *Women Leaders in College Sports* (WLCS), formerly known as the National Association of Collegiate Women Athletics Administrators (NACWAA), focus is to develop and advocate for female collegiate athletic administrators. WLCS in partnership with the National Collegiate Athletic Association (NCAA) offers four annual leadership development symposiums that fit every level of athletic administration (Women Leaders in College Sport, 2017). The shared missions of these women's sports organizations are to advocate for women as a collective; however, Black sportswomen need their voices to be heard separately from the collective due of the distinctiveness of their sporting experiences.

Meeting at the Intersection of Race and Gender

To date, there is only one organization devoted to the Black sportswoman, the *Black Women in Sports Foundation* (BWSF). The BWSF, founded in 1992 by Tina Sloan Green, Dr. Alpha Alexander, Dr. Nikki Franke, and Linda Greene, Esq., maintains a mission to "increase the involvement of Black women and girls in all aspects of sport, including athletics, coaching, and administration" (BWSF, n.d.). This grassroots level organization seeks to redress social inequities of Black girls and women through a range of "hands-on" developmental programs for youth (e.g., Amazing Grace, Go Girl Go) and professionals (e.g., Next Step Mini-Forum). Moreover, they "sow seeds" through scholarship offerings (e.g., The Madeline Kountze Dugger-Kelly Scholarship, The Angela Murphy Scholarship) for Black college women specifically, and women of color broadly, at the undergraduate and graduate levels. Through these programs, the BWSF has actively engaged the community for over twenty-five years; however, their programming reach is limited to girls and women from largely marginalized neighborhoods in Philadelphia, Pennsylvania. Despite their limitations, the BWSF provides a platform for Black girls and sportswomen to feel supported through understanding their challenges and providing strategic avenues to overcome current and potential barriers in sport and society.

Strategic Implications of Community Othermothering

Employing the principles of community othermothering, again, purports the awareness of issues and trials for the communities' children. Embodying the Black feminist thought standpoint serves as a mainstay "arguing that group location in hierarchical power relations produces common challenges for individuals in those groups"; and that "shared experiences can foster similar angles of vision leading to group knowledge or standpoint deemed essential for informed political action" (Collins, 2000, p. 300). Therefore, having awareness of the four aforementioned barriers that Black female participants face can fuel Black sportswomen's community othermothering agenda and efforts.

However, the barriers for Black female coaches and administrators located within historically Black and historically White institutions like higher education can not only pose challenges for career advancement, but for carrying out community othermothering efforts based on their race and gender, and akin to Black female participants, socioeconomic status, gender stereotyping, and cultural barriers. Hence, Abney and Richey (1991) consciously crafted a list of eight (8) strategies as a guide for Black women professionals to overcome the identified barriers. (See Table 2.) And, we would be remiss if we did not also include that Black female sport scholars experience similar challenges like coaches and administrators; thus, Dr. Robertha Abney and Dorothy Richey's strategic foresight can assist Black women connected to sport and physical activity for mutual benefits (e.g., understand issues, analyze issues, write policy).

Table 2. Strategies to Overcome Barriers of Marginalization

(1) Black women aspiring to coaching and athletic administrative positions should start support groups, organizations, and/or programs to exchange ideas and share experiences

(2) Black women and other minorities should investigate initiating formal and informal mentoring programs within the athletic arena of the governing bodies of sport

(3) Black women must be confident, competent, determined, and willing to persevere when unpleasant experiences arise

(4) Black women must develop and maintain positive sense of self while remaining in sport

(5) Black women must be inspired to meet sports' challenges

(6) Black women must be qualified and compete for leadership roles at all levels in sport

(7) Black women must become actively involved in sport associations, organizations, committees, and/or governing bodies

(8) Black women presently in athletic administration and coaching positions must help interested Black women grow professionally in sport

Note: This table is adapted from Abney and Richey (1991, p. 21).

Reviewing the eight strategies, four directly speak to the ideals of Black women serving as community othermothers; and consequently, these strategies incorporate efforts to "uplift the race" (James, 1993, p. 49) through "collective action" (James, 1993, p. 47). First, strategy one proposes Black women "start support groups, organizations, and/or programs to exchange ideas and share experiences" (Abney & Richey, 1991, p. 21). Initiating support groups, organization, and/or programs solely for Black women can provide a "safe cultural space" (Collins, 2000) to educate each other and provide coping strategies to endure discriminatory practices in their quest for advancement within majority institutions.

Second, strategy two suggest Black women begin "formal and informal mentoring programs within the athletic arena of the governing bodies of sport" (Abney & Richey, 1991, p. 21). Developing formal mentor programs often pairs a senior level professional with a junior level professional, and can aid Black women with learning how to navigate the institutional politics (i.e., networking, institution and/or position expectations) that can and have hindered Black women's advancement. Comparatively, developing informal mentor programs lack formal structure, but allow the freedom and flexibility to communicate as needed. However, we raise caution with this strategy due to (a) limited Black female professionals (e.g., coaches, administrators; TIDES—The Racial and Gender Report Cards, 2016) and (b) mentor fit, Black women are not a monolithic culture (Collins, 2000); and thus, not every Black woman can identify with the other [Sistahs of the Academy].

Third, strategy seven advises Black women to "become actively involved in sport associations, organizations, committees, and/or governing bodies" (Abney & Richey, 1991, p. 21). According to the principles of community othermothering, obtaining a "power position of respect" can allow Black sportswomen to serve as a representative authority on the "conditions and situations that may affect the well-being of her community" (James, 1993, p. 48). Attaining an assignment in local/regional/national/international groups, or having a "seat at the table," allows Black women to have a voice and an opportunity to effect change (i.e., cultural, legislative, social). For example, serving on boards and/or committees in organizations such as the International Olympic Committee (IOC), North American Society for Sport Management (NASSS), North American Society for the Sociology of Sport (NASSS) as well as the aforementioned MOAA, NCAA, and WSF.

While fourth, strategy eight commands that Black women "must help interested Black women grow professionally in sport" (Abney & Richey, 1991,

p. 21). This directive assumes that Black women have embraced the episte-mological aspects for an ethic of caring (i.e., individual expressiveness, appro-priateness of emotions, capacity for empathy) such that a connective knowledge base is made through lived experiences (Collins, 2000). Forging this kind of relationship provides support in addition to—or in lieu of—col-lective support groups, mentorship, or sport association affiliation. For exam-ple, Black sportswomen like Felicia Hall Allen (President and CEO, Felicia Hall Allen & Associates), Dawn Staley (Head women's basketball coach, Uni-versity of South Carolina), Katrina Adams (President, United States Tennis Association), Andrea Williams (Commissioner, Big Sky Conference), Felicia Martin (Vice President of Eligibility, NCAA), and Lisa Borders (Commis-sioner, Women's National Basketball Association [WNBA]) we feel have adopted this strategy and used their wisdom to assist and guide aspiring Black sportswomen. This commanding ideal speaks to the notion of "lift as we climb" and the community othermothering essence of Mary Church Ter-rell who eloquently stated:

> And so, lifting as we climb, onward and upward we go, struggling and striving, and hoping that the buds and blossoms of our desires will burst into glorious fruition ere long. With courage, born of success achieved in the past, with a keen sense of the responsibility which we shall continue to assume, we look forward to a future large with promise and hope. Seeking no favors because of our color, nor patronage because of our needs, we knock at the bar of justice, asking an equal chance [Church Terrell, 1898].

Thus, the purposeful engagement of Black sportswomen with one another at all levels ensures that we are not without understanding, wisdom, and guidance from other Black sportswomen.

Conclusion

The purpose of this essay was to illuminate the role that community othermothering has, does, and can play in Black sportswomen's lives. More specifically, this essay conveys how community othermothering is the catalyst of #BlackGirlMagic; and, how Black sportswomen have endured despite the barriers of underrepresentation and the lack of organizations that solely speak on their behalf. As presented, community othermothers to include coaches, academic and career advisors, academic instructors, and high school, college, professional, and recreational administrators serve as mentors, strength sources, and a *living bridge* of hope for young Black sportswomen that aspire to lead. Likewise, carrying the title of community othermothers communicates a breadth of knowledge, a willingness to guide, and a duty to engage in activist efforts that promote ideological notions of equality and equity. Therefore, it is our hope that this essay not only serves as an information source documenting the valuable role of community othermothers for Black sportswomen, but that it also serves as a guide on the efforts and strategic methods, rooted in Black feminist standpoint, that can provide ways to overcome systemic barriers, persevere, and achieve individually *and* as a collective.

NOTE

1. The ethic of caring is an epistemological framework and practice utilized by Black women (Collins, 2000) and incorporates three components that promote knowledge validation: personal expressiveness and uniqueness, engaging in emotional dialogues, and cultivating the ability for empathy. This notion was found to be an appropriate framework for Black female college athletes' holistic development (Carter-Francique, 2014).

REFERENCES

Abney, R. (2007). African American women in intercollegiate coaching and athletic administration: Unequal access. In D. Brooks and R. Althouse (Eds.), *Diversity and social justice in college sports: Sport management and the student athlete* (pp. 51–76). Morgantown, WV: FIT.

Abney, R., & Richey, D. (1991). Barriers encountered by Black female athletic administrators and coaches. *Journal of Physical Education, Recreation & Dance*, 62(6), 19–21.

Associated Press. (2016 October 15). Nonprofit focused on promoting minority coaches will dissolve. *ESPN*. Retrieved from_http://www.espn.com/college-sports/story/_/id/17796619/advocates-athletic-equity-non-profit-focused-promoting-minority-coaches-going-business.

Barnett, B.M. (1993). Invisible southern black women leaders in the civil rights movement: The triple constraints of gender, race, and class. *Gender & Society*, 7(2), 162–182. Black Women in Sports Foundation.

Borland, J.F., & Bruening, J.E. (2010). Navigating barriers: A qualitative examination of the under-representation of Black females as head coaches in collegiate basketball. *Sport Management Review*, 13(4), 407–420.

Bruening, J.E. (2005). Gender and racial analysis in sport: Are all the women White and all the Blacks men? *Quest*, 57(3), 330–349.

Carter, A.R. (2012). A reflection of revolution and its significance for Black women in sport. In F.G. Polite and B. Hawkins (Ed.), *Sport, race, activism, and social change: The impact of Dr. Harry Edwards' scholarship and service* (pp.125–144). San Diego: Cognella.

Carter-Francique, A.R. (2014). An ethic of care: Black female college athletes and development. In Conyers, J.L., Jr. (Ed.), *Race in American sports: Essays* (pp. 35–58). Jefferson, NC: McFarland.

Carter-Francique, A.R. (2016). The impact of sport participation on African American girls' health. In P. Larke, G. Webb-Hasan, J. Young (Eds.), *Cultivating achievement, respect, and empowerment (CARE) for African American girls in PreK? 12 settings: Implications for access, equity and achievement* (pp. 303–336). Charlotte, NC: Information Age.

Carter-Francique, and Cavil, J.K. (Eds.), *The athletic experience at historically black colleges and universities: Past, present, and persistence* (pp. 61–83). Lanham, MD: Rowman & Littlefield.

Carter-Francique, A.R., & Flowers, C.L. (2013). Intersections of race, ethnicity, and gender in sport. In *Gender relations in sport* (pp. 73–93). Rotterdam: SensePublishers.

Carter-Francique, A.R., & Richardson, F.M. (2015). (2015). Black female athlete experiences at historically black colleges and universities. In B. Hawkins, J.N., & Cooper, A.R.

Church Terrell, M. (1898 February 13). The progress of Colored women. *National American Women's Suffrage Association*. Columbia Theater, Washington, D.C.

Collins, P.H. (2000). What's going on? Black feminist thought and the politics of postmodernism. *Working the ruins: Feminist poststructural theory and methods in education*, 41–73.

Collins, P.H. (2004). *Black sexual politics: African Americans, gender, and the new racism.* New York: Routledge.

Davis, M.D. (1992). *Black American women in Olympic track and field: A complete illustrated reference.* Jefferson, NC: McFarland.

Giddings, P. (1984). *When and where I enter: The impact of Black women on race and sex in America.* New York: Bantam.

Hattery, A.J. (2012). They play like girls: Gender and race (In) equity in NCAA sports. *Wake Forest Journal of Law and Policy, 2,* 247.

hooks, b. (1981). *Ain't I a woman: Black women and feminism.* Boston: South End Press.

hooks, b. (n.d.). *Understanding patriarchy.* Louisville, KY: No Borders.

Houzer, S.P. (1974). Black women in athletics. *The Physical Educator, 31,* 208–209.

James, S.M. (1993). Mothering: A possible Black feminist link to social transformation? In S.M. James and A.P.A. Busia (Eds.), *Theorizing Black feminism: The visionary pragmatism of Black women* (pp. 44–54). New York: Routledge.

Lapchick, R., Balasundaram, B., Bello-Malabu, A., Bloom, A., Cotta, T., Liang, K., Marfatia, S., Morrison, E., Mueller, M., Mulcahy, M., & Taylor-Chase, T. (2016). Assessing diversity among campus and conference leaders for Football Subdivison (FBS) schools in the 2016–2017 academic year. *The Institute for Diversity and Ethics in Sport.* Retrieved from http://www.tidesport.org/div-i-leadership.html.

Lapchick, R., Marfatia, S., Bloom, A., Sylverian, S. (2017). The 2016 racial and gender report card: college sports. The Institute for Diversity and Ethics in Sports. http://nebula. wsimg.com/38d2d0480373afd027ca38308220711f?AccessKeyId=DAC3A56D8FB782449 D2A&disposition=0&alloworigin=1.

Mathewson, A.D. (1995). Black women, gender equity and the function at the junction. *Marquette Sports Law Journal, 6*(2), 239–266.

McDowell, J., & Carter-Francique, A.R. (2016). Experiences of female athletes of color. In E.J. Staurowsky (Ed.), *Women and Sport: From Liberation to Celebration* (pp. 95–116). Champaign, IL: Human Kinetics.

Naples, N.A. (1991). "Just what needed to be done": The political practice of women community workers in low-income neighborhoods. *Gender & Society, 5*(4), 478–494.

Naples, N.A. (1992). Activist mothering: Cross-generational continuity in the community work of women from low-income urban neighborhoods. *Gender & Society, 6*(3), 441–463.

Naples, N.A. (1996). A feminist revisiting of the insider/outsider debate: The "outsider phenomenon" in rural Iowa. *Qualitative Sociology, 19*(1), 83–106.

National Association of Collegiate Directors of Athletics (NACDA) (2017). What is NACDA and what does it do? *NACDA Mission Statement.* Retrieved from http://www.nacda.com/nacda/nacda-overview.html.

The National Center for Public Policy Research. (n.d.). *Brown v. Board of Education, 347 U.S. 483 (1954) (USSC+).* Retrieved from http://www.nationalcenter.org/brown.html.

Newman, R. (2000). *African American quotations.* New York: The Onyx Press.

Oglesby, C.A. (1981). Myths and realities of Black women in sport. In T.S. Green, C.A. Oglesby, Alexander, A., and Franke, N. (Eds.). *Black women in sport* (pp. 1–13). Reston, VA: American Alliance for Health, Physical Education, Recreation, and Dance.

Orem, B. (2012). 40 years after Title IX women in Utah still pushing. *The Salt Lake Tribune.* Retrieved from http://archive.sltrib.com/story.php?ref=/sltrib/sports/54350932-77/women-sports-title-utah.html.csp.

Osborne, B., & Yarbrough, M.V. (2000). Pay equity for coaches and athletic administrators: An Element of Title IX. *Michigan Journal of Law Reform, 34,* 231.

Osgood, M. (2016 August 15). Sports history forgot about Tidye Pickett and Louise Stokes, two Black Olympians who never got their shot. Smithsonianwww. Retrieved from http://www.smithsonianmag.com/history/sports-history-forgot-about-tidye-pickett-and-louise-stokes-two-black-olympians-who-never-got-their-shot-glory-180960138/.

Pastore, D.L. (2003). A different lens to view mentoring in sport management. *Journal of Sport Management, 17*(1), 1–12.

Reid, J. (2016 August 18). Black women are heroes in Rio. But they're not just fighting to win gold. *The Washington Post*. Retrieved from https://www.washingtonpost.com/postevery thing/wp/2016/08/18/black-women-are-heroes-in-rio-but-theyre-not-just-fighting-to-win-gold/?utm_term=.cca3afda3382.

The Reliable Source (2013). How Venus Williams got equal pay for women at Wimbledon. *The Washington Post*. Retrieved from https://www.washingtonpost.com/news/reliable-source/wp/2013/07/02/how-venus-williams-got-equal-pay-for-women-at-wimble don/?utm_term=.e975ab046720.

Rhoden, W. (2012). Black and White women far from equal under Title IX. *New York Times*. Retrieved from http://www.nytimes.com/2012/06/11/sports/title-ix-has-not-given-black-female-athletes-equal-opportunity.html.

Smith, Y. (1992). Women of color in society and sport. *Quest, 44*(2), 228–250.

Smith, Y. (2000). Sociohistorical influences of African American elite sportswomen. In D. Brooks and R. Althouse (Eds.), *Racism in college athletics: The African American Athlete experience* (2d ed.) (pp. 173–197). Morgantown, WV: Fitness.

Staurowsky, E. (2012). Is multiple jeopardy the name of the game for Black women in sport? In F.G. Polite and B. Hawkins (Ed.), *Sport, race, activism, and social change: The impact of Dr. Harry Edwards' scholarship and service* (pp. 113–124). San Diego: Cognella.

The United States Department of Education (2015). Title IX and sex discrimination. *Office for Civil Rights*. Retrieved from https://www2.ed.gov/about/offices/list/ocr/docs/tix_dis.html.

The United States Department of Justice (2016). *Title VI of the Civil Rights Act of 1964 42 U.S.C. § 2000D ET SEQ.* Retrieved from https://www.justice.gov/crt/fcs/TitleVI-Over view.

The United States Department of Labor (n.d.). Affirmative action. *Department of Labor.* Retrieved from https://www.dol.gov/general/topic/hiring/affirmativeact.

Vertinsky, P., & Captain, G. (1998). More myth than history: American culture and representations of the black female's athletic ability. *Journal of Sport History, 25*(3), 532–561.

Weaver, M.A., & Chelladurai, P. (1999). A mentoring model for management in sport and physical education. *Quest, 51*(1), 24–38.

Williams, V. (2006). Wimbledon has sent me a message: I'm only a second-class champion. *London Times*. Retrieved from:http://www.thetimes.co.uk/tto/sport/tennis/article2369 985.ece.

Women Leaders in College Sport (2017). Women leaders in college sport. Retrieved from https://www.womenleadersincollegesports.org/.

Women's Sports Foundation (n.d.). *About the Women's Sports Foundation.* Retrieved from https://www.womenssportsfoundation.org/about-us/.

The Stories of Boobie Miles and Rysheed Jordan

How the Institution of Sports Is Failing Black Male Athletes

DREW D. BROWN *and* CHRISTINA KANU

Introduction

Scholars have detailed countless narratives regarding the success of contemporary Black male athletes. These stories consist of the hurdles that were overcome during childhood or the struggle-filled journey on the way to become a collegiate or professional athlete (Carrington 2; Smith 25; Hartmann 302; Pope 325; Rodgers and Rodgers 353). However, in sports, there are more players than available positions for their labor; thus, many players will not receive an athletic scholarship or be selected by a team from the National Football League (NFL) or the National Basketball Association (NBA). Many of these athletes do not develop non-athletic skills and are subsequently unable to take advantage of alternative opportunities that would help support their descent from athletic relevance. Several scholars have identified this as "identity foreclosure" and claims that it is one of the major hindrances for Black male athletes (Beamon 125). L. Harrison et al. state, "Identity foreclosure is defined as making a commitment to an identity role without exploring other role possibilities" (99). Additionally, these authors suggest, "Although, being viewed as an athlete is not necessarily detrimental. There is a negative connotation attached to being perceived mainly as an athlete as it fails to acknowledge other coexisting identities and magnifies prevailing stereotypical views" (L. Harrison 98).

This disproportionately affects Black players for several reasons. First, many Black males often find themselves in lower socioeconomic conditions due to factors of race and racism and desperately seek the expedited social and economic mobility that making it to the NBA or NFL can provide. Second, the lack of alternative opportunities outside of sports has highlighted the success Black males have found in sports. Many Black males recognize sports as one of very few sources of salvation from the cycles of oppression and poverty. McCallum concurs, "[we] have a society now where every black kid in the country thinks the only way he can be successful is through athletics" (6). Third, sports is promoted as a meritocracy and the playing field is a place of equal opportunity, which has allowed Blacks to ostensibly find success. Many Black male athletes look to model the sporting success of others. Last, Black males have been socialized to play and excel at sports through social stereotyping that views Black males as athletic and the celebration of athletes by their own community. These factors contribute the desire for Black athletes to take up, primarily and exclusively, an athletic identity and leaves them with identity foreclosure (Woolfolk and Perry 528).

The two significant narratives of Boobie Miles and Rysheed Jordan involving Black male athletes exemplify the damaging results of identity foreclosure. Miles's plan for success was contingent upon his athletic ability. When his high school football career prematurely ended, he did not have an alternative plan. Limited attention was given to academics which resulted in life-long hardship for Miles. Similarly, Jordan was ill-equipped to handle the academic rigors of college and was misadvised by administrators during his transitional years out of school. His unsuccessful professional career and minimal academic skills led him down a precarious path to prison. Both narratives highlight the systemic problems that continuously hinder Black male athletes from achieving success in life. By briefly examining the narratives of Boobie Miles and Rysheed Jordan, this essay identifies some of the causes of identity foreclosure and offers mentorship as an adequate solution for the subsequent struggles many Black male athletes face during their transition out of sports.

Identity Foreclosure

While building upon the research of psychologist Eric Erikson, James Marcia developed the Theory of Identity Development (Woolfolk and Perry 528). The four parts to Marcia's Theory of Development include identity achieved, identity foreclosed, identity diffused, and moratorium. Most closely related to Black student athletes is identity foreclosure. Persons who do not identify with additional definitions of who they are typically have a foreclosed identity. Identity foreclosure is defined as "a commitment to an identity before one has meaningfully explored other options or engaged in exploratory behavior, such as career exploration, talent development, or joining social clubs or interest groups" (Beamon 196). Athletes are often socialized to commit to their athletic personas.

There are many reasons why a person experiences identity foreclosure. Typically, it is a result of "encouragement from parents, peers, and close significant others" (Beamon 196). Beamon asserts that identity foreclosure is highly prevalent among Black males. She writes, "Black males are socialized intensely into sports by family, peers, media, and community; and there tends to be an overemphasis on sports amongst Blacks in general" (Beamon 196). For athletes, this leads to an identity foreclosure that heavily identifies with the athletic part of one's being. Beamon also writes, "In terms of athletic identity foreclosure, athletes tend to choose this self-identity before they have considered other possible roles and statuses. They forgo exploration of other talents, interests, hobbies, or occupations and center their identity on an athletic participation and achievement" (Beamon 196). L. Harrison et al. mention, "The prospect of entering professional football and the sizeable salaries professional athletes may attain provide ample fuel for the development and sustaining of a persistent athletic identity" (99).

The lack of career exploration is dangerous because in a sports career, where it is extremely common to fall short of the NBA or NFL, players who do not make it to the professional level find that their success is very limited. As Beamon argues, there is an overemphasis of sports within the Black community. This does not mean that sports are negative (Beamon 196). This means that some Blacks openly display their affection for sports more than other facets of life. It is imperative that Black athletes are exposed to other roles and activities to prevent sports from eclipsing their entire identity. However, America's obsession with sports and the exploitation of Black male athletes creates challenges for them to combat the pressure and desire to pursue an athletic career at all costs.

Background: American Sports Culture

In order to fuel one's obsession with sports, Americans are willing to spend an exorbitant amount of money. The sky is truly the limit. People will invest money for game tickets, tailgate parties, athletic gear, or opportunities to meet sports stars. For example, starting ticket prices for the Super Bowl in 2018 was $4,000, according to Ticketmaster. Yet, the Super Bowl is a sold-out event every year. Professional sporting events are not the only events people will pay to attend. College sports are extremely popular as well. From March Madness to College Football Bowl Games, fans are invested in attending. For the fans who do not have the opportunity to attend, they are certainly watching in the comfort of their own homes. In *Power and Ideology in American Sport*, George Sage discusses the connection between sports and the media. Sage writes, "More than half of the 25 top rated television programs of all time are sport events" (Sage 168). These figures prove how much value is placed on sports.

A majority of the Division I college football and basketball teams consist of teams where Blacks make up a majority of the team (Hawkins 142). According to the 2009–2010 NCAA Student Athlete Ethnicity Report, 45.8 percent of Black male students are NCAA FBS Football Bowl Subdivision (FBS) players. Blacks account for 60.9 percent of NCAA Men's Division I basketball players (Smith 104). Anyone who watches college revenue-generating sports (football and men's basketball) is aware that Blacks play an important role. In the book, *The New Plantation*, race and sports scholar Dr. Billy Hawkins states, "Black male athletes are the 'bread winners' or 'workhorses' for PWIs athletic departments across this nation" (Hawkins 116). Said differently, these athletes carry the burden of ensuring success for their teams. Athletes are often expected to be fully invested and giving their best of everything they have to contribute to the team, in order to make sure they progress in rankings and even make it to tournaments and bowl games. The more successful a team is, the more revenue gets generated for a university. The value of an athlete often depends upon how well they compete during the game. Fans love the athletes when they have a great game or are having a great season. These fans are obsessed with the athletes' athletic abilities. However, without athletic notoriety and stardom, the obsession would be non-existent.

Some athletes are aware of this and are able to maintain a positive self-worth that is independent from their athletic success. Many athletes are not fortunate enough to keep a positive self-worth intact independent from their athletic success. George Sage emphasizes, "Hence, athletes are willing participants whose self-worth and self-esteem have largely become synonymous with their athletic prowess. Their main impulse is to mind their own business while striving to be successful as athletes. In the work world, this is referred to as pragmatic role acceptance" (Sage 248). Instead of being able to see the other attributes they possess, they hold closely to their athletic talent. It is their talent that has people cheering them on in sold-out stadiums. It is that gift that has people spending thousands of dollars for tickets. Without that talent, would these people feel the same?

Adler and Adler (1991) highlight the relationship between athletes and college boosters. This relationship is often contingent upon the performance of the athlete. One athlete states, "I thought I had close relations with some boosters, but it turns out it wasn't the way I thought it was. I liked a couple of boosters a lot, and I thought they really cared for me. But as soon as I went down on my knee, it was like unbelievable. They, like turned the n***er off, and shit. And that kind of hurt me. No question, you are forgotten once you are out" (Adler and Adler 191). Young Black males see the praise that these athletes receive. The amount of praise athletes receive is not equal to the praise that Black doctors receive. Why would one want to pursue a career in medicine instead of majoring in dunking? Society has glorified the Black athlete to the extent to where there is an obvious cultural currency associated with being an athlete instead of other professions. This notion makes it challenging for a Black athlete to avoid identity foreclosure.

The Disappointing Story of James Earl Miles, Jr., aka Boobie Miles

Although football is widely popular across the United States, it has been a cultural staple, particularly in the state of Texas. High school football games in Texas, also referred to as "Friday Night Lights." The grand attendance found at high school football games is an indication of the way football has captured the hearts of people in Texas for decades (Hawkins 147). Journalist H.G. Bissinger took an interest in this phenomenon and wrote a literary masterpiece titled *Friday Night Lights a Town, a Team, and a Dream*. This *New York Times* bestseller captures the true story of Odessa, Texas, and their beloved high school football team, the Permian Panthers. In the book, the audience is introduced to many athletes and community members. Dr. Billy Hawkins explains how this text demonstrates a remarkable adoration for high school football and displays the problematic culture of masculinity in sports (Hawkins 147). However, one cannot discuss Friday Night Lights without discussing the team's star Black player, Boobie Miles.

James Earl Miles, Jr., also known as Boobie Miles, was widely known during the 1980s era of high school football. *Texas Football* magazine "named Boobie a blue-chip recruiting prospect and one of the ten best running backs in the state" (Bissinger 64). Boobie Miles is symbolic of many young Black male athletes (Burnett 1; Gatmen 562). Their stories are synonymous. Miles was a talented tailback who was heavily recruited by Division I universities across the country. Although wildly gifted on the field, Boobie was far from skilled in the classroom. Bissinger explains, "Some teachers worked diligently and patiently with Boobie, aware of how hard it was for him to concentrate. Others just seemed to let go, doing little more than babysitting this kid who, as one acknowledged, was destined to become the next Great Black Hope of the Permian football team" (Bissinger 66). These educators believed that his athleticism would sustain him in life. L. Harrison et al. assert, "When both faculty and fellow students viewed a student-athlete 'mainly as an athlete,' it was likely to cause appreciable damage to the athlete's self-esteem and academic identity" (99). The community that praised him for his athleticism also doubted his intellectual abilities. Bissinger writes, "On other occasions, some whites offered another suggestion for Boobie's life if he no longer had football; just do to him what a trainer did to a horse that had pulled up lame at the track, just take out a gun and shoot him to put him out of the misery of a life that no longer had any value" (67). This quote suggests that, according to some Whites, the mere purpose of Boobie's existence was to entertain with his athletic gift (Hoberman 4; Simiyu 58). This explains why Miles also did not see the necessity in pursuing academics. He could only see himself as an athlete.

As a result of identity foreclosure, Miles was not interested in pursuing other identities or career paths. However, on the tragic day that ultimately ended Boobie's career, it would have been ideal to have a plan disparate to football. If Boobie would have had alternate plans that did not solely rely on his physicality, this day would have been less of a tragedy. Boobie was injured during a preseason game. Bissinger writes,

> Boobie lay down and several student managers took off his pads. In his uniform, with all the different pads he fancied, he looked like a little Robo cop. But stripped of all the accouterments, reduced to a gray shirt soaked with sweat, he had lost his persona. Boobie said, "I won't be able to play college football man…. It's real important. It's all I ever wanted to do. I want to make it in the pros" [57].

He did not fully recover from his injury. He never made it to the "pros" or even played college football. Instead of fulfilling his dreams he had multiple children, lacked stable employment, and ended up in prison (Moore n.p.). Identity foreclosure disabled the endless possibilities Miles could have had. If Boobie would have explored other activities or identities, his identity would not have been solely linked to athletics. Without healthy exploration in other areas of his life Boobie's life did not progress after his injury. Miles is a prominent example of what a foreclosed identity can do to an adolescent.

Athletes are often the heroes of children—especially young Black boys (Gates n.p.). In his dissertation titled "Dream Chasers: An Exploration of How Role Identity is related to Career Development Attitudes among Black Male Collegiate Athletes," Charles Small elucidates,

> In particular, the boys relate to professional athletes who serve as role models for attaining the American Dream. These dynamics help to further develop and solidify a boy's athletic identity. Many of the student-athletes view their parents as being role models. However, they also referenced college student-athletes and NBA players as serving as role models. Specifically, they view professional athletes as being not only successful in their sport but also wealthy. As the student-athletes develop their skills, they view being a professional athlete as a career that is achievable and realistic. If they are not able to play sports professionally, basketball is viewed as an avenue to

accessing college. As a result, collegiate and professional athletes serve as role models for attaining the American Dream. When family members excel athletically at the collegiate and professional level, the message is reinforced further [160].

Children place the athlete on a pedestal and often want to emulate the athlete's lifestyle. The child may not know what it took for the athlete to reach that level of success. Additionally, the child is not aware that the likelihood of playing a professional sport is extremely unlikely. However, because the media is constantly pushing images of Black male athletes, it is easy for one to believe that this dream is attainable. This creates a never-ending cycle to want to mimic the behavior of the athlete and commit to an athletic identity without the exploration of other possibilities.

It is critical that one understands the emotional relationship between athletes and their sport. If a person understands this relationship, it will be easy to understand why an athlete is so foreclosed to developing their non-athletic identities. It is necessary at every level for athletes to be exposed to alternatives routes to success or to even discuss backup plans for their future. It is unrealistic to believe that every person who wants to play a sport will be successful in sports. Scholar Henry Louis Gates suggests,

> Too many of our children have come to believe that it's easier to become a black professional athlete than a doctor or lawyer. Reality check: according to the 2000 census, there were more than 31,000 black physicians and surgeons, 33,000 black lawyers, and 5,000 black dentists. Guess how many black athletes are playing professional basketball, football and baseball combined. About 1,400. In fact, there are more board-certified black cardiologists than there are black professional basketball players [qtd. in Smith 122].

Sports sociologist Earl Smith suggests that retirement and death are synonymous terms in the sports world (Smith 174). Athletes need an example that it is possible to live a life when the last shot is made, and the last touchdown is scored. If retirement is synonymous with death, then athletes experience grief post playing a sport (Beamon 204). This notion is not to be taken lightly. There is already a stigma in the Black community about Black men discussing their emotions. The physicality that is associated with Black athletes practically eliminates the possibility that they may have feelings, too. Therefore, it must be difficult for an athlete to share their sentiments about not being able to play professionally or being worried about their future. Instead, the emotions become masked with facades of false dreams that may never come to pass. This situation describes the Kareem Abdul Jabbar Curse. This curse is a result of "athletes ending up in a dust bin when the end of their careers come" (Smith 89). During their time as athletes they are simply used accolades and achievement. It is difficult to transition out of that lifestyle if the only identity one has been associated with is related to sports. One athlete described the transition as such: "It's like I said football and playing at each level, pretty much everything's done for you, I mean you used to people waiting on you hand and foot, you used to being the big man around campus, and whatever you did you're pretty much god. Losing that status, that was the most depressing thing to me" (qtd. in Beamon 204). Another athlete stated, "I really didn't know how to be a regular dude, how to not be a basketball player, what that means even" (qtd. in Beamon 204).

The undeveloped student identity of Black athletes suffering from identity foreclosure denies them of opportunities once their athletic careers are over. The academic failures of Miles are structurally set up at both the high school and collegiate levels. The failures in U.S. sports institution are no better exemplified than in an infamous photo of former NBA player and college graduate Kevin Ross. In this photo, the illiterate Ross is surrounded by elementary-school aged children raising their hands, presumably to answer a question. Ross is seated in the back of the classroom in a chair meant for the elementary school students. There is a book in his hand, and he appears focused on the front of the classroom. This picture of a college graduate from Creighton University sitting in an elementary school classroom learning how to read is heavily problematic and difficult to comprehend. Hawkins asserts,

Although he was denied admission by the university, the athletic department was able to reverse their decision and have Ross admitted as a special admit. Ross played four years of college basketball at Creighton University majoring in eligibility. After his eligibility ran out, he had no offers to play professional basketball, and he lacked the educational skills equivalent to attending four years at a university [68].

The first problem in Ross's situation is that he was admitted to the university without meeting the admission requirements. This set the trajectory for Kevin Ross's failure in his academic pursuits. Secondly, when Hawkins states, "he was majoring in eligibility" (68), this meant the athletic department made sure he was taking classes that would easily pass him. Ross came to college illiterate and he left illiterate. This forced him to go back to elementary school in order to gain the necessary skills in order to read. His attachment to basketball removed him from the other necessary part in college—academics. As a result, Kevin Ross is another example of an athlete with a foreclosed identity.

The problematic relationship between athletes and education does not begin at the university level. These problems arise in high school, with a greater emphasis placed on the athletic achievements of an athlete and not their academic pursuits. However, this becomes complex when a high school athlete prepares for signing day. Signing day is a national day when student athletes commit to universities to play a sport. In order to commit to a school, one must be academically eligible. However, scholar activist Harry Edwards states, "on average, Black athletes are the least prepared of all students entering the university system" (qtd. in Smith 86). This lack of academic preparation during high school leads to scandalous situations in order to recruit the desired athlete.

Rysheed Jordan: The Prince of North Philadelphia

When examining the challenges Black athletes, specifically males face, it is important to note that the struggles of many Black players are linked to the deep structural and systemic issues that pervade U.S. society. This is apparent in the case of Rysheed Jordan, who was charged with robbery and attempted murder after a disappointing basketball career ("Ex–St. Johns Player" par. 3; Forgrave par. 3). Like many other Black male athletes, Jordan was plagued by a host of challenges that contributed to his incarceration. He grew up in Philadelphia, which has a poverty rate over 25 percent (U.S. Dept. of Commerce) and a crime rate that is 101 percent higher than the rest of the state of Pennsylvania (Neighborhood Scout). The structural issues within Philadelphia are exacerbated in areas where a majority of the residents is Black such as North Philadelphia, where Jordan grew up. Many Black males in cities like Philadelphia around the country place their hopes and dreams on being extremely successful in sports. A survey given to high school athletes indicated that 51 percent of high school athletes believe they can play a professional sport (Sage 98). Many scholars and community leaders, such as scholar activist Harry Edwards, have articulated the extremely low odds of playing in one of the major professional sports leagues. Edwards notes, "You have a better chance of getting hit by a meteorite in the next ten years then getting work as an athlete" (qtd. in Sage 98). However, for Black athletes who suffer from identity foreclosure, reaching the NFL or NBA remains the primary objective, regardless of the low probability of success. Their extreme desire leaves them vulnerable to exploitation.

Universities have been scrutinized for their exploitation of Black football players (Singer 368). When a university fails to develop athletes academically, it leaves them ill-prepared to take on future career or academic opportunities, which enhances their dependence on their athletic identity. Their athletic identity is also fed by the challenges they face academically and their success athletically. Continuing to participate in sports allows Black athletes to participate in perhaps the only thing they are comfortable doing as a primary job, and it allows them to be more than "normal" or "regular" members of their family and community (Beamon 204). Family members and friends can severely contribute to the development of Black athletes' identity foreclosure by valuing them based on their athletic achievements (Beamon 205). For many Black athletes like Jordan, their families and friends become enthralled in their athletic participation and success (Beamon 203). Jordan was known as the "Prince of North Philly" (Tanenbaum par. 3). This type of community support and celebration of Jordan's athletic ability helped inflate his athletic talent and left little room for alternative ones, which contributed to his identity foreclosure.

In the areas of academics and career preparation, the underachievement of Black players is often caused partly by university and high school athletic programs and administrators. Instead of focusing on advancing the academic development of Black males, many universities merely focus on developing the athletic-related contributions Black players can make to the school. According to a study by Shaun R. Harper, at many universities Black men represent around 3 percent of undergraduate students but around 60 percent of the basketball and football players (1). This further communicates to Black male athletes that they are more valuable as athletes than as students. Subsequently, Black male athletes tend to gamble their future on making it to the NFL or NBA. The media also influences the consciousness of Black males by constantly associating wealth with Black male professional athletics. This conditions them to accept the exploitation of the NFL or NBA (Gaston 373; C.K. Harrison 99). Jordan was no different. He pursued his athletic goals and by 2013 Jordan was one of the top high school recruits in the country (Forgrave par. 4). Jordan went on to defy the odds by playing collegiate basketball for St. John's University in Queens, New York. Unfortunately, he did not develop a plan or skills for a future that did not include playing in the NBA.

While in college, Jordan joined an athletic culture that focused more on basketball than academic progress, which contributed to his identity foreclosure. In this type of environment, rather than focusing on the full academic development and career preparation of athletes, careless coaches are too concerned with having eligible players who meet the minimal academic requirements to play. Beamon argues that the current student-athlete in a revenue-generating sport does not have adequate time to succeed academically because of their athletic-related activities. She states, "Student athletes often participate in athletic activity at the equivalent level of a full work week and this is often year-round" (197). In an interview with the National Football League Players Association (NFLPA), Seattle Seahawks Richard Sherman discussed the plight of student athletes. Sherman stated, "No I do not believe that student athletes are given the opportunity to take advantage of the free education that they are given and it is frustrating" (Sherman). He also emphasizes that this is not a topic that many people are concerned with; therefore, it is rarely discussed. Richard Sherman had the opportunity to attend one of the Ivy League institutions, Stanford University. If a person is not prepared for the level of academic rigor that is expected of college students, it will be difficult to balance their academic pursuits and athletic demands.

In 2015, Jordan initially planned to enter the NBA draft after his sophomore year and skipped his final exams that semester. This poor academic decision speaks to the exploitative mentality of schools' athletic programs that are concerned with pulling the most athletic talent out of players and keeping them academically eligible, but not providing them with much guidance once they appear to have depleted their eligibility or moved on from the team. Jordan later changed his mind and decided to stay at St. John's to play for the new head coach, Chis Mullin, only to discover that he was academically ineligible and could not play because of his missed exams. This academic blunder cannot be viewed solely as an individual failure. This was caused by a combination of poor academic counseling and a disregard for players whose talents appeared to be of no more use to the school. Jordan was forced to withdraw from classes, ending his collegiate playing career. He joined a semi-pro D-League where he was drafted in the first round by the Delaware 87ers. He was later released after playing only 11 games (Burton par. 1; Forgrave par. 37).

Jordan was done playing in the D-League but had no alternative plan or goals outside of basketball. Like many Black male athletes, Jordan's identity was dominated by his athletic identity. This terminal point in an athlete's career can provide many hardships and highlight the worst parts of identity foreclosure. In the *Huffington Post* article "The Reasons Ex Athletes Can't Move Past Their Sport," Jennie Shulkin addresses the issues of identity athletes face. Athletic identity has been a part of athletes since they started their athletic careers. It is during childhood that a person's identity is forming. Shulkin writes, "Ex-professional and ex-college athletes alike describe leaving their sports with a sense of grieving, as though much of their identity is buried underneath the pile of athletic gear collecting dust in the closet. Recovery from such a loss is a daunting task" (par. 2). Shulkin provides another example of the trials that athletes face when they stop playing a sport. Athletes tend to part from their sport due to age, injury, or by force. It is not rare for athletes to continue to participate in some career choice linked to athletics (Shulkin pars. 9–10). Choosing this path instead of a different career choice allows the former athlete to still be connected to their past as an athlete.

Not only do many Black athletes have to cope with the pressures of basketball and college courses, but they also have home and family struggles. Many Black athletes come from families of poverty where, in some cases, they are the primary breadwinner. For Black athletes, the added burden of playing professional sports in order to financially support their family could further contribute to their identity foreclosure. Financial stability for anyone is an appealing endeavor, but for those growing up at or near the poverty line, like 28 percent of Blacks, according to the 2012 U.S. census, financial stability is a severe struggle. For Black athletes in poverty, there is a need for some type of income while playing collegiate sports, but the NCAA does not allow schools to provide adequate financial support for student athletes. Seeking financial stability through sports does carry an extreme risk. Guttmann warns, "Sports alone do almost nothing to enhance a person's career—unless that career is in sports. A career in sports is, however, enormously risky" (Guttmann 137). Statistically, only about 1 in 10,000 will succeed in the professional ranks (Guttmann 138).

Throughout high school and college, Jordan accepted financial support from local members of his North Philadelphia community, who assumed that he would return the funds or favors once he reached the NBA. Once his playing career came to an end, his financial supporters demanded that he return the funds. With a limited education and no career opportunities outside of sports, Jordan was unable to pay back what he owed through legal employment. According to police reports, on May 27, 2016, Jordan allegedly arranged a meeting with three men to sell marijuana but attempted to rob the three men of their cell phones. Jordan shot one of the men in the arm ("Ex–St. Johns Player" par. 3; Forgrave par. 3). He remains incarcerated and is awaiting trial.

Jordan's experience was not only a result of his childhood environment, but also the impact of a collegiate system that did little to prepare its Black student athletes for athletic retirement. In addition, the social expectations of becoming a significant member of society in ways approved by cultural exaggerations under the guise of manhood called for Jordan to seek extreme forms of wealth and fame. He eventually fell victim to what I call "The Playing Field-to-Prison Pipeline," which describes the cyclical nature that keeps Black males striving to make it to the NFL or NBA and engaging in identity foreclosure, while leaving them with a lack of employable skills and drives them to engage in criminal behavior. This pipeline perpetuates the poverty and culture of Black communities, which contributes to a greater number of Black male athletes with identity foreclosure. Had Jordan invested more in education or career development, he would have been in a better position to acquire employment and possibly pay off his debts. This would have allowed him to avoid the confrontation that landed him in prison. To eliminate the issues that plague Black male athletes like Jordan, institutional change must be implemented in the system, structure, and culture of sports, as well as in society as a whole.

Solutions for Change

For the few athletes who end up playing professionally, there is still uncertainty in the game. Athletes have to stop playing sports due to injuries, being cut from a team, lack of performance, or other unforeseen circumstances. George Sage reports, "The average professional athlete remains at the top level of competition for less than five years" (98). This statistic is unfortunate. What happens to the college athletes who never make it to the pros? And what happens to the athletes who make it to the pros and their careers are short-lived? If a person has been focusing solely on athletic abilities for a majority of his life, it is going to challenging to find success in other avenues. This is why academics are extremely critical for student athletes. Without some level of academic achievement, it is going to be difficult to succeed after graduating from college. The job market is competitive, and jobs are scarce. Even with this knowledge, members of the Black community are still adamant about pushing our children to perfect their athletic craft. In his essay "We Need to Educate our Athletes," Lloyd Hackley provides a plea to the Black community: "If we as Black people don't teach our children the difference between athletics and academics, and explain to them the difference between preparing for life and entertaining fans on Saturday afternoon, then it is not cultural identity they will need, but mental maturity" (Hackley 335). The paradigm needs to shift in the community. There is nothing wrong with encouraging Black youth to play sports. However, if sports is the sole being of their existence and doing well in school is secondary, that is a problem.

One of the first solutions to eliminating the foreclosed identity of an athlete is a proper education. With education, a person can go from being in poverty to the President of a company. A person's education should never be taken for granted or placed in jeopardy. There are attempts to ensure that the education of student athletes is not taken for granted. These attempts to preserve the integrity of collegiate athletics are made by The National Collegiate Athletic Association (NCAA). The NCAA is "a membership driven-organization dedicated to safe guarding the well-being of student-athletes and equipping them with the skills to succeed on the playing field, in the classroom and throughout life" (NCAA).

Another solution that would help eliminate identity foreclosure is to increase the number of Black male mentors available to Black players. As mentioned previously, the percentage of Black student athletes is very high at the university level. The percentage of Black student athletes does not correlate with the percentage of Black coaches. For example, "The Football Bowl Subdivision (FBS) consists of 120 colleges and universities. The percentage of white head football coaches is 89.1%, the percentage of Black head football coaches is 9%" (Smith 177). Racial representation is imperative. It is necessary for the athletes to have someone talk to and to whom they can relate. These relationships provide mentoring and guidance during their collegiate athlete journey. In 2014 President Obama launched the My Brother's Keeper Initiative.

This report provides an array of statistics such as health and wellness, education, incarceration rates, and socioeconomic status. One of the most significant findings in the report is the importance of mentoring in the lives of boys:

> In addition to parents, other caring adults have a pronounced impact on young people's lives. Many successful adults credit a teacher, coach, faith leader or some other mentor with helping them raise their aspirations or navigate difficult times. Specifically, youth with high-quality, sustained mentors are more likely to engage in positive behaviors and less likely to engage in negative behaviors [White House 25].

Having a Black man serve not only as a coach but as a mentor would provide aspiration as to what one could be. The lack of a Black presence on the other side of sports is a hindrance to the journey of Black athletes.

Conclusion

Boobie Miles and Rysheed Jordan are only two examples of Black male athletes who are victims of the current athletic system. There are countless others who have suffered from a poor athletic system that is not set up for the success of Black males who face the challenges of structural oppression that includes poverty, poor education systems, and a lack of opportunities for advancement outside of sports. It is essential that Black male athletes are exposed to opportunities, resources, and people who are interested in their non-athletic development. All athletes should be cognizant that there is a life after sports. Without this understanding, athletes will constantly seek sports as their only means of success in life. We need to develop mentorship programs or culture that eliminates this epidemic. By creating a healthy culture that embraces other identities for athletes, we are progressing towards the possibility eliminating identity foreclosure for Black male athletes.

REFERENCES

Adler, Patricia A., and Peter Adler. *Backboards and Blackboards: College Athletics and Role Engulfment.* Columbia University Press, 1991.
Beamon, Krystal. "Are Sports Overemphasized in the Socialization Process of African American Males? a Qualitative Analysis of Former Collegiate Athletes' Perception of Sport Socialization." *Journal of Black Studies,* vol. 41, no. 2, 2010, pp. 281–300.
_____. "'I'm a Baller': Athletic Identity Foreclosure Among African-American Former Student-Athletes." *Journal of African American Studies,* no. 16, 2012, pp. 195–208.
Bissinger, H.G. *Friday Night Lights: A Town, a Team, and a Dream.* Da Capo Press, 2015.
Burnett, Michael A. "One Strike and You're Out: An Analysis of No Pass/No Play Policies." *High School Journal,* vol. 84, no. 2, 2001, pp. 1–6.
Burton, Roy. *Rysheed Jordan, Myck Kabongo Lead Delaware 87ers' Draft Class,* 31 October 2015, https://www.libertyballers.com/2015/10/31/9651842/rysheed-jordan-myck-kabongo-lead-sevens-draft-class-delaware-87ers-nba-dleague. Accessed 30 November 2017.
Carrington, Ben. *Race, Sport, and Politics: The Sporting Black Diaspora.* Sage, 2010.

"Ex–St. John's Player Rysheed Jordan Charged with Attempted Murder." 1 June 2016. https://www.si.com/college-basketball/2016/06/01/rysheed-jordan-gun-related-charges-robbery-st-johns-red-storm. Accessed 30 November 2017.

Forgrave, Reid. "The Fall of Rysheed Jordan: How the Streets of Philly Swallowed an NBA Prospect." 6 September 2016. Bleacher Report. http://bleacherreport.com/articles/2730989-the-fall-of-rysheed-jordan-how-the-streets-of-philly-swallowed-an-nba-prospect. Accessed 30 November 2017.

Gaston, John C. "The Destruction of the Young Black Male: The Impact of Popular Culture and Organized Sports." *Journal of Black Studies*, vol. 16, no. 4, 1986, pp. 369–384.

Gates, Henry Louis. "Delusions of Grandeur." *Sports Illustrated*, 19 August 1991.

Gatmen, Elisia J.P. "Academic Exploitation: The Adverse Impact of College Athletics on the Educational Success of Minority Student-athletes." *Seattle Journal for Social Justice*, vol. 10, no. 1, 2011, Article 31.

Guttmann, Allen. *A Whole New Ball Game: An Interpretation of American Sports*. UNC Press, 1988.

Hackley, Lloyd V. "We Need to Educate Our Athletes." *The Unlevel Playing Field*, edited by David Kenneth Wiggins and Patrick B. Miller, University of Illinois Press, 2003, pp. 332–335.

Harper, Shaun R. *Black Male Student-athletes and Racial Inequities in NCAA Division I College Sports: Edition*. University of Pennsylvania Center for the Study of Race and Equity in Education, 2016. https://equity.gse.upenn.edu/sites/default/files/publications/Harper_Sports_2016.pdf. Accessed 15 January 2018.

Harrison, C. Keith. "The Assassination of the Black Male Image in Sport." *Journal of African American Studies*, vol. 3, no. 3, 1998, pp. 45–56.

Harrison, Louis, et al. "Living the Dream or Awakening from the Nightmare: Race and Athletic Identity." *Race Ethnicity and Education*, vol. 14, no. 1, 2011, pp. 91–103.

Hartmann, Doug. "Bound by Blackness or Above It? Michael Jordan and the Paradoxes of Post-Civil Rights American Race Relations." *Out of the Shadows: A Biographical History of African American Athletes*, edited by David K. Wiggins, University of Arkansas Press, 2006, pp. 301–323.

Hawkins, Billy. *The New Plantation: Black Athletes, College Sports, and Predominantly White NCAA Institutions*. Palgrave Macmillan, 2013.

Hoberman, John. *Darwin's Athletes: How Sport Has Damaged Black America and Preserved the Myth of Race*. Mariner Books, 1997.

Moore, James. "Boobie Miles Lives On in Aldon Smith." *Los Angeles Post-Examiner*, 16 September 2015. http://lapostexaminer.com/boobie-miles-lives-on-in-aldon-smith/2015/09/16. Accessed 30 November 2017.

NCAA. (2018). "Who We Are." Retrieved 11 25, 2018, from NCAA.org: http://www.ncaa.org/about/who-we-are.

Neighborhood Scout. "Philadelphia, PA Crime Rates." https://www.neighborhoodscout.com/pa/philadelphia/crime. Accessed 29 November 2017.

Pope, Stephen. "Race, Family, and Nation: The Significance of Tiger Woods in American Culture." *Out of the Shadows: A Biographical History of African American Athletes*, edited by David K. Wiggins, University of Arkansas Press, 2006, pp. 325–352.

Rodgers, Pierre R., and Ellen B. Rodgers. "Race, Family, and Nation: The Significance of Tiger Woods in American Culture." *Out of the Shadows: A Biographical History of African American Athletes*, edited by David K. Wiggins, University of Arkansas Press, 2006, pp. 353–372.

Sage, George H. *Power and Ideology in American Sport: A Critical Perspective*. Human Kinetics Publishers, 1990.

Sherman, Richard. "Richard Sherman: Student Athlete Education." *Sports Illustrated*, 1 February 2015.

Shulkin, Jennie. "The Reason Ex Athletes Can't Move Past Their Sport." *Huffington Post*, 31 August 2015.

Simiyu, Wycliffe W. Njororai. "Challenges of Being a Black Student Athlete on US College Campuses." *Journal of Issues in Intercollegiate Athletics*, vol. 5, 2012, pp. 40–63.

Singer, John N. "Understanding Racism Through the Eyes of African American Male Student-Athletes." *Race Ethnicity and Education,* vol. 8, no. 4, 2005, pp. 365–86.

Small, Charles Lamar. "Dream Chasers: An Exploration of How Role Identity Is Related to Career Development Attitudes Among African American Male Collegiate Athletes." Dissertation. 2013.

Smith, Earl. *Race, Sport and the American Dream.* Carolina Academic Press, 2007.

Tanenbaum, Michael. "'Prince of North Philly,' Former Hoops Star, Nears Fateful Trial Date." 14 September 2017. http://www.phillyvoice.com/prince-north-philly-former-hoops-star-nears-fateful-trial/. Accessed 8 December 2017.

"ticketmaster.com." 2018. ticketmaster.com. Website. 15 January 2018.

United States Department of Commerce. (2017). *Persons in Poverty (Data File).* Retrieved January 15, 18, from https://www.census.gov/quickfacts/fact/table/philadelphiacounty pennsylvania/IPE120216#viewtop.

White House. *My Brother's Keeper Task Force Report to the President.* United States Department of Education, 2014. https://obamawhitehouse.archives.gov/sites/default/files/docs/053014_mbk_report.pdf. Accessed 15 January 2018.

Woolfolk, Anita, and Nancy Perry. *Child and Adolescent Development.* Pearson Higher Ed, 2013.

"Man up"

Sport, Masculinity and African American Communities

BRUCE LEE HAZELWOOD

Introduction

Turn on ESPN, specifically any of their shows on the National Football League (NFL), and you will undoubtedly hear the phrase, "You need to man up," or some derivative of this statement. This leads to the question, "What does it mean to be a man?" To all men and boys, this may be problematic scenario. However, conceptions of manhood and masculinity are undoubtedly unique amongst populations, affecting the way each man and boy receives this message. For African American and Black communities, how do stereotypes regarding Black masculinity and manhood influence how Black men and boys, as well as their communities, interpret messages such as the one above? How do these interpretations define the masculinities sought, embodied, and reified by many young Black men and boys? What avenues can all of us take to invoke other interpretations and iterations of masculinity and manhood? While there is no one answer to each question, I will attempt to provide some thoughts through the examples and discussion in this essay.

Roadmap

Through the use of both a critical anti-racist and masculinity studies framework, I will argue sport may be the most effective avenue with which to expose and explore different conceptions and portrayals of masculinity and manhood. It may be the most effective tool in educating students and communities on social justice issues. Sport, because of its pervasiveness and relatability to a swath of people, may prove to be the most effective medium to have difficult conversations around race, gender, and masculinity. For example, so much of sport, particularly contact sports, revolves around the ability of athletes to play through pain and injury under the masculine notion that men either do not feel pain, or can push right through said pain. Therefore, common phrases in sport such as, "Are you hurt, or are you injured?" must be explored through a critical lens of masculinity. Because Black male athletes (and Black men in general) are often stereotyped as indestructible and able to push past their bodily limits, this calls for a more critical examination through a racial lens.

To explore and analyze these issues, I turn to scholars/activists in the fields of Critical Race Theory (CRT) and Critical Masculinity Studies (CMS). These scholars/activists include Patricia Hill Collins (2000; 2005), Mark Anthony Neal (2005), Byron Hurt (2006), William C. Rhoden (2006), Bell (1983), and Crenshaw (1989); along with R.W. Connell (2005), Michael A. Messner (1992; 2009), Michael Kimmel (2004; 2011), C.J. Pascoe (2006), and Cyd Zeigler (2016), among others. Turning to these scholars allows for conversations through two of the most powerful social factors in our society: race and gender, specifically on the gendered deployment of masculinity. I will take a specific focus on the effects this may have on African American and Black communities, both in the hegemonic way we discuss sport and masculinity, and in the potential of sport to create new imaginings of manhood and masculinity. This does not mean that I have "solved" the issue of the problematics in conceptions of Black masculinity, but rather an attempt to highlight how different Black men embody their own sense of masculinity.

Critical Race Theory

Critical Race Theory (CRT) is a body of legal scholarship with members who are both people of color and ideologically committed to the struggle against racism (Taylor et al, 2009, p. 40). Derrick Bell, credited as one of the founders of CRT, writes white CRT scholars usually are cognizant of and committed to the overthrow of their own racial privilege. To guide this struggle against racism, CRT has a few agreed-upon core tenets.

CRT theorist Gloria Ladson-Billings argues some of the tenets of CRT are the acknowledgment that racism is normal in everyday society, to the point whites do not realize or take it for granted; the employment of storytelling as counter-narrative; a critique of liberalism; and that whites have been the main beneficiaries of civil rights legislation (as cited in Taylor et al, 2009, pp. 21–22). Bell's (1980, p. 523) "interest-convergence," where the oppressor gives concessions to the oppressed only when it benefits the oppressor, may account for this phenomenon. Lastly, Kimberle Crenshaw (1991) introduces "intersectionality" as a critique to both CRT and feminism; intersectionality argues for the critique of social issues through multiple lenses, rather than a single issue (race, gender, sexuality, etc.) because people constitute various social categories simultaneously.

Exploration of a Few Tenets of CRT

The normalization of racism in the United States gave birth to modern rhetoric to explain away any connection to racial injustice in the post–Civil Rights era: color-blindness. Eduardo Bonilla-Silva (2014) argues the shift from overt to covert racism necessitated a language shift, leading to color-blind racism. While color-blind racism is a different form of racism, it functions at both the systemic and individual level, thus affecting people of color in a white supremacist society. CRT theorists start with the acknowledgment that racism is present and everyday.

Storytelling is a critical tool for many CRT theorists. Storytelling is an important tool because too often, these are the voices and stories that are silenced and erased. Perhaps the most well-known example is Anzaldua (2012), who used storytelling (as well as poetry and Spanish) to write on the experiences of being a queer Chicana feminist. On the fiction side, writers such as Paul Beatty (1996; 2001), Khaled Hosseini (2003), James Baldwin (1956), Toni Morrison (1970; 1987), and Sherman Alexie (1993, 2007) employ storytelling to reveal readers to some of the experiences, themes, histories, and realities of various subjugate groups. There are also the growing number of spoken word artists (through access with *Def Poetry Jam* and others) and musicians employing storytelling as counter-narrative (KRS-One, Nas, Jean Grae, Angel Haze, and others).

Critiquing the abstract values of liberalism trumpeted by dominant narratives is another important tenet to explore, particularly in the way liberalism narratives transpose in sports. Ladson-Billings (as cited in Taylor et al, 2009) argues the slow, liberal approach to political change (arguing precedence over citizen rights) fails because of its emphasis on incrementalism. Rather, CRT argues that racism requires sweeping changes in order to eradicate systemic and institutional racism. Liberalism also trumpets individualism and meritocracy, leading to view each case as individual and separated from any larger contextual history and reality. Liberalism, through meritocracy and notions of hard-work, brainwashes people to believe the only change that need happen is that of yourself; it deflects any critique of the very systems liberalism helps to uphold.

Interest convergence, as Bell (1980) coined, is the principle in which, "The interest of blacks in achieving racial equality will be accommodated only when it converges with the interests of whites" (p. 523). Most people believe civil rights legislation (such as affirmative action) benefit only people of color and in fact, acts as a form of reverse discrimination (Bonilla-Silva, 2014). Rather, in the case of affirmative action, for instance, research shows white, middle-class women are the main beneficiaries of affirmative action policies (Allan et al, 2009). Yet there are constantly cases of people claiming they or someone they know lost out on a job or college opportunity to a person of color due to affirmative action (Bonilla-Silva, 2014), but these same people rarely account for the fact white women benefit most from affirmative action. This principle finds many examples in sport, with arguably the most egregious discussed later.

When it comes to intersectionality, Crenshaw (1989) argues, "Because the intersectional experience is greater than the sum of racism and sexism, any analysis that does not take intersectionality into account cannot sufficiently address the particular manner in which Black women are subordinated" (p. 140). What intersectionality is, then, is examining social justice issues through *multiple* social lenses/constructions. For example, as Crenshaw argues, it is futile to examine the experiences of African American women solely through the lens of race; what about the presence of gender, class, sexuality, ability, education, environment, and/or other categories? People are not *just* raced or classed or gendered individuals, but they are all of these (and more) simultaneously in a society built on social constructions. I am a multiracial and multiethnic individual who identifies as a Korean American, heterosexual, non-religious, and a working-class male; examining my experiences only through my racial/ethnic or gendered identity would disavow who I am as an individual.

Critical Masculinity Studies

(Critical) masculinity studies is a theory focusing on the ways in which power, patriarchy, and privilege function in society (oftentimes simultaneously) at the systemic, institutional, social, cultural, and individual levels. It is an intersectional analysis accounting for race, class, privilege, sexuality, ability, religion/spirituality, culture, and more (mensstudies.org). However, it should be noted that the viewpoint in (critical) masculinity studies most often is written from the White male stance, much like many other theories (or in the case of feminism, White women). Furthermore, (critical) masculinity studies also analyzes the ways biologically sexed males undergo a socialization regiment to become socially masculine and thus, seen as men (Kimmel, 2004). As such, the theory acknowledges masculinity/manhood is a *socialization process* as well the effects of various oppressions (including patriarchy) on identities.

These acknowledgments are crucial, and the reasoning why I use Critical

Masculinity Studies (CMS). One of the affirmations proclaimed by the AMSA is men's studies includes, "scholarly, critical, and activist endeavors engaging men and masculinities as social-historical-cultural constructors reflexively embedded in the material and bodily realities of men's and women's lives" (mensstudies.org). Furthermore, what seems to be lacking in the AMSA goals are the presence of non-hetero identities, and CMS includes non-hetero identity and issues into the intersectional analyses.

There are several core theorizations of CMS applicable to this paper. First, gender is socially constructed (Kimmel, 2004, 2011). Second, we live in a system of patriarchy with patriarchal dividend (Johnson, 2014). Third, the mind/body split (Messner, 1992). Fourth, as argued by scholars such as Neal (2006), Yang (2006), Collins (2005), Todd Boyd (2004), Pascoe (2007), Fred Fejes (2000), and Mary Bucholtz (1999) are subordinated/alternative masculinities. These subordinated masculinities offer young boys and men alternative embodiments of masculinity.

EXCURSION THROUGH A FEW THEORIES OF CMS

Kimmel (2011) provides four reasons for the power and hold biological explanations have on gender differences and inequality. First, biological explanations have the look and sound of "true" science, providing credibility to the masses. Two, they tend to reinforce what people see with their own eyes—men and women do seem so different. Three, the biological explanations reinforce that what *is* is the way it should be, and what is social is natural. Fourth, maybe most salient, is biological explanations provide a tidy reason for inequality, that it is the fault of nobody and is natural. However, "men" and "masculinity" are socially constructed performances (Butler, 1990).

Men also have to uphold highly unattainable masculine ideals. A quick list of typical things a young male may hear or see reinforcing masculinity: never show emotion, unless it is anger or violence; never show pain and/or work through the pain (Messner's mind/body split); always be dominant (read: win) at everything; always provide for the household (generally solo); violence is a perfect first response to anyone and anything; television glorifying masculine images such as sport or military, or relegating women to background sexual images; and so much more. As Hurt says in his groundbreaking documentary *Hip-Hop: Beyond Beats & Rhymes* (2006), "Violent masculinity is at the heart of American identity." This socialization process of masculinity is violent (in extreme ways) to both men and women: women in their relegation to objects of desire & conquest, and the violent measure taken against women by men; and men, in their self-destructive and dominate-at-all-costs actions which prevents an honest connection to one's self and others.

As Allan G. Johnson (2014) argues, "And if we cannot talk about a problem, we make it all but impossible to understand it, much less discover what to do about it" (p. 4). The problem Johnson is addressing is patriarchy, and the domination of society by males. To define patriarchy critically yet simply, Johnson argues societies are "...patriarchal to the degree that it promotes male privilege by being *male dominated, male identified*, and *male centered*. It is also organized around an obsession with control and involves as one of its key aspects the oppression of women" (pp. 5–6). Though we hate to admit it, institutions and systems (such as patriarchy) ingrain in us racist/gendered/homophobic and other tendencies. While others may argue family and friends are larger influences than schools or church, the question then to ask is, "Well, who influences them?" Rather, as Johnson states, "We need to see and deal with the social roots that generate and nurture the *social* problems that are reflected in and manifested through the behavior of individuals" (p. 28).

Next, as discussed in *Power at Play* (1992), Messner writes of how the athlete's mind and body are disconnected, and finds that for most male athletes, the primary use of their body is to be an instrument with clear goals and objects to be destroyed/conquered. As such, every hindrance needs negation. This leads to the splitting of the mind and body, where the mind finds ways to push the body beyond its limits to achieve the goals of the masculine individual. "Athletes attempt to 'use' their minds in order to 'get the most out of their bodies'" (p. 64). This may come in a form of the question, "Are you hurt, or are you injured?" Essentially, play/work through the damn pain.

On a more general plane, this concept may prove insightful for those of subordinated masculinities (race, gender, sex, ability). For example, many African American scholars have written of the hypermasculinity and hypersexualization embodied and expressed by African American male youth in particular (Neal, 2005; Collins, 2005; hooks, 2004). Shows such as *Oz* (1997–2002) and *The Wire* (2002–2008) highlight the struggles of masculinity and sexuality among black males in prison (the former) and the ghetto (the latter). Neal (2005) attempts to synthesize all the stereotypes and embodiments of masculine identity by black males, along with the non-stereotypical aspects that he himself embodies (such as academic/scholar, middle-class) to hypothesize what he terms the new black man. The mind/body split can further this discussion by analyzing the cognitive maneuvers that reinforce those stereotypes and hides the aspects that threaten masculinity.

Sport and Intersectionality: "We're just forty million-dollar slaves"

The above quote are the words of former NBA veteran Larry Johnson, speaking to a group of reporters during a mandatory media session (Rhoden, 2006). Because of his status as a prominent multi-millionaire black athlete in a post-racial era, this quote became target of harsh criticisms of Johnson's equation of slavery to professional athletes from the media and the upper echelons of the NBA. Many also took the opportunity to reinforce the belief of living in a post-racial/color-blind era and the measures taken since the Civil Rights Era to bring equality. Yet, the failure of these criticisms is in their inability to acknowledge the distinct dimension of Johnson's remarks: the power dynamic of teams/NBA over players such as Johnson.

During the era of slavery in the U.S. South, Rhoden (2006) argues the utilization of sport on the plantations by slaveholders "…were used as diversion to dull the revolutionary instinct" (p.47). Fearing a potential slave rebellion, slaveholders felt athletic contest would expel the anger, aggression, and hostility suppressing inside the slave. Instead, the release of those emotions came against fellow slaves. In these arenas, the reclamation of a sense of humanity and selfhood also brought the rebirthing of masculine identities for male slaves Further, fellow slaves spectating the events were also able to reclaim a sense of humanity by seeing fellow slaves take *control* of their own bodies. Certain competitions and athletes could expect rewards (whether small monetary rewards or others, such as marbles or food). Yet, these small triumphs did nothing to change the power dynamics of the plantation.

Johnson's greater critique in his comments is the very little power athletes hold in comparison to the coaches, management/ownership, and leagues. The likely actions following an athlete speaking out about the team, ownership, coaching, success/failure, or league is usually: benching, suspension/fine, trade, or outright release from contract. Yet coaches/management tend to lose jobs only when losses mount, clashes with team personnel, or retiring/asking for release. Owners essentially run the league, only facing repercussions for the most egregious offenses, such as the decades-long acts of racist discrimination and prejudice of former Los Angeles Clippers owner Donald Sterling (nba.com, 2014).

Sport is not the only realm facing this power dynamic. Rather, nearly every institution in the West faces this same power dynamic. Few white males hold unyielding power in most institutions, benefiting more than others do from the policies and resulting spoils. A larger percentage of people are the main workforce keeping these institutions afloat, yet receive a tiny fraction of the spoils. Since sport is relatable to a large swath of people, it seems to be a prime arena to discuss social issues. Below are a few examples of analyzing sport through an intersectional lens.

Intersections of Storytelling as Counter-Narrative in Sport

Perhaps the most popular athlete of last century, Muhammad Ali is a unique example of counter-narrative. Utilizing the bombast and braggadocio unseen since the days of Jack Johnson (the first black heavyweight pugilist to receive the recognition from white boxing), the former Cassius Clay became an educative (and vindicated) authority on social issues in the U.S. and around the world. His conversion to Islam, refusing to serve in the Vietnam War, his battle with Parkinson's, his comments on race/religion/politics, and other actions carry more power because of his status as a prominent former athlete and celebrity. Many identify Ali as the first activist-athlete, giving birth to space allowing for activist-athletes such as John Carlos & Tommie Smith, Etan Thomas, Earvin "Magic" Johnson, and more contemporary activist-athletes such as LeBron James, the 2015 University of Missouri football team, and many more.

Athletes that are more prominent tend to release autobiographies, using this space to expose readers to their life outside of what they see on television. A sampling of a few athlete autobiographies include Jackie Robinson's *I Never had it Made* (1972); Brittney Griner's *In My Skin* (2014); Mike Tyson's *Undisputed Truth* (2013); and Arthur Ashe's *Days of Grace* (1994). There are situations where, rather than an autobiography of a single individual, a researcher seeks a collection of voices. Rhoden's *Third and a Mile* (2007) details the trials and triumph of the black quarterback in football, using the voices of black quarterbacks both past and present. There are also the fantastic documentary works of Ken Burns, including *Unforgivable Blackness* (2004) and *Jackie Robinson* (2016). The proper utilization of works such as these can help humanize athletes and their struggles, which may aid students in understanding larger social issues (such as HIV/AIDS or segregation and integration). Though each athlete highlighted in this essay, or in sports generally, may not explicitly state they are engaging in counter-narrative, their presence, experiences, voices, and actions all constitute counter-narratives because they are representative of just a few of the identities left out of mainstream notion and narratives.

INTEREST CONVERGENCE AND SPORTS

The integration of Jackie Robinson into baseball is similar to the *Brown* case in the sense of romanticizing the event through time, as well as taking place in a similar period (about a decade before the *Brown* decision). As Newman & Rosen (2014) argue, the Negro Leagues were drawing attendance away from the major White ball clubs. Although the fleeing attendance was mostly African Americans relegated to the worst seats away from White spectators, the absence made enough of an impact monetarily for the White clubs to consider integration. On top of the monetary value, some within White baseball also recognized the talent gap, pace of play, and excitement present within the Negro Leagues, and wanted to capitalize. Signing Robinson and integrating baseball benefited White baseball on two levels: incorporating new (arguably better) talent and style of play into white baseball and winning the money of African American fans once again. Maybe Branch Rickey, the man who signed Robinson to play with the Brooklyn Dodgers, did have altruistic and well-meaning intentions, but that does not take away from the fact that the *business* of baseball matters more than the potential social implications. As with the integration of public schools, it was Black people integrating into White institutions, leveling a catastrophic blow to Black economics for the betterment of the White supremacist structure. The next example, about two decades after Robinson, highlights a gendered iteration of interest-convergence, but on the non-professional level.

Hailed as a landmark piece of legislation, Title IX grants all individuals access to any public institution receiving federal funding. The legislation aims to better the gender inequality in higher education and by extension, the place of women in society. Interestingly enough, although many people associate Title IX with sports, not one word of Title IX includes the words "sport" or "sports," as it states, "No person in the United States shall, on the basis of sex, be excluded from participation in, be denied the benefits of, or be subjected to discrimination under any educational program or activity receiving Federal financial assistance" (Allan et al, 2010). One would assume this also means the integration of educational and public institutions receiving federal funding based on gender; however, in college athletics (and mostly all organized sports), sports remain segregated on the basis of gender. The message to men and women is that physically, men still dominate women, and women maintain a secondary place to men in the athletic field. While allowing women into organized sport seems altruistic, keeping sport gender-segregated works to maintain a patriarchal system lending credence to the biological arguments of male domination over others.

These two examples can hold much power in terms of discussing masculinity/femininity. For instance, many people know that Jackie Robinsons was *chosen* to integrate baseball because of his "demeanor" and "turn-the-other-cheek" attitude (Rhoden, 2006; Helgeland, 2013; Newman & Rosen, 2014; Burns, 2016), rather than other Negro League greats such as Cool Papa Bell or Satchel Paige who had a little more flair. The connection to Michael Jordan is then apparent, through what Rhoden terms "the dilemma of neutrality," that is, how a Black athlete has to navigate being Black while catering to a mostly White audience; could Allen Iverson or Randy Moss have been who all the children wanted to "be like"?

Alternative Masculinities

Alternative masculinities are a space for men (and women) to assert a masculine identity unfound in the stringent identities of hegemonic masculinities, which very few men actually attain. It may be easiest for people to think about this topic through raced/ethnic, sexed, and classed masculinities, among others. More critically (or provocatively) are the introductions of female masculinities to this discussion. Masculinity is not solely the domain of men, just as femininity is not solely the domain of women.

To better contextualize and highlight this concept, I will examine a homosexual and African American masculinity. I have a few reasons for choosing these two masculinities. First, race and gender issues are central to sport, as well as many other institutions. Second, sport is a hypermasculine arena governed by and through hegemonic and hypermasculinity. Third, the most recent decade is full of discussions in sport surrounding race and/or sexuality (Granderson, 2005; Borden, 2013; Collins, 2013; Leonard & Hazelwood, 2014; Borges, 2016). Lastly, in a "post-racial" society (Bonilla-Silva, 2014) and one in which LGBTIQ+ people can legally marry, using these two masculinities to expose the ignorance and fallacy of society regarding these issues may prove highly effective in breaking down common-sense notions of masculinity, identity, and equality. This by no means suggests these are the only two subordinate masculinities to analyze, but rather how I will proceed.

Homosexual and Black Masculinity

As Zeigler (2016) argues, there have always been LGBT athletes in sport; he argues those athletes are just a little more comfortable now to be open than before, though the numbers indicate the level of comfortability is low. With Sheryl Swoopes, Brittney Griner, Michael Sam, Derrick Gordon, and Jason Collins among the "first" of the recent generations of athletes to be open about their sexuality, it opens discussions about sexuality *and* race. In the scripted yet athletic world of professional wrestling, Fred Rosser III (better known as "Darren Young"), formerly of World Wrestling Entertainment (WWE), was the only openly gay male wrestler in the WWE, and he is Black (though the Young character is not gay). This is particularly important for many Black communities because, as Cathy J. Cohen (1999) and Collins (2005) have argued, there has been a longstanding narrative saying there are no gay Black men. As we know, there are gay men of every race, ethnicity, religion, etc., and these athletes disrupt not just the notions in many Black communities surrounding race and sexuality, but also the mainstream notions. Other popular culture portrayals of gay Black men, such as Omar Little of the acclaimed show *The Wire* (Simon, 2002–2008), create discussions for many viewers they probably would not have had if not for the portrayal.

Why are these discussions important? Black men, particularly in sports, become valued for only what they can physically accomplish; even the discussion surrounding LeBron James' "basketball IQ" only came after a decade of dissecting his physical attributes. The presence of athletes such as Collins, Gordon, and Sam present a disjuncture to common narratives and norms particularly because they challenge these predominant notions of what it means to be a Black man. Because of the emphasis on the body, the fact that all these well-known athletes have or are earning college degrees dispels notions of mental inferiority. The lack of "scandal" associated with these athletes, in terms of sex/violence/drugs, also helps to create alternate images of Black men, keeping in mind White and Black athletes are treated differently for the same transgressions. Further, although flamboyance and flashiness are what I enjoy in athletes and sports, dominant traditions (particularly in baseball) penalize these acts, particularly towards Black and Brown athletes. Having a mixture of Black athletes up and down the spectrum allows people to have a greater imagination and understanding of Black people.

Further, as Zeigler (2016) argues, there is a longstanding stereotype of gay men as effeminate, and as such, lacking athletic skill. Aside from the WWE (where there have been a litany of "gay/androgynous" characters such as Adrian Adonis and Goldust), mainstream representations of gay athletes have not been too kind nor prevalent. Most athletes who are open about their non-hetero sexuality, but not all (like Sam and Gordon), are only open after their playing days, if at all. This is probably most notable through examples like former Olympic diver Greg Louganis (Zaccardi, 2015), former NBA player John Amaechi (Zeigler, 2007), former NFL players Esera Tualolo and Wade Davis (Klemko, 2013), and Collins. Seeing these athletes be open during their playing days, and to see that many are Black gay men, should open doors for Black men, gay Black men, and everyone else opportunities to interrogate their own notions of the intersections of race and sexuality in sports.

A DIFFERENT LOOK AT BLACK MASCULINITY THROUGH FATHERHOOD

Too often, our media and sociocultural narratives about Black men is that they are absentee fathers who only care about their own pleasure and satisfaction, with some of these narratives perpetuated by some Black people as well (Screven, *WRNB Philly*). Most, if not all of these discussions, remove the fact that several generations of Black men are incarcerated through the farcical "War on Drugs" (Mouzon, in McClure & Harris, 2018; Doude, in McClure & Harris, 2018). Although there are studies indicating the stereotypes we have of Black communities may actually apply more to comparable White communities (Price-Boham & Skeen, 1979; Thomas et al, 1996); books seeking to interrogate Black fatherhood for both fathers and sons (Connor & White, 2006); or popular media articles dispelling stereotypical notions of Black men and/or fatherhood (Donaldson, 2015; Hager, 2015; Smith, 2017), preexisting sociocultural narratives reign supreme.

Rather than focus on superstar athletes lauded for their fathering, I want to turn to someone many sports fans may not be aware of: Thaddeus Bullard, Sr., or "Titus O'Neil" in the WWE. A former University of Florida football national champion, he has received the most recognition for his role as a single father to his two sons. As mentioned above, he was a central celebrity figure in the Fatherhood.gov campaign in 2015. He ultimately won the "MEGA Dads Celebrity Dad of the Year" award in 2015 as well (WWE.com). He openly discusses his love for his sons, and how he wants to set a good example for them both as a man and as a father (Mooneyham, 2018). In the community, Bullard focuses on assisting children, particularly those living in impoverished areas or under-funded schools (Mooneyham, 2018).

Because Black masculinity is so often portrayed as hypermasculine, hypersexual, aggressive, violent, and a peculiar sense of caring (for the homies, but a lack of true intimacy and emotion), Bullard and other Black fathers such as LeBron James and Dwyane Wade dispel mainstream notions of Black fatherhood and masculinity. They show that truly caring for others through love and empathy, particularly your family, is not only acceptable, but wanted. Their presence also fights against portrayals of Black fathers as strict, abusive, and detached.

This does not mean one has to be a father to incorporate these aspects into their identity as most everyone has people they care for and love, both family and non-family alike. Rather, it should allow for a reconceptualization of relationships for Black men and boys where, rather than domination and physical/sexual/economic prowess, relationships can be built through love, care, empathy, and intimacy. Being able to have more of these portrayals (Black fathers and positive representations of Black men in general) will only serve to fight against Donaldson's (2015) argument because there should be more of an array of portrayals of Black representation and should work to help everyone begin to unravel the tropes of masculinity many hold as paragons of "true" manhood.

Conclusion: Alternative Masculinities in Sport

Recent years have seen an increase in the visibility of non-hegemonic masculinities. As Zeigler (2016) writes, the examples of Michael Sam, Derrick Gordon, Abby Wambach, and Fallon Fox show the intersections of race, sexuality, gender, and masculinity/femininity. Further, Black athletes such as Vernon Davis (who regularly engages in the traditional art community); Martellus Bennett (a writer and illustrator of children's books); Odell Beckham, Jr. (notable for his flamboyance both on and off the field); LeBron James,

Dwyane Wade, and Steph Curry (family men in powerful positions); and James, Wade, Chris Paul, Carmelo Anthony, Colin Kaepernick, and countless college and K–12 student-athletes (#BlackLivesMatter and other social justice issues pertaining to Black communities specifically), show there are many Black athletes already providing alternative notions of manhood and masculinity.

For another example from a non–Black, non-male athlete, there is Ultimate Fighting Championship (UFC) fighter and former Marine Liz "Girl-Rilla" Carmouche. She occupies a hypermasculine arena. However, she represents a subordinate masculinity, as Carmouche is a woman and a lesbian. With Carmouche, her physical appearance embodies a masculine aspect. While fighting at 135 pounds, she is fairly muscular, something attributed to men and undesirable in women. She also engages in prizefighting, an endeavor long open only to men.

By placing the gender modifier in front of gorilla, she blatantly indicates her gender identification to the masses. However, by reimagining a traditionally masculine animal (in mainstream conception) to fit her masculinity, she is subtly asserting and gaining recognition of her masculinity (at least, that is the hope). Third, she openly discusses her sexuality, and utilized a rainbow mouthpiece for her training and fights (until a uniform policy in July 2015), an ode to the Rainbow Pride flag for many in the LGBTIQ community (Buzinski, 2013).

One of the big difficulties is having conversations about sports that go beyond fandom and loyalty, but to these critical aspects including race, gender, sexuality, masculinity, etc. This does not mean we should not attempt to engage in these conversations. As Johnson (2014) noted earlier, we cannot solve or work to better problems if we do not identify and discuss these problems. We also must strive to remove the common tropes and narrative associated with sport, including meritocracy, so we can look at how the systems affect the individuals, and how individuals can affect the systems.

For Black communities, particularly because of the stereotypes of hypermasculinity and hypersexuality, highlighting and discussing alternative forms of masculinity may help many young Black boys and men find a sense of "manhood" in things other than violence and aggression, but this holds true for all boys and men. One can occupy different levels and embodiments of masculinity, and one can create their own, hybridizing their masculinity through many of the examples throughout this essay. One can even eschew masculinity all together. At the same time, we as individuals need to be willing and able to discuss these issues with young boys and men while working for better, more diverse and accurate portrayals of masculinity and Black masculinity more specifically.

REFERENCES

Alexie, S. (1993). *The Lone Ranger and Tonto fistfight in heaven*. New York: Grove/Atlantic, Inc.
Alexie, S. (2007). *The absolutely true diary of a part-time indian*. Boston: Little, Brown and Company.
Allan, E.J., Iverson, S.V.D., & Ropers-Huilman, R. (2009). *Reconstructing policy in higher education: Feminist poststructural perspectives* (Kindle). New York: Routledge.
Anzaldua, G. (2012). *Borderlands/La frontera: The new mestiza* (4th ed.). San Francisco: Aunt Lute Books.
AP. (n.d.). Clippers owner Sterling banned for life by the NBA. Retrieved January 8, 2017, from //www.nba.com/2014/news/04/29/nba-bans-donald-sterling.ap/.
Ashe, A., & Rampersad, A. (1994). *Days of grace: A memoir*. New York: Random House Publishing.
Baldwin, J. (1953). *Go tell it on the mountain*. New York: Knopf Doubleday.
Battista, J. (2016). NFL hopes Rooney Rule for women will improve organization. Retrieved January 8, 2017, from http://www.nfl.com/news/story/0ap3000000632517/article/nfl-hopes-rooney-rule-for-women-will-improve-organization.
Beatty, P. (1996). *The white boy shuffle*. New York: Picador.
Beatty, P. (2001). *Tuff*. New York: Anchor Books.
Bell, D. (1980). Brown v. Board of Education and the interest-convergence dilemma. *Harvard Law Review*, 93(3), 518–533.
Bernhard, J. (n.d.). SLPOA condemns Rams display. Retrieved January 3, 2017, from http://www.ksdk.com/news/local/slpoa-condemns-rams-display/278759364.
Bonilla-Silva, E. (2014). *Racism without racists: Color-blind racism and the persistence of racial inequality in America* (4th ed.). Maryland: Rowman & Littlefield Publishers, Inc.
Borden, S. (2013, April 18). Brittney griner comes out, and sports world shrugs. *New York Times*. Retrieved from http://www.nytimes.com/2013/04/19/sports/ncaabasketball/brittney-griner-comes-out-and-sports-world-shrugs.html.
Borges, R. (2016, February 3). With Cam Newton, it's not always black & white. Retrieved January 8, 2017, from http://www.bostonherald.com/sports/patriots/2016/02/borges_with_cam_newton_its_not_always_black_white.
Boyd, T. (2004). *The new H.N.I.C: The death of civil rights and the reign of hip hop*. New York: NYU Press.
Brown_vs._Board_of_Education_and_the_Interest-Convergence_Dilemma_-_Derrick_Bell.pdf. (n.d.). Retrieved from http://www.kyoolee.net/Brown_vs._Board_of_Education_and_the_Interest-Convergence_Dilemma_-_Derrick_Bell.pdf.
Bucholz, M. (1999). You da man: Narrating the racial other in the production of white masculinity. *Journal of Sociolinguistics*, 3(4), 443–460.
Burke, T. (n.d.). Rams players enter field with "hands up, don't shoot." Retrieved January 3, 2017, from http://deadspin.com/rams-players-enter-field-with-hands-up-dont-shoot-1664860731.
Burns, K. (2004). *Unforgivable blackness: The rise and fall of Jack Johnson*. PBS.
Burns, K., Burns, S., & McMahon, D. (2016). *Jackie Robinson*. PBS.
Butler, J. (1990). *Gender trouble: Feminism and the subversion of identity*. New York: Routledge.
Buzinski, J. (2013, February 13). Openly gay mixed martial artist Liz Carmouche to fight for first UFC women's title. Retrieved January 8, 2017, from http://www.outsports.com/2013/2/13/4054318/openly-gay-mixed-martial-artist-liz-carmouche-to-fight-for-first-ufc.
Carey, I. (2018). Titus O'Neil collecting boycotted Nike shoes for charity. *SEScoops*. Retrieved from http://www.sescoops.com/titus-oneil-collecting-boycotted-nike-shoes-for-charity/.
Cohen, C.J. (1999). *Boundaries of blackness: AIDS and the breakdown of Black politics*. USA: University of Chicago Press.

Collins, J. (n.d.). Why NBA center Jason Collins is coming out now. Retrieved January 8, 2017, from http://www.si.com/more-sports/2013/04/29/jason-collins-gay-nba-player.

Collins, P.H. (2000). *Black feminist thought* (2d ed.). New York: Routledge.

Collins, P.H. (2005). *Black sexual politics: African Americans, gender, and the new racism.* New York: Routledge.

Connell, R.W., & Messerschmidt, J.W. (2005). Hegemonic masculinity: Rethinking the concept. *Gender & Society, 19*(6), 829–859.

Connell_-_Hegemonic_Masculinity.pdf. (n.d.).

Conner, M., & White, J. (2006). *Black fathers: An invisible presence in America.* Mahwah, NJ: Lawrence Erlbaum Associates, Inc.

Crenshaw, K. (1991). Mapping the margins: Intersectionality, identity politics, and violence against women of color. *Stanford Law Review, 43*(6), 1241–1299.

Crenshaw, K. (1997). Demarginalizing the intersection of race and sex: A Black feminist critique of antidiscrimination doctrine, feminist theory and antiracist politics. In *Critical race feminism: A reader* (2d ed., pp. 23–33). New York: NYU Press.

Crenshaw, Demarginalizing the intersection of race and sex.pdf. (n.d.). Retrieved from http://www.faculty.umb.edu/heike.schotten/readings/Crenshaw,%20Demarginalizing%20the%20Intersection%20of%20Race%20and%20Sex.pdf.

Dekernion, G. (2014). *Chozen.* FX.

Donaldson, L. (2015). When the media misrepresents Black men, the effects are felt in the real World. *The Guardian.* Retrieved from http://www.theguardian.com/commentisfree/2015/aug/12/media-misrepresents-black-men-effects-felt-real-world.

Doude, S. (2018). "If Black people aren't criminals, then why are so many of them in prison?": Confronting racial biases in perceptions of crime and criminals. In *Getting real about race* (2d ed.). Los Angeles: SAGE Publishing.

Ewing, H., & Grady, R. (2013). *Branded.* ESPN Films.

Fejes, F. (2000). Making a gay masculinity. *Critical Studies in Media Communication, 17*(1), 113–116.

Fontana, T. (1997, 2002). *Oz.* Home Box Office.

Goodnough, A. (2009, July 20). Harvard professor jailed; Officer is accused of bias. *New York Times.* Retrieved from http://www.nytimes.com/2009/07/21/us/21gates.html.

Granderson, L. (2005, October 27). Three-time MVP "tired of having to hide my feelings." Retrieved January 8, 2017, from http://www.espn.com/wnba/news/story?id=2203853.

Griner, B. (2014). *In my skin.* New York: Dey Street Books.

Hagler, J. (2015). The media narrative of Black men in America is all wrong. *Newsweek.* Retrieved from http://www.newsweek.com/black-men-today-dont-fit-old-stereotype-314877.

Helgeland, B. (2013). *42.* Warner Bros.

hooks, bell. (2004). *We real cool: Black men and masculinity.* New York: Routledge.

Hosseini, K. (2004). *The kite runner.* USA: Riverhead Books.

Hurt, B. (2006). *Hip-hop: Beyond beats & rhymes.* ITVS.

Johnson, A.G. (n.d.). *The gender knot: Unraveling our patriarchal legacy* (3d ed.). Philadelphia: Temple University Press.

Kimmel, M. (2011). *Manhood in America: A cultural history* (3d ed.). Oxford: Oxford University Press.

Kimmel, M.S., Hearn, J., & Connell, R.W. (2004). *Handbook of studies on men and masculinities.* New York: SAGE Publishing.

Klemko, R. (2013). Gay in the NFL. *Sports Illustrated.* Retrieved from http://www.si.com/2013/07/23/gay-in-the-nfl.

Koerner, C. (n.d.). LeBron James, other nba players wear "i can't breathe" shirts before game. Retrieved January 3, 2017, from http://www.buzzfeed.com/claudiakoerner/lebron-james-kyrie-irving-wear-i-cant-breathe-shirts-before.

Kozol, J. (2005). *The shame of the nation: The restoration of apartheid schooling in America.* New York: Crown Publishers.

Leitch, W. (2014a). Athletes are speaking up now more than ever. *Sports on Earth.* Retrieved from http://www.sportsonearth.com/article/103438006/i-cant-breathe-shirt-eric-garner-derrick-rose-lebron-james.

Leitch, W. (2014b, December 12). "I can't breathe': Will sports TV viewers and sponsors be turned off by activist athletes? Retrieved January 3, 2017, from http://www.sportingnews.com/nba/news/eli-manning-lebron-james-eric-garner-michael-brown-nfl-nba-activist-athletes-new-york-giants-cleveland-cavaliers-georgetown-hoyas/1iu8uywczsueill8vyyjgoi3u5.

Leonard, D.J., & Hazelwood, B.L. (2014). The race denial card: The NBA lockout, LeBron James, and the politics of new racism. In *The colorblind screen: Television in post-racial America*. New York: NYU Press.

Mapping the Margins. (n.d.). Retrieved from http://socialdifference.columbia.edu/files/socialdiff/projects/Article.

Martin, J. (n.d.). Threats after Rams "Hands up don't shoot" protest. CNN.com. Retrieved January 3, 2017, from http://www.cnn.com/2014/12/04/us/rams-threats-ferguson/index.html.

Messner, M.A. (1992). *Power at play: Sport and the problem of masculinity*. Boston: Beacon Press.

Messner, M.A. (2009). *It's all for the kids: Gender, families, and youth sports*. Berkeley: University of California Press.

Mooneyham, M. (2018). WWE's Titus O'Neil: The power of a life changed. *The Post and Courier*. Retrieved from http://www.postandcourier.com/sports/wrestling/wwe-s-titus-o-neil-the-power-of-a-life/article_d198a9fe-2ea7–11e8–98e7-ef259441f66a.html.

Morrison, T. (1970). *The bluest eye*. California: Holt McDougal.

Morrison, T. (1987). *Beloved*. New York: Knopf Doubleday.

Mouzon, D. (2014). "Black people don't value marriage as much as others": Examining structural inequalities in Black marriage patterns. In *Getting real about race* (2d ed.). Los Angeles: SAGE Publishing.

Neal, M.A. (2005). *New Black man*. New York: Routledge.

New York Times Snapshot. (n.d.). Retrieved from http://www.nytimes.com/2009/07/21/us/21gates.html?_r=0.

Newman, R.J., & Rosen, J.N. (20014). *Black baseball, Black business: Race enterprise and the fate of the segregated dollar*. Jackson: University Press of Mississippi.

Pascoe, C.J. (2012). *Dude, you're a fag: Masculinity and sexuality in high school* (2d ed.). Berkeley: University of California Press.

Payne, M. (n.d.). President Obama endorses LeBron James's "I can't breathe" shirt. Retrieved January 3, 2017, from http://www.washingtonpost.com/news/early-lead/wp/2014/12/19/president-obama-endorses-lebron-jamess-i-cant-breathe-shirt/.

Price-Bonham, S., & Skeen, P. (1979). A comparison of Black and White fathers with implications for parent education. *The Family Coordinator*. Retrieved from http://www.jstor.org/stable/583268?seq=1#metadata_info_tab_contents.

Rhoden, W.C. (2006). *Forty million dollar slaves: The rise, fall, and redemption of the Black athlete*. New York: Three Rivers Press.

Rhoden, W.C. (2007). *Third and a mile: The trials and triumph of the Black quarterback*. United States: ESPN Books.

Robinson, J., & Duckett, A. (1972). *I never had it made*. New York: Ecco Press.

Screven, N. (n.d.). Who's your daddy: The epidemic of absent Black fathers. *WRNB Philly*. Retrieved from http://rnbphilly.com/2585634/whos-your-daddy-absent-black-fathers/.

Simon, D. (2002, 2008). *The Wire*. Home Box Office.

Smith, M. (2017). The dangerous myth of the "missing Black father." *The Washington Post*. Retrieved from http://www.washingtonpost.com/posteverything/wp/2017/01/10/the-dangerous-myth-of-the-missing-black-father/?noredirect=on&utm_term=.92c78d7d1069.

Sohi, S. (n.d.). The NBA and "I can't breathe": A controversy at a crossroads. Retrieved January 3, 2017, from http://www.rollingstone.com/culture/features/the-nba-and-i-cant-breathe-a-controversy-at-a-crossroads-20141211.

Taylor, E., Gillborn, D., & Ladson-Billings, G. (2009). *Foundations of critical race theory in education*. New York: Routledge.

Thomas, G. et al. (1996). Fathers on delinquency and substance abuse in Black and White adolescents. *Journal of Marriage and Family*. Retrieved from http://www.jstor.org/stable/353977?seq=1#metadata_info_tab_contents.

Trujillo. (2009). Henry Louis Gates, Jr., arrested, police accused of racial bias. *The Huffington Post*. Retrieved from http://www.huffingtonpost.com/2009/07/20/henry-louis-gates-jr-arre_n_241407.html.

Tyson, M. (2013). *Undisputed truth*. New York: Blue River Press.

Wire, S.I. (n.d.). St. Louis Rams players used the "Hands up, don't shoot" pose while taking the field today. Retrieved January 3, 2017, from http://www.si.com/nfl/2014/11/30/st-louis-rams-ferguson-protests.

WWE (n.d.). Titus O'Neil receives celebrity of the year award. *WWE*. Retrieved from http://community.wwe.com/diversity/gallery/titus-oneil-receives-celebrity-dad-year-award-photos.

Yang, G.L. (2006). *American born Chinese*. New York: First Second Books.

Zaccardi, N. (2015). Greg Louganis recalls Olympic diving, HIV, coming out in "Back on Board" Film. *NBC Sports*. Retrieved from http://olympics.nbcsports.com/2015/08/04/greg-louganis-documentary-back-on-board-olympics-diving/.

Zeigler, C. (2007). John Amaechi comes out publicly. *Out Sports*. Retrieved from http://www.outsports.com/2013/2/20/4009716/john-amaechi-comes-out-gay.

Zeigler, C. (2016). *Fair play: How LGTB athletes are claiming their rightful place in sports*.

PART IV

Media and Art

Identity Construction

Media, Myth and Perception in Football Recruiting

Travis R. Bell

College football is the overwhelming income for Division I university athletic departments. Through revenue-generating bowl games and billion-dollar television contracts, college athletic departments, especially those situated in a Power Five conference, operate as a Fortune 500 company disguised as a non-profit organization. Research has focused on concern for the players who are the primary generators of this revenue despite receiving minimal financial return through scholarships. These players, especially black athletes, are at the center of much of this research that problematizes college athletics through exploitation (Van Rheenen 20), disproportionate graduation rates and limited academic opportunities (Siegel 220; Southall et al. 408), and position segregation (Pitts and Yost 227). These studies provide just a sample of what Harry Edwards predicted as college athletics' "spiraling 'athletic arms race' wherein student-athletes are both the most strategic material and chief causalities" (7) of the economic boom of college football.

The feeder system for college football is the expansive, yet undertheorized, elite high school football players who are situated in a unique and disconcerting space. On one end, these teenagers compete for district and state championships and possibly mythical national titles while utilizing sport as a portal to a college education at highly sought-after, predominately white institutions (PWI). On the other end, they balance life away from the field that includes family, school, and recruiting. The time away from football that should prioritize academics is often usurped by recruiting, which requires abundant time and energy. Recruiting is ever-present in online spaces to fuel daily fan usage (Love et al. 238; Mudrick and Lupinek 73) and enrich media corporations. Thus, it is through this online space that stretches high school football beyond the myth of community and purity (Hardin and Corrigan 89) perpetuated through the context of Friday night lights and moves it into a space of improper focus.

This essay explores the recruiting process through the lens of interest-convergence, which Derrick Bell asserts is when "the interests of blacks in achieving racial equality will be accommodated only when it converges with the interests of whites" (523). While black athletes account for more than two-thirds of NFL players, the chance of making it to the professional ranks is minuscule, yet recruiting websites assist in constructing an athletic identity for elite high school football players that overemphasizes future football potential for the financial gain of PWIs and the media corporations that own the recruiting websites. Those statistics create dissolution with a focus on athletics over academics beginning at the grassroots level, which lead to adolescent health risk and the detriment of academic potential (McDougal and Capers 74). Therefore, this essay explores how recruiting exposure benefits the player in the short-term through heightened publicity but problematizes the process and the ranking of athletes where black athletes are commodified (Ferber 12) by a mostly white system that operates under the guise of perceived colorblindness (Bimper 237).

Interest-Convergence and Sport

Interest-convergence is the theoretical context utilized in this essay to analyze recruiting websites. However, interest-convergence must be understood within the larger context of critical race theory (CRT), which originated in the 1970s in legal scholarship with a focus on "transforming the relationship among race, racism, and power" (Delgado and Stefancic 3). CRT expanded into education and other disciplines with an activist approach intended to promote change through social justice (DeCuir and Dixson 27). The goal for CRT studies is to expose social and hierarchical imbalances that favor whites over blacks through opportunity situated in specific narrative examples embedded within systemic analysis (Tate 210).

Derrick Bell is considered one of the founding fathers of CRT and is specifically the mind behind interest-convergence. Through this theoretical approach, Bell's analysis of the 1954 Supreme Court case *Brown v. Board of Education* argues that the case was focused less on the advancement for blacks in education and more on the political and economic growth for whites. These converged interests intersected as an ideological, positive perception of the U.S. in a global context against the backdrop of the battle against Communism and a reassurance for blacks that the World War II fight grounded in the tenets of equality and freedom was not just lip service (524). The issue for Bell regarding integration of schools was not a knock against equal access to classrooms but that a lack of effective schools was provided for black students. Thus, a substantial disparity in quality of education, despite a perceived racial balance in access, favored white students to the detriment of black students (532–533). Therefore, interest-convergence argues that concessions can be made for blacks that provide little substantive difference while also not disrupting the status quo for whites (DeCuir and Dixson 28).

CRT and interest-convergence have fit into sport scholarship connected to football. Amy and Robert McCormick argue that racial integration in collegiate athletics was not through a beneficent desire on the part of universities. Instead, integration was recognized as an opportunity for economic growth. Their study of interest-convergence focused on the integration of three major bowl games based in southern cities. The Cotton Bowl in Dallas, the Sugar Bowl in New Orleans, and the Orange Bowl in Miami each allowed black athletes to compete for northern schools against Jim Crow segregation laws in the 1940s and 1950s. Despite protests from the southern school counterparts, the economic gain for participating in these lucrative bowl games outweighed segregation so the rules were bent to allow minimal access for black athletes to maximize financial profits for the schools (27–28).

Jamel Donnor explicates how the National Letter of Intent (NLI) signed by high school athletes adds to the commercialization of college football while situating the student-athlete as institutional property. The NLI offers a scholarship "opportunity" that binds the athlete by creating a non-negotiable contract that favors the institution. Donnor explores two legal cases, *Taylor v. Wake Forest University* and *Ross v. Creighton University*, that describe the NLI as weighing sport over the value of education regarding student-athlete contracts (54–56). *Ross v. Creighton* provides evidence of how a black athlete's "physical talent and academic development can be manipulated for the competitive interests of other educational stakeholders" (57). Donnor and the McCormicks provide two significant examples that examine sport-as-institution through a critical lens that avoids the naïveté often linked to the benefits of sport, especially related to individual athletes (Edwards 9). This summary of interest-convergence in sport allows a better understanding to explain the construction of the "student-athlete" identity specific to black male athletes.

Student-Athlete Identity

The formation of a student-athlete identity is a malleable construction among a group that includes an individual athlete, their family, coaches, teachers, and other personal mentors in church or other influential groups (Harrison et al., 2011, 99). However, that group formation is primarily a private construction. The public identity and perception is difficult to navigate and control, especially at the intersection of recruiting, due to the confluence of media, legislation, and fans who fuel an interdependent relationship that initiates when an athlete is identified by an institution as a possible recruit (Hawkins 45). This "socialization process" (Harrison et al., 2002, 122) begins at an adolescent age of understanding racial stereotypes, especially through immersive participation in pop culture and sport (130–131). College coaches, fans, and media further perpetuate stereotypes of black "athletic" identity (Love et al. 242; Thomas et al. 250).

Edwards outlines this immersive process influenced in four parts. First, mass media makes black athletes mostly visible to black youth. Second, black communities reward sport achievement at earlier adolescent times. Third, black athletes are filtered into select sports (e.g., football, basketball) that intensifies competition for opportunity. Finally, sport is a space for the construction of black masculine identity (10). Abby Ferber centralizes these ideas as a mainstream construction that situates black athletes through illusory violent stereotypes that "naturalize and reinforce racial inequality" (22) within systematic practices of primarily white institutions. In an age of the Internet and social media, this mainstream construction of black athlete identity is oversaturated through systematic media representation that reinforces a focus on athletics over academics and creates the "dumb jock" (Edwards 7).

Proposition 48 legislation promulgated this academically inferior ideology in college athletics. Implemented by the NCAA in 1986, recruits required a minimum 2.0 grade point average in core courses and scores of either a 700 on the SAT or a 15 on the ACT. Failure to accomplish these minimum standards resulted in "partial qualifier" status to prove academic competence in college without athletic participation. What Prop 48 afforded was for dominant athletic departments to allow students with minimal academic qualifications into higher education based solely on athletic prowess. Prop 48 focused on access and nothing to emphasize retention or graduation once the student started college (Edwards 17; Siegel 220). The notion of the "student-athlete" further shifted to a "profit-athlete" in revenue-generating sports that further deemphasize academic opportunities specifically for black athletes at PWIs (Southall et al. 408).

The NCAA has since implemented regulations such as the 40/60/80 rule and Academic Progress Rate (APR) penalties. An athlete must incrementally progress toward degree completion in their second (40 percent), third (60 percent), and fourth years (80 percent), respectively, in college (Sulentic 129). Additionally, schools can be penalized with less practice time and competition bans if they do not maintain a specific APR for student-athlete progress ("Academic Progress"). These NCAA mandates offer some protection for student-athletes by forcing colleges to attain certain minimum standards toward graduation. However, these rules do not influence what academic major an athlete can be directed toward or how much assistance is provided once an athlete finishes their playing career.

Billy Hawkins describes this as a reciprocal relationship of exploitation (43). The exploitation of student-athletes occurs through colorblind ideological practices of equal opportunity and choice of select academic programs that do not require too much work outside of class (Bimper 230–231) and implementation of programs such as Prop 48 (Shropshire 141). This naturalized process reinforces "racism within the athletic enterprise" (Rhodes and Butler 922). However, minimal research has examined the exploitation of these athletes prior to their college participation when the myth of the "student-athlete" is perpetuated as "one of the cruelest sociological hoaxes" (Patterson 104) that emphasizes athletic opportunities for employment and mobility over statistical evidence of minuscule opportunities through an obsessed mediated identity. Therefore, this essay exposes the football recruiting process as a critical space of interest-convergence that functions as a site of identity construction for the nation's top-ranked high school football players, who are overwhelmingly black, due to the significant economic gains made possible through this heightened construction for PWIs and media corporations that fuel the process.

The Recruiting Process

The football recruiting process officially begins when a college coach contacts a potential recruit either in person, by phone, or online. The mediated identity for a football recruit predominately starts as a high school freshman through recruiting websites but players have received scholarship offers from college coaches as early as seventh grade (Farrell par. 1). Four primary websites drive recruiting news and information. These websites are *espn.com*, *247sports.com*, *rivals.com*, and *scout.com*. The last three websites primary business models are centered on recruiting, and all provide searchable databases beginning with high school freshmen. They provide biographical information that includes a player's name, position, hometown, and high school. Physical information about each athlete includes height, weight, and often a 40-yard dash time. These bits of information are included in analysis by recruiting "experts" who then produce subjective star-rankings with five-star as the highest possible ranking down to two stars.

The websites *247sports.com* and *scout.com* provide star values for players before their sophomore season begins while *scout.com* and *espn.com* begin ranking players as juniors (Lewis et al. 1). Each website provides a searchable database that includes freshmen (*espn.com* is the exception beginning only with juniors) to sort by any of the biographical or physical markers. While *espn.com* is a small subset of the larger ESPN television network brand, the ESPN brand garners significant national attention in the recruiting process (Bell et al. 48). The final information included in a player's profile is what colleges are recruiting them and which of those colleges the player is most interested, often through an updated "top five" provided by the athlete to recruiting reporters.

These websites provide the national platform for the recruiting process. However, every Division I football program has a website specific to that school that caters coverage of the recruiting process to the individual school. The school-specific website operates under the umbrella of the national platform and provides updated content through recruiting reporters for each school. These reporters contact recruits daily and weekly for updated information on recruiting visits to different campuses to identify any changes to the player's top five. Additionally, the reporters contact family members, high school coaches, and college coaches.

This 24/7 process ends for seniors (or in some cases for junior college athletes) with National Signing Day (NSD), which is annually held on the first Wednesday in February when athletes officially sign their NLI. The NCAA started allowing a 72-hour early signing period in December 2017. Signing day events include players signing the NLI in front of a public audience that includes coaches, family members, and teammates. Recruiting reporters and local media attend as well for highly ranked players. For four- and five-star recruits, national media outlets may televise the player's announcement of where he will attend college. Colleges announce their respective recruiting classes online and through press releases and often host signing day parties for fans to visit with the head coach to talk about the recruits. College coaches are forbidden by the NCAA to discuss any player by name until they have officially signed a NLI. Finally, the recruiting websites provide analysis after NSD to rank the cumulative college recruiting classes. Then the process begins again for the juniors who will be the center of attention in the recruiting process over the following 12 months. Now with a brief overview of the recruiting process, it is significant to outline how the interests of high school football recruits, PWIs, and media corporations converge in the recruiting process.

Interests for High School Recruits

Recruiting is a racially dominated space by minority (mostly black) athletes as evident by 82 of ESPN's top 100 recruits in the 2016 class occupied by people of color. The recruitment of high school football players has become a media spectacle through the advent of the Internet and creation of recruiting websites (Dumond et al. 73; Kian et al. 682; May 51). Alongside the explosion of online recruiting information, social media allows athletes to self-promote in a way that generates mass media attention from recruiting websites and national media outlets. For example, the top 10 recruits in the 2017 class each had Twitter accounts with thousands of followers before NSD. Mississippi running back Cam Akers led the way and provided an example of how recruiting immediately generated new connections. Before Akers committed to Florida State on December 27, 2016, he had over 16,000 Twitter followers. In the week after his commitment, Akers added nearly 2,000 more followers, presumably FSU boosters, fans, and media who cover the Seminoles. This space provides a unique opportunity for these high school athletes to break recruiting news for themselves, teammates, and other nationally recruited players who they meet during national scouting combines and all-star games.

With this distinct space for identity construction, top-ranked recruits receive previously unavailable national exposure. This increased exposure creates notoriety and celebrity status that result in lavish recruiting trips, televised interviews, all-star game trips sponsored by apparel companies, and appearances in commercials, on marketing material, and in mass media programs including highlight shows and documentaries. These often-isolated opportunities for heavily recruited high school athletes result in short-term gains for the individual athlete but feed into the economic machines that drive these gains that are outlined in the next section of this essay. The possibility of incremental gains results in unexpected consequences for the athlete.

The first notable consequence is loss of personal and academic time. The time spent doing excessive interviews with recruiting reporters, texting with coaches, and connecting through social media is exponential, not just in hours but in weeks and months inundated with requests. This time spent in the recruiting process is a detriment to time that could focus on academic achievement in high school classes, preparation for standardized tests, or planning for the rigor of balancing academics and athletics at the collegiate level that research has shown can result in social isolation (Harrison et al., 2011, 95; Van Rheenen 12) caused by the hours required for practice, training, travel, and games as well as attending colleges geographically distant away from family (Southall et al. 399). The mediated construction of identity in the recruiting process focuses so much attention on athletic ability that removes the "student" out of "student-athlete" and creates a perception that the student is only in college because of athletics and the labor intensive, economically-focused model (Harrison et al., 2011, 98).

The second notable consequence is backlash from coaches and fans when a player does not sign a NLI. Through message boards on recruiting websites, Kian et al. identified racist language directed at recruits based on college choice. The study indicates that other fans did police the racist language (693–694), but that does not remove the space that is available for fans to target these teenage athletes that is accessible for any subscriber to read. Love et al. identify overt racism in message boards is being replaced by colorblind racism through more implicit references that nevertheless reinforce racial stereotypes (Love et al. 244). Defensive tackle Rashan Gary is an extreme example of direct racism in recruiting that reverted to a traditional form of communication. The consensus No. 1 recruit in the 2016 class received a voicemail prior to a visit to Clemson from a person self-identified as "Clemson Dan" who said, "If you're coming down here, you gotta do just like the KKK and be serious about your football. Clemson and the KKK, the two things we love the most" (Cooper par. 2). Gary signed with Michigan, but his story is sadly not an isolated case.

A final consequence of the recruiting process in the interests of high school athletes is injury. If an athlete is significantly injured during his high school career, his perceived "value" as an athletic commodity rapidly diminishes (Hawkins 83) followed by fading notoriety and decreased public status that is only propped by verbal agreements with coaches (Ivins par. 2). A scholarship offer can be pulled at any moment and any promises made by coaches may look like fraudulent misrepresentation (Sulentic 157) but is a reality of recruiting. The pressure placed on an athlete in the recruiting process is staggering and as described in this section, alters reality for what is expected of a recruit and the challenges faced in a system that favors white institutions that construct the recruiting process.

Interests for PWIs and Media Companies

Three primarily white institutions reap significant economic gain through the recruiting process. These institutions are the recruiting websites, the PWI schools who maximize financial opportunities with the free publicity garnered through heightened recruiting coverage, and other corporations who utilize the recruiting information to generate mediated financial opportunities. Recruiting has been the backbone of college football since its inception. However, scholarship limitations in 1992 to the current level of 85 players per Football Bowl Series (formerly Division I-A) school and 63 for a Football Championship Series (former Division I-AA) school intensified focus on the significance of the process. The interests for these institutions regarding the recruiting process exploded with the Internet and its opportunity for economic growth.

Recruiting websites vaulted the recruiting process into a year-round media cycle through a "market niche" (Dumond et al. 73) for maximum economic gain generated by the online space with minimal financial overhead. The business model is simple and produces guaranteed content every year because of the annual recruiting cycle. It is also financially brilliant in that it targets a fervent fan base with disposable income willing to pay $10 per month for information about high school athletes and access to message boards for fan discussion of where the various athletes are considering attending college, which is fueled by the abundance of information generated by recruiting reporters through constant contact with the athletes. This fan base is predominately white and male (Kian et al. 684; Love et al. 239). As outlined in the section discussing the recruiting process, these websites devote countless hours and column inches in reporting content that appears online, on-air, and across mobile platforms that aid in the athletic identity construction that benefits the player during the short-term status as a marquee recruit. Ultimately, this "high stakes" recruiting drives coaches, subscribers, and other media outlets to use this content in discussing the athlete's overall recruitment (Thomas et al. 241).

These recruiting websites were independently launched but were purchased by major media corporations before the 2008 economic downturn in the U.S. For example, News Corp. bought *scout.com* for a reported $60 million in 2005, and Yahoo! acquired *rivals.com* for $100 million in 2007, thus filling the pockets of the white owners and investors in the websites. North American Media Group purchased *scout.com* in 2013 for reportedly less than News Corp. but bought the website to create a self-described digital network as "the destination for brands to speak with men in a premium environment" ("Company Overview"). Despite ownership changes, the goal is still to profit off black teenagers to produce content consumed by the white, male target market with disposable income craved by advertisers.

During this rise of recruiting websites, PWIs have economically capitalized on the mediated construction of recruits (Mudrick and Lupinek 73). The constant cycle of information provides free national exposure for the university that would cost millions in advertising dollars. Instead, many schools spend those millions in cost savings for recruiting high school athletes (Brady et al. par. 3). Recruiting rankings are utilized by the colleges to create promotional materials that highlight the off-field success of the program. For example, a press release for Alabama football released after NSD 2016 mentions a near consensus top-ranked recruiting class (*espn.com* ranked them second) that breaks down the recruits, where the websites ranked them individually and collectively, and offers interview archives with the recruits produced during online-specific shows generated by the university. Fans can track the "Big Board" as recruits NLIs are received and watch video highlight reels of what the school hopes will be the next star athletes of the program ("Crimson Tide").

NSD provides another point of financial and media access for PWIs. The schools host events with the head coach to discuss the team's recruiting success and introduce fans to the next batch of players. Michigan took this idea to a new level in 2016 with the "Signing of the Stars" event. The Wolverines and head coach Jim Harbaugh welcomed the new signees in the on-campus performance auditorium where 3,500 fans attended the celebration. The star-studded event included appearance by New England Patriots quarterback Tom Brady, former Heisman Trophy winner Desmond Howard, and Michigan native and former New York Yankees captain Derek Jeter. Fans were greeted by cardboard cutouts of the team's premier recruits ("Signing of the Stars"). The 2017 event was moved to the school's basketball facility, Crisler Arena, with a seating capacity over 13,000.

The rise of recruiting aided in the construction of new media opportunities for television networks, college conferences, and apparel companies. ESPN, in conjunction with its own recruiting website, annually hosts 11 hours of signing day television programming with dozens of reporters situated on college campuses all day to discuss the culmination of the recruiting process (Bell et al. 61–62). Other regional sports channels host similar shows to maximize viewership and revenue. College conferences have created their own sports channels (e.g., Big Ten Network, SEC Network) to promote the conference schools and offer programming opportunities for non-revenue sports. However, these networks also capitalize on NSD by hosting shows that discuss the impact of recruiting for conference schools. In 2016, the SEC Network produced 10 hours of content devoted to this one-day event, and the Big Ten Network provided eight hours of content.

Non-media companies have partnered with recruiting websites and television networks to construct events specifically highlighting the recruiting process. Under Armour sponsors regional and national scouting combines with *rivals.com* and partners with ESPN for a nationally-televised all-star game with several athletes announcing their college selection live on-air. The United States Army hosts an all-star game televised by NBC that also creates a space for announcing college decisions. Nike hosts "The Opening" in the summer where elite 7-on-7 football teams compete, and individual athletes participate in skills competitions and various drills that are televised and promoted by ESPN. The "Elite 11" competition among the nation's best quarterback airs on ESPN with the production of a 2016 documentary hosted by former Super Bowl-winning quarterback Trent Dilfer. Additionally, college quarterbacks (and former top-ranked high school recruits) like Clemson's DeShaun Watson and Tennessee's Josh Dobbs served as "counselors" to the competitors but received no financial compensation to avoid impacting their

NCAA Eligibility. These are just a few examples of how recruiting websites spawned economic opportunities for corporations to capitalize on the recruiting process of high school athletes that are all part of the commodification process of recruiting and the players who often are not even yet on campus minus a few early enrollees.

Conclusion

Football recruiting produces a multimillion-dollar industry created as a profitable space of interest-convergence that offers fans and media a place to meet and engage with the nation's best high school football players. Coaches, the universities, the NCAA, and other affiliated corporations operate under notions of colorblindness in this "dysfunctional" process (May 61) that emphasize access to college and opportunity for national exposure offered through recruiting without any recognition of the impact or detriment to a teenage athlete who is navigating his own identity construction under a microscope. The converged interests reach the PWIs that utilize their respective recruiting success to promote a program and create an environment that explicitly emphasize football over academics after an athlete signs a NLI (Donnor 49). This de-emphasis of academics originally promulgated through the recruiting rankings further commodifies the high school athlete and commercializes the process with a sole focus on physical attributes like height, strength, and speed with little-to-no recognition of—or emphasis on—academic success for a prospective recruit (Hawkins 14).

The trickle-down effect of athletics over academics begins in the recruiting process where a recruit's college choice is not affected by the school's history of graduating players (Dumond et al. 83) but is instead based on a school's success in NFL draft placement. This problem manifests the unrealistic goal that athletics is perceived as a viable and profitable professional experience (McDougle and Capers 72). Instead, athletes use up their most productive years providing free labor at the high school and college levels in what Hawkins calls the "athletic industrial complex" (19). The addition of high school combines, all-star games, and events such as "Elite 11" add to a faster breakdown of the body and, thus, the commodity that is used by the white institutions discussed in this essay until they are no longer valued enough to participate in the economic creation of content.

CRT focuses on race as the central starting point of critique and is significant for this research due to the racialized space of football recruiting. However, this research recognizes that social class and gender are not explicitly excluded from the analysis. Instead, it is understood that social class and gender operate in direct relation with race regarding football recruiting to the exclusion of opportunities for women and people of color who are not athletically inclined. Additionally, while recruiting websites offer similar database characteristics for white athletes, it is through the converged interests for black males that this analysis relies on CRT to critique how coaches, media, universities, and their affiliated corporations perpetuate stereotypical practice and policies (DeCuir and Dixson 30; Love et al. 241–242; Thomas et al. 252) of recruiting that are covertly racist by emphasizing physical ability of black athletes—and intellect for white athletes—for the benefit of these primarily white institutions that serve to gain economically and build up the myth of the minuscule possibility of professional athletics for the high school athlete.

REFERENCES

"Academic Progress Rate Explained." http://www.ncaa.org/aboutresources/research/academic-progress-rate-explained. Accessed 20 December 2016.
Bell, Derrick A., Jr. "*Brown v. Board of Education* and the Interest-Convergence Dilemma." *Harvard Law Review*, vol. 93, 1980, pp. 518–533.
Bell, Travis R., Melvin Lewis, Andrew C. Billings, and Kenon A. Brown. "'It Just Means More?': Depiction of the Southeastern Conference (SEC) in ESPN Signing Day Coverage (2015–2018)." *Southern Quarterly*, vol. 56, no. 3, 2019, pp. 48–67.
Bimper, Albert Y., Jr. "Lifting the Veil: Exploring Colorblind Racism in Black Student Athlete Experiences." *Journal of Sport and Social Issues*, vol. 39, no. 3, 2015, pp. 225–243.
Brady, Erik, John Kelly, and Steve Berkowitz. "Schools in Power Conferences Spending More on Recruiting." *USA Today*, 3 February 2015, https://www.usatoday.com/story/sports/ncaaf/recruiting/2015/02/03/college-football-recruiting-signing-day-sec-power-conferences/22813887/. Accessed 8 August 2018.
"Company Overview." http://www.scout.com/corporate/3/about.html. Accessed 5 January 2017.
Cooper, Darren. "Racist Reference in Voice Mail Left for Recruit from Paramus Catholic a Disturbing Reality." *The Record*, 16 April 2016, https://www.northjersey.com/story/sports/2016/04/16/cooper-racist-reference-in-voice-mail-left-for-recruit-from-paramus-catholic-a-disturbing-reality/94639142/. Accessed 20 December 2016.
"Crimson Tide Finish with No. 1 Recruiting Class in 2016." 3 February 2016, http://www.rolltide.com/news/2016/2/3/Crimson_Tide_Finish_with_No_1_Recruiting_Class_in_2016.aspx?path=football. Accessed 5 January 2017.
DeCuir, Jessica T., and Adrienne D. Dixson. "'So When it comes out, they aren't that surprised that it is there': Using Critical Race Theory as a Tool of Analysis of Race and Racism in Education." *Educational Researcher*, vol. 33, no. 5, 2004, pp. 26–31.
Delgado, Richard, and Jean Stefancic. *Critical Race Theory: An Introduction*, 2012, New York University Press, 2012.
Donnor, Jamel K. "Toward an Interest-Convergence in the Education of African-American Football Student Athletes in Major College Sports." *Race, Ethnicity and Education*, vol. 8, no. 1, 2005, pp. 45–67.
Dumond, J. Michael, Allen K. Lynch, and Jennifer Platania. "An Economic Model of the College Football Recruiting Process." *Journal of Sports Economics*, vol. 9, no. 1, 2008, pp. 67–87.
Edwards, Harry. "The Collegiate Athletic Arms Race: Origins and Implications of the 'Rule 48' Controversy." *Journal of Sport and Social Issues*, vol. 8, no. 1, 1984, pp. 4–22.
Farrell, Perry A. "Jim Harbaugh, Michigan Football Offer Scholarship to Seventh-Grade Quarterback." *USA Today*, 20 June 2018, https://www.usatoday.com/story/sports/ncaaf/bigten/2018/06/20/jim-harbaugh-michigan-football-scholarship/717049002/. Accessed 8 August 2018.
Ferber, Abby L. "The Construction of Black Masculinity: White Supremacy Now and Then." *Journal of Sport & Social Issues*, vol. 31, no. 1, 2007, pp. 11–24.

Hardin, Marie, and Thomas F. Corrigan. "Media and the Business of High School Sports: A Case for Closer Scrutiny." *Journal of Sports Media*, vol. 3, no. 2, 2008, pp. 89–94.

Harrison, Louis, C. Keith Harrison, and Leonard N. Moore. "African American Racial Identity and Sport." *Sport, Education and Society*, vol. 7, no. 2, 2002, pp. 121–133.

Harrison, Louis, Gary Sailes, Willy K. Rotich, and Albert Y. Bimper. "Living the Dream or Awakening from the Nightmare: Race and Athletic Identity." *Race Ethnicity and Education*, vo. 14, no. 1, 2011, pp. 91–103.

Hawkins, Billy. *The New Plantation: Black Athletes, College Sports, and Predominately White NCAA Institutions*. Palgrave, 2010.

Ivins, Andrew. "Athletes Face Uncertainty After Injuries Hurt Their Recruiting Plans." *Sun-Sentinel*, 26 January 2014, http://articles.sun-sentinel.com/2014-01-26/sports/fl-recruiting-injury-0127-20140126_1_william-jeanlys-college-football-recruiting-college-scholarships. Accessed 20 December 2016.

Kian, Edward M., Galen Clavio, John Vincent, and Stephanie D. Shaw. "Homophobic and Sexist Yet Uncontested: Examining Football Fan Postings on Internet Message Boards." *Journal of Homosexuality*, vol. 58, no. 5, 2011, pp. 680–699.

Lewis, Melvin, Travis R. Bell, Andrew C. Billings, and Kenon A. Brown. "White Sportscasters, Black Athletes: Race and ESPN's Coverage of College Football's National Signing Day." *Howard Journal of Communications*, vol. 31, no. 3, 2020, pp. 1–14. https://doi.org/10.1080/10646175.2019.1608482.

Love, Adam, Bianca Gonzalez-Sobrino, and Matthew W. Hughey. "Excessive Celebration? the Racialization of Recruiting Comments on College Football Internet Message Boards." *Sociology of Sport Journal*, vol. 34, no. 3, 2017, pp. 235–247.

May, Vaughn. "'Planes Don't Fly North': College Football Recruiting and the Oppositional South." *Studies in Popular Culture*, vol. 34, no. 2, 2012, pp. 49–71.

McDougle, Leon, and Quinn Capers, IV. (2012). Establishing priorities for student-athletes: Balancing academics and sports. *Spectrum: A Journal on Black Men, 1*(1), 71–77.

Mudrick, Michael, and Joshua Lupinek. (2015). Craving the scoop: An examination of highly identified fans' utilization of subscription-based college-recruiting networks. *Journal of Sports Media*, 10(1), 51–77.

Patterson, Orlando. *The Cultural Matrix: Understanding Black Youth*. Harvard University Press, 2015.

Pitts, Joshua. D., and Daniel M. Yost. "Racial Position Segregation in Intercollegiate Football: Do Players Become More Racially Segregated as They Transition from High School to College?" *The Review of Black Political Economy*, vol. 40, no. 2, 2013, pp. 207–230.

Rhodes, Lodis, and Johnny S. Butler. "Sport and Racism: A Contribution to Theory Building in Race Relations?" *Social Science Quarterly*, vol. 55, no. 4, 1975, pp. 919–925.

Shropshire, Kenneth L. "Colorblind Propositions: Race, the SAT, and the NCAA." *Stanford Law and Policy Review*, 1997, vol. 8, pp. 141–157.

Siegel, Donald. "Higher Education and the Plight of the Black Male Athlete." *Journal of Sport and Social Issues*, vol. 18, no. 3, 1994, pp. 207–223.

Signing of the Stars. http://www.theplayerstribune.com/signing-of-the-stars-michigan-football/. Accessed 5 January 2017.

Southall, Richard M., E. Woodrow Eckard, Mark S. Nagel, and Morgan H. Randall. "Athletic Success and NCAA Profit-Athletes' Adjusted Graduation Gaps." *Social of Sport Journal*, vol. 32, 2015, pp. 395–414.

Sulentic, Katherine. "Running Backs, Recruiting, and Remedies: College Football Coaches, Recruits, and the Torts of Negligent and Fraudulent Misrepresentation." *Roger Williams University Law Review*, vol. 14, no. 1, 2009, pp. 127–162.

Tate, William F., IV. "Critical Race Theory and Education: History, Theory, and Implications." *Review of Research in Education*, vol. 22, 1997, pp. 195–247.

Thomas, Grant, Jessica J. Good, and Alexi R. Gross. "Racial Athletic Stereotype Confirmation in College Football Recruiting." *The Journal of Social Psychology*, vol. 155, 2015, pp. 238–254.

Van Rheenen, Derek. "Exploitation in the American Academy: College Athletes and Self-Perceptions of Value." *The International Journal of Sport & Society*, vol. 2, no. 4, 2011, pp. 11–26.

The (African) American Dream
Spectacle and Post-Racial Teleology
in U.S. Sports Films

Nathan Kalman-Lamb

This essay will explore the ways in which narrative and documentary films repeatedly rehearse what I will refer to as an (African) American Dream. Close readings of the films *Glory Road* (2006), *Remember the Titans* (2000), *Through the Fire* (2006), and *Hoop Dreams* (2004) reveal that sport is persistently positioned as a site of economic opportunity and a mechanism for the amelioration of racial conflict and injustice through the discipline and hard-work of individual athletic actors. These films about sport are most intelligible when understood as a form of racial spectacle that endorse the promise of the American Dream for African Americans—the idea that sport provides realistic opportunities to achieve socio-economic upward mobility even as the actual probability of such success is minute. Thus, they obfuscate the structural impediments to such opportunity that exist within a late capitalist American political economy. Further, this spectacle produces a liberal teleology that diminishes the significance of on-going structural racial inequality by suggesting that racism has been consigned to a historical past in the progressive march towards a just society. Thus, sport films have a particularly significant ideological impact in the way that they frame the nature of American society and the life chances and opportunities available to African Americans. There are considerable implications to this as it functions to both reproduce the illusory promise of the American Dream, particularly for African Americans, and obfuscate the continued existence of structural racial inequality for the society at large.

Structural Racism and the American Dream

Representations of sport, race, and the American Dream must be understood within the material context in which they circulate. The American Dream is widely understood to be the idea that the freedom to achieve economic opportunity and advancement exist in the United States for all who are willing to work hard enough to achieve them. Musick and Wilson argue, "the most important part of the American Dream is not its promise of opportunity but the way it connects effort and reward," (1998, p. 17). Likewise, Hochschild suggests that "the American Dream is joyously liberating in its message that people may aspire to control their own destiny rather than merely acquiesce in the vagaries of fate or an overlord" (Hochschild, 1995, p. 252). The American Dream is fundamentally a liberal fantasy that no structural constraints exist in the United States to obstruct individual opportunity and agency. Yet, this mythical notion of American freedom and equality contrasts sharply with the data on structural inequality in the country, particularly for African Americans. Indeed, the United States is a nation built on concrete differences in terms of freedom and access to economic resources according to a logic of racialization. Feagin and Bennefield write,

> The U.S. is a country with systemic oppression and centuries of genocide, 336 years of slavery and legal segregation, about 85 percent of U.S. history. Since the 17th century a white elite has played the central role in maintaining racialized institutions and a rationalizing white framing, while ordinary whites have usually supported oppression because of white privilege. Over about 20 generations, whites have inherited socioeconomic resources from ancestors who benefitted unjustly from slavery, segregation, and other racial oppression. Unjust enrichment of whites from this oppression brought unjust impoverishment for people of color [2014, pp. 7–8].

This brief historical synthesis testifies to the bankruptcy of the American Dream as a lived reality for racialized Americans. Generations of slavery and economic exploitation and discrimination have produced a society that distributes resources and opportunities based on racial status rather than effort, aptitude, or a basic principle of equity. For these reasons, in the essay I use the expression (African) American Dream to indicate the very particular ways in which the conventional American Dream narrative is experienced by African Americans.

Myriad examples exist that testify to the way in which structural racism functions in the United States today to undermine the (African) American Dream. Segregation persists in both housing and labor markets, affording higher property values, better-funded education, and more economic opportunities to white Americans. Ovadia writes,

> In urban America, two areas in which segregation remains extensive are the housing and labor markets. Blacks and whites typically do not live in the same neighborhoods in metropolitan areas ... and black workers continue to be "crowded" into a limited set of occupations that are, in turn, de-valued on the labor market [2003, p. 313].

In 2010, in 35 of the largest U.S. cities, unemployment for African Americans peaked at between 30 to 35 percent, the same rate as during the Great Depression. Further, African Americans and Latinos are three times as likely to live in poverty as whites, while 90 percent of Black children will depend on food stamps at some point. Indeed, for each dollar of net worth owned by whites in the U.S., African Americans possess 10 cents and Latinxs 12 (McNally, 2011). African Americans also experience higher rates of mortality and morbidity than whites due to structural racism in the U.S. healthcare system (Feagin & Bennefield, 2014).

Similar structural discrimination exists with respect to the criminal justice system wherein African Americans are two-and-a-half times more likely to be killed by police than whites, while unarmed African Americans are five times more likely to be killed by police (Lowery, 2015, July 11). Two-thirds of all incarcerated people in the United States are African American or Latinx, including one-third of all Black men in the country (McNally, 2011). For African Americans, then, the American Dream continues to exist as little more than a fetishistic myth disguising the persistence of structural racism. There is nothing post-racial about U.S. society today given that race continues to frame the opportunities and life chances of U.S. citizens.

> In urban America, two areas in which segregation remains extensive are the housing and labor markets. Blacks and whites typically do not live in the same neighborhoods in metropolitan areas (Massey and Denton, 1993; Lewis Mumford Center, 2001) and black workers continue to be "crowded" into a limited set of occupations that are, in turn, de-valued on the labor market [Jacobsen, 1997; Reid, 1998].

In 2010, in thirty-five of the largest U.S. cities, unemployment for African Americans peaked at between 30 to 35 percent, the same rate as during the Great Depression. Further, African Americans and Latinxs are three times as likely to live in poverty as whites, while 90 percent of Black children will depend on food stamps at some point. Indeed, for each dollar of net worth owned by whites in the U.S., African Americans possess ten cents and Latinxs twelve (McNally, 2011). African Americans also experience higher rates of mortality and morbidity than whites due to structural racism in the U.S. healthcare system (Feagin & Bennefield, 2014).

Yet, the American Dream persists as a myth that the United States is a meritocracy in which upward mobility can be achieved by anyone, through discipline and hard work. This ideology is dangerous and misleading. The myth of meritocracy obscures and de-legitimizes the constraints facing individuals in subordinated subject positions, be they predicated on class, race, gender, or sexuality, thus diminishing both the potential for the redistribution of resources by those with power and—in some (but certainly far from all) cases, when this myth is interpellated as an aspirational telos, radical political resistance by the marginalized. At the same time, the hope provided by the myth facilitates the reproduction of the cycle of economic stratification, as it contributes to the production of a racialized work force that is disciplined and hard working in the service of corporate capital.

Nowhere is the myth of the American Dream more persistently rehearsed than in the world of sport. This is particularly evident in the narratives constructed around and about the games, which, stripped of all the accouterments of their culture, remain relatively benign. Today, perhaps the most prevalent source of these narratives is film. I argue that the version of the American Dream most commonly disseminated through sports film can be understood as an (African) American Dream in that it implicitly suggests that the American Dream is most available to African Americans through the opportunities offered by high performance sport. The promise of this Dream is belied by the basic reality that confronts any aspiring professional athlete. For instance, a recent study by the NCAA (*Probability of competing beyond high school*, 2017, March 10) suggests that for young basketball players, the probability of reaching the NBA is minute. Only 3.4 percent of high school basketball players in the United States will play in the NCAA (and only 1 percent will play in Division One, the level of college basketball from which nearly all professional players are drawn). Additionally, only 1.1 percent of NCAA men's basketball players will ultimately play in the NBA. These basic figures highlight the exceptional improbability—indeed, the near-impossibility—of the prospect of playing professional basketball for any young American, let alone those confronted with structural constraints inhibiting access to resources that might help cultivate one's abilities. Yet, despite these stark realities, again and again, sport is figured as an effective vehicle for economic opportunity in U.S. popular culture, particularly film.

Although there have been countless such films, I will restrict my analysis here to a handful of films that are presented under the guise of verisimilitude. I am particularly concerned with films attesting to be "based on a true story" or documentary, because they stake a claim to truth. Debord argues that spectacle creates a "self-representation" of actual material conditions that is "superior to the world," (1994, p. 22). This self-representation is a utopian interpretation of the world that masquerades as reality. Verisimilar and documentary films about the experience of the American Dream for young African American athletes can be understood as self-representations. Certainly, much or even most of what they say may have occurred. My point, however, is that the decision to share *these* uplifting stories leaves myriad tales of exploitation and "failure" submerged. Even more significant is the way in which these stories are told, for the persistent accumulation of narrative upon narrative of the American Dream has a tangible effect: it creates the sense that the American Dream is a reality and that structural racism does not exist as a barrier to individual accomplishment. It produces the idea that America is a post-racial society, wherein individual aptitude and effort are the only determining factors in the pursuit of opportunity. This is why the sports film, particularly the "true" sports film, is one of the most persistent and efficacious forms of racial spectacle in contemporary American society. Ultimately, these spectacles legitimize a racialized capitalist order, presenting America as a utopian realization of liberal teleology rather than a site of oppression and structural racism.

Structure and Representation

I have argued elsewhere (Kalman-Lamb, 2013; Kalman-Lamb, 2015) that representation (the cultural realm of texts) and structure are inextricably linked. Departing from a vulgar Marxist notion of base-superstructure that figures material (structural) conditions as inherently determinative of the cultural (textual) realm, I argue instead, building on the work and cultural studies approach of Stuart Hall, that representation plays an active role in reproducing structure by naturalizing and legitimizing it. This makes representation both a vital object of inquiry and also a site of genuine political praxis. Hall argues that we must always think in terms of

> the culture and society paradigm—not culture isolated, because by itself culture becomes another thing, a rarified realm of the aesthetic et cetera; and not society in some sort of determinist way in which society tells culture what to do, but in the complicated interrelationships between the social and the cultural, between the social and the symbolic—because culture is in some way always constitutive [MacCabe, 2007, p. 21].

Hall instructs us here to understand that culture cannot be excised from the realm of the structural, as in some myopic cultural studies analysis that becomes preoccupied with texts as self-contained objects divorced from the material world. Yet, likewise is it a mistake to understand texts only as superstructural manifestations of political economic conditions. Instead, Hall exhorts us to view the representational realm as an active agent in the production and reproduction of social structure. Textual analysis of works of representation provide us with a window into the way in which structure is formed and maintained through ideas about what forms of social relations are and are not legitimate. The (African) American Dream, then, should be understood as a complex set of ideas about the social world that, through their circulation in the cultural sphere of representation, help to reify that world and its structures.

Hall is also useful here for the way in which he provides a methodological foundation for understanding how to unpack the relationship between the text and the broader social realm it circulates within. For Hall, "we may describe the whole repertoire of imagery and visual effects through which difference is represented at any one historical moment as a *regime of representation*" (1997, p. 232). Another way of putting this is that texts become comprehensible because they always already operate within an inter-textual context that affords them legibility. A film produced in a cultural vacuum would produce meaning entirely based on the significations found within it. However, no film is produced in such a context. Rather, all films (all texts) are produced in "regimes of representation," cultural systems comprised of myriad other concrete texts that serve to anchor meaning according to the logic of widely-held norms. Capitalism and structural racism produce a regime of representation that romanticizes the possibility of economic opportunity through sport, while at the same time essentializing Blackness as inherently linked to physicality. These assumptions, rehearsed through countless texts, naturalize the (African) American Dream and largely (although not absolutely) foreclose other interpretations of the Black experience in sport. The textual readings that follow are guided by the assumption that ideas about the American Dream and Blackness *already exist*. Thus, these films do not need to offer fully explicit articulations of these ideological constructs in order to reproduce their logic. Rather, they draw upon the inter-textual logic of the (African) American Dream to consolidate an idea that already has considerable currency: that Black people in America should, can, and will achieve upward mobility through hard work because structural racism no longer confronts them as a barrier to such opportunity.

Verisimilar Narrative Film and the (African) American Dream: Glory Road *and* Remember the Titans

James Gartner's film *Glory Road* (2006) is the story of the unheralded 1966 Texas Western team that became the first to win an NCAA basketball championship with an all-Black starting lineup. The film is spectacular in that it provides both a teleological American capitalist meta-narrative and a conventional rags-to-riches story. The meta-narrative is indexed right from the opening montage of the film. Upbeat, optimistic background music accompanies a radio announcer's pronouncement that "times are changing." These aural signifiers are accompanied by illustrative visual images, including astronauts, basketball players, and the Beatles. These relatively palatable signifiers of progress are linked to an image of soldiers in Vietnam and then protestors marching alongside Martin Luther King, Jr. The parallelism of the montage reciprocally imbues the Vietnam War with the pristine ethics of King, redeeming it as a valiant struggle to contain the sinister insurgent specter of communism, while simultaneously framing the Civil Rights movement as part of American capitalism's righteous struggle towards progress. The final images of a basketball and then a child in a classroom contribute to the overall sense that capitalism, race, and basketball are all linked as part of a lockstep march towards progress and opportunity. Debord (1994) writes that "the spectacle manifests itself as an enormous positivity, out of reach and beyond dispute" (p. 15). This preliminary sequence of *Glory Road* is an example of such a spectacle. Capitalism and racial justice are framed as the aims and objectives of history, as progress itself; no rational justifications for these assertions are necessary, for we have already been informed that this is a true story. Soon after, Coach Haskins explicitly invokes the ideology of the American Dream when he attempts to convince Bobby Joe Hill that he should come to play for Texas Western. Hill is reluctant, espousing a realist vision based on his experiences of racial subordination. At one point he concludes, "You sign me up, like your token Negro, bury me at the end of the bench, I'd rather hang it up, do something else." Haskins dismisses the challenges faced by young African American men, asserting instead the equal-opportunity ideology of the American Dream by stating, "You just told me about a big 'ole dream you have. I can let you play. I can help you make your dream come true faster than a twist will take your socks off."

Later, soon after the players have arrived in their residences in El Paso, Flournoy looks at a book by Malcolm X that he picked up off of the bed of his roommate Worsley. Worsley enters the room and tells Flournoy not to touch his things. The potentially subversive socialistic connotations of residence life are here deftly repressed through a reassertion of the sanctity of property rights. Black resistance, moreover, is appropriated to capital. Indeed, this is a crucial thematic implication of the film: improved "race-relations" and capital go hand-in-hand; continued racial inequalities are neatly glossed over. On the eve of the climactic national championship game between Texas Western and all-white Kentucky, melodramatic, gospel-esque music plays as we see a shot framing Haskins looking up at an immense American flag that hangs over the court. The flag fills most of the screen, implying that Texas Western's improbable season and America are in some way connected. This connection is not difficult to make: the team is a living testament to the (African) American Dream. The promise of America extends to racial justice, not simply economic opportunity. In fact, a capitalist logic is embedded in Haskins' pep talk to his team with two minutes remaining in the final game. He tells them: "Now, they've been there before, so they're not going to give it to us. We've gotta go out there and we've got to take it. Right? Take it! I want you to go out there and take it! One ... two ... three...," which leads to the whole team shouting, "Take it!" The persistent repetition of the command to "take it" is an all-too-appropriate mantra for a film that consistently advocates individualistic materialism.

Glory Road is more than an abstract meditation on the merits of capitalism; it also mimetically represents the rags-to-riches American Dream in action. When viewers are first introduced to Haskins, he is at the bottom of the coaching hierarchy, guiding a girls' high school basketball team. Notably, the emphasis on the fact that it is a girls' team signifies that he has started at the *very* bottom of the coaching ladder, in this way re-inscribing gender hierarchy. Soon after, Haskins is offered a position at Texas Western. Although this is an upgrade, it becomes evident that it is as poor a position as one can find coaching at the highest level of college basketball. He is informed that if he takes the job, he will not receive a salary other than accommodation in the men's dormitory and free meals in the school cafeteria. As Haskins tours his new school, he discovers just how impoverished it is by the standards of major college basketball. His assistant coach tells him that the "cupboard" is "a little bare," suggesting that they lack talented players. While walking through the gymnasium, Haskins notices that a floorboard is loose and birds are roosting in the rafters. When he attempts to recruit a player at a Kansas summer league, the athlete rejects his overtures, informing Haskins that he is "partial to winning." Like Haskins and the school itself, most of the (Black) Texas Western players recruited by the coach hail from impoverished origins. Flournoy and Artis are first seen playing basketball at the United Steel Mill in Gary, Indiana. Similarly, Worsley, Cager, and Shed are found playing "in the street" in the South Bronx, New York.

Fortuitously, the viewer is provided with a clear blueprint for how to ascend from rags-to-riches in America. Haskins tells his players, "You're here to learn disciplined, defensive basketball. Now, that means discipline both on and off the courts. No girls, no booze, no late nights, nothing besides fundamental basketball. I speak, you listen." Haskins conditions his players— and viewers of the film—to be disciplined capitalist subjects who work hard and follow orders under the pretext that this will lead to material prosperity. Further, he makes an implicit argument that the racialized nature of poverty in the United States is a function of apathy and indolence on the part of racialized people, rather than structural constraints. This argument that individual discipline and hard work can overcome any institutional and systemic barriers is justified in the film by the ultimate end of winning a national championship and achieving the glory that comes with it. Submerged in this triumphalist narrative, however, is the reality that nearly every other team—and those watching the film and aspiring to similar goals—is conditioned in the same way, yet will never achieve the glory promised in the title of the film. Instead, by following the dictums of Haskins and other coaches like him, they will become the unquestioning and diligent proletarian labor force that a racialized capitalist system demands. Nowhere in the film is the logic of disciplinary capitalism more pronounced than in a speech delivered by Haskins to his star Hill:

> My old man drove a truck for the better half of his life. Now, there ain't nothing wrong with that other than the fact that he hated it. But Hill, that's the only way he knew to put food on the table and give his kids a chance to do something they loved. I love this game. I *love* this game. I never was the greatest player, but I busted my butt and I outworked better players. I ain't the smartest coach, but I bust my butt and I outwork smarter coaches.

Haskins is framed as the archetypal everyman who has successfully lived the American Dream through perseverance, tenacity, and effort. His ability to do so implies that the same possibility exists for all of us. Yet, his whiteness (in contrast to the Blackness of his players) remains unacknowledged.

Haskins' disciplinary model *is* contested midway through the film, when, while trailing to Iowa, Hill challenges him to allow the players to "play our game." Haskins compromises: "All right, Hill, you play your game … and you play my game." This seems to be a more liberating version of capitalism, as the players are invited to cultivate entrepreneurial tendencies within the system. Yet, this can also be read as a metaphor for race in America. As the opening montage first suggested, genuine liberation for African Americans must come from within American capitalism, not from an alternative radical social system. The systemic constraints confronting African Americans are in this way completely elided, leaving viewers with the impression that Black Americans have absolute agency as to whether or not they achieve material prosperity. By the end of the film, disciplinary capitalist ethos has returned to the fore. After a blatantly unjust—possibly even racist—foul is called against him, Lattin knocks over a garbage can. Haskins chastises him, scolding, "You hold yourself together, son. You keep that anger inside of you and I'll let you know when you can let it go, you understand me?" The consistently favorable portrayal of Haskins throughout the film codes his paternalistic and authoritarian disciplinary message as truth. The truth value of this white capitalist ideology is "proven" by the final scenes of the film, as Texas Western defeats Kentucky to win the National Championship. Subsequently, viewers learn that nearly every player on the team was able to "win" in life as well, ascending to the middle class, be it as gas executives, teachers, or police detectives, no doubt owing to the valuable lessons imparted by Haskins. (The fact that none graduated from college is noteworthy foreshadowing, however, for the future adaptation of revenue college sport into a system adept at exploiting Black labor under the guise of institutional benevolence.) Thus, the ultimate message of the film is that the American Dream is available to all in America, regardless of race. Indeed, the constant emphasis on discipline and hard work in the teachings of Coach Haskins to his African American players implies that economic success is a function of individual responsibility and agency, not structural discrimination. The triumph of Texas Western also suggests that the era of racial injustice in American sport is firmly in the rearview mirror.

Boaz Yakin's film *Remember the Titans* (2000) provides a different, but equally spectacular, spin on the (African) American Dream. The film depicts the 1971 struggle to integrate Black and white Alexandria, Virginia, high schools into a single school, with a single football team under the leadership of African American coach Herman Boone. Although this is not a traditional rags-to-riches story, it is a variation on the same theme: instead of poverty, it is racism that must be overcome. As we shall see, the vision of America as a society teleologically advancing towards progress guided by the logic of liberal individualism is no different than that embedded in *Glory Road*. Indeed, it is appropriate that both were produced by Disney: each is a fairy tale version of life in America.

The first quarter of *Remember the Titans* consistently foregrounds the extent to which racism pervades the Alexandria community. At the very beginning of the film, viewers are informed that during the summer before the integration of T.C. Williams was to take place, a Black teenager was killed by a white storeowner, leaving the city "on the verge of an explosion." Immediately after this information is conveyed, white members of the football team are shown rallying to protect the store owner from an enraged Black crowd, foreshadowing the racial tensions that will ensue. Soon after, the star of the white football team unabashedly declares, in the presence of Coach Boone, that he does not want to play with "Black animals." As Coach Boone's family moves into an all-white community, neighbors are shown deriding the new arrivals. By the time white parents refer to the coach as "Coach Coon," it has become abundantly clear that Alexandria is rife with prejudice. As one might expect, the first attempts to integrate the team are largely unsuccessful. At training camp, a white player expels Rev from a bunk bed that they are supposed to share. White star Gary then refuses to look at African American Julius' poster of the 1968 Olympic Black pride salute, engendering a team-wide brawl. On the field, Gary singles out Julius for playing poorly, while a white player tells a Black player who is trying to get water to "wait your turn, boy." Both of these incidents precipitate fights. The climactic racist moment of the film comes when someone screams "hey Coach Coon" and then hurls a brick through the window of the Boones' house. There is little question that Alexandria is plagued by racial discord.

Although the challenge confronting him is slightly different, Coach Boone employs the same methods employed by Haskins to create a unified, successful football team. When Boone is introduced to his black players, he immediately makes it clear how he expects them to behave. He forces Petey, heretofore a fun-loving and jovial young man, to proclaim that football is not supposed to be fun. Although this is a stern message, it is portrayed as legitimate: Boone's ethical authority has already been established as a person who marched with Martin Luther King, Jr., and stood up to the Ku Klux Klan. The sanctity of discipline is reasserted in Boone's subsequent speech to the team: "We leave for camp, Gettysburg College, August fifteenth, seven-twenty-nine a.m. If you report at seven-thirty, you will not be playing football this season. You will be watching. You will wear a jacket, shirt, and tie. This is no democracy, it is a dictatorship. I am the law." Boone's insistence on uniform attire is a logical product of his attempt to create an efficient, integrated, conformist team/work force. His emphasis on punctuality is also part of the project to produce workers whose lives are entirely structured by the demands of capital. Rose (1999) argues that such governmental practices largely determine the way in which we experience and cognize the world, normalizing the disciplinary regime of the working day. This is the process of subject-formation that the film serves to justify.

However, *Remember the Titans* does raise the question of the legitimacy of Boone's tactics. After he subjects his players to a grueling three a.m. run, Yoates, the former coach of the white team and assistant under Boone, tells him that he is dealing with a football team, not the marines. Yet, Boone's authority is not called into question for long. The film ultimately sides with his disciplinary regime by framing Yoates' interventions as racist. Yoates tells Boone, "Some of the boys just don't respond well to public criticism. I tell them what they need to know, but I don't humiliate them in front of the team." Boone leaps to respond:

> Which boys you talking about? Which ones you talking about? I come down on [white] Bertier, I don't see you coddle him, come down on Sunshine, don't see you grab his hand, take him to the side. Which boys you talking about? Now, I may be a mean cuss, but I'm the same mean cuss with everybody out there on that football field. The world don't give a damn about how sensitive these kids are, especially the young black kids. You ain't doing these kids a favor by patronizing them. You're crippling them, crippling them for life.

Boone simultaneously codes Yoates' behavior as paternalistic, thus dismissing its legitimacy, and rehearses the notion that disciplinary conditioning will create the possibility of upward mobility for the Black players on the team. Near the end of the film, Yoates levels a critique of capitalism and its disciplinary ideology: "Everything's not always about winning and losing." Boone, however, reaffirms the validity of his philosophy, "I'm a winner. I'm going to win." Improbable as it may seem, at the very end of the film, Boone's ideology is absolved by the assistant, who admits: "I know football.... What you did with those boys: you were the right man for the job, coach."

Confirmation of the efficacy of Boone's disciplinarity also comes from the successful integration of the team and the town. The first sign that attitudes have begun to change comes after Boone tells his team not to end up like the soldiers who fought at Gettysburg. In the next scene, white and Black players sing together and exchange "yo momma" jokes in the change room. Later, Julius is stopped by a police car while walking through Gary's neighborhood in an apparent instance of racial profiling. Instead, the officer rolls down his window and remarks, "Heck of a game you boys played last night. Best defense I've seen in twenty years. Tell that coach of yours to keep up the good work." Near the end of the film, the neighborhood that originally shunned the Boones comes out en masse to celebrate their triumphs. This moment is particularly spectacular given the persistent problem with residential segregation and white flight in the latter half of the twentieth century in America (Sugrue, 2005). The swift resolution of this problem in the film obfuscates the traumatic experiences of countless families less fortunate than the Boones. The film's ultimate moment of racial reconciliation comes in the final game, when T.C. Williams is able to score the winning touchdown on a play in which a white player blocks for a Black player on a play that the white coach gave to the Black coach. Like *Glory Road*, *Remember the Titans* "proves" that all obstacles to a post-racial society can be overcome through discipline and hard work.

The most spectacular aspect of *Remember the Titans*, however, is the fact that it obscures the dire contemporary racial dynamics of America with its teleological narrative. Legions of viewers (particularly white viewers who do not have to confront the realities of racism everyday)—the film grossed an astounding $115M at the box office (McCallum, 2001, February 5, p. 106)—are left with the impression that a utopian, integrated, egalitarian society has already been achieved in the United States. Yet since 1971, T.C. Williams has subsequently deteriorated into almost complete segregation. By 2001, only six of the forty-two players on the Titans football team were white, and of those, only three regularly played at all (Layden, 2001, October 15, p. 75). At the time portrayed in the film, Alexandria's population was 85 percent white and the school was comprised of 77 percent white students. In 2001, despite an only marginal increase in overall population, the city's population was only 60 percent white, and the school's had fallen to 27 percent white. Moreover, whereas 21,000 white couples owned property in Alexandria in 1971, only 14,500 did in 2001. The explanation for these statistics is simple: white flight. The increased presence of Black families in the community prompted white families to move to suburban areas and send their children to private schools (p. 77). As of 2001, the experience for those white students who remained at T.C. Williams was in many ways radically different than that of the Black students at the school. Black athletes continued to play football on a team that received approximately $12,500 per year in funding. Conversely, most white athletes at the school participated in crew, a team which received a brand new $27,000 shell every year and enjoyed "a sprawling weight room that, by comparison, humbles the football team's musty basement facility" (pp. 79–80). Despite the film's assertion that Boone's disciplinary approach would produce a new generation of young Black men capable of overcoming racial oppression to achieve material success, white graduates of T.C. Williams—the boosters who fund crew—evidently continued to enjoy a dramatic material advantage. A former white football player at T.C. Williams put it this way: "'To make a generalization, the crew parents represent where the money and power are. The parents in the football program are not in the same position'" (p. 80). Thus, the overall experience of Alexandria since 1971 has been, in many ways, *exactly the opposite* of the experience depicted in the film. This is precisely why *Remember the Titans* is the epitome of spectacle.

Documentary Film and the (African) American Dream: Through the Fire *and* Hoop Dreams

I would now like to shift to an examination of a pair of documentary films in order to demonstrate that although they attest to be mirrors of reality, they too function as spectacle. The first film I will discuss is Jonathan Hock's *Through the Fire* (2005). *Through the Fire* is a chronicle of the final high school basketball season of Brooklyn prodigy Sebastian Telfair, a story that ends with his triumphant selection as an NBA draft pick. Like *Glory Road*, *Through the Fire* stridently attempts to convey the abject nature of the poverty experienced by its protagonist. This tactic is particularly noteworthy in the case of *Through the Fire*, since most viewers of the film would already have been cognizant of Telfair's successful entry into the NBA. Thus, even as the viewer surveys the destitution of Telfair's origins, they are almost reflexively forced to frame these origins as the backdrop for his later success; the (African) American Dream suffuses the film. Immediately after the credits, viewers are greeted, in sequence, with shots of men wearing dirty white undershirts, rundown businesses, the title of the film framed against a barren field with housing projects looming in the background, and, finally, an aerial shot of public housing. Soon after, Telfair explains that the local court on which he plays beside his Coney Island home is referred to as "MSG" or "The Garden." It is named after New York City's famous Madison Square Garden, prompting the viewer to juxtapose this modest court with the affluence and glory that ultimately await Telfair. Soon after, Telfair describes the difficult circumstances of his youth: "When we would say coming up that we was poor, it was not like poor like 'we live in the projects.' We was poor meaning 'we ain't have nothing'... It was times when I didn't have no sneakers. I would have a pair of boots, but I ain't have no sneakers." Although there is little question that Telfair and his family once experienced severe poverty, by the time the film is made, they are on the socioeconomic ascent. Telfair has at this point been in the national spotlight for years, his team is sponsored by Adidas and, most basically, his imminent success is the very reason why this film is being made. Consequently, nearly all of the adversity portrayed in the film is contrived in order to make the rags-to-riches American Dream narrative seem compelling. Thus, in footage the film shows of one of Telfair's games being broadcast on ESPN2—again, a high school game on national television is not the hallmark of a player toiling in obscurity—an announcer disingenuously asks, "Is he the greatest, or simply the latest?" When Telfair suffers a sprained ankle early in the season, the film accentuates the severity of the injury in order to create the illusion that it will be a serious obstacle. Yet, after extended footage of Telfair writhing in pain on the court and his brother nervously pacing, the young star returns in the second half to dominate the game.

The film makes it very clear that for racialized and impoverished families like the Telfairs, opportunities do exist for material advancement in America through sport. An anonymous Coney Island resident improbably informs viewers that everyone has the agency to achieve the American Dream: "You gotta sleep with the ball, man, when you growing up, just put it under your arm, go to sleep on it. And your dream come true." Telfair's brother Daniel Turner reinforces the notion that hard work is the ticket to prosperity when he tells Sebastian's team: "I ain't go to college. All my brothers went to college, though, 'cause I put my foot in they ass. All of them." Towards the very end of the film, Telfair himself legitimizes the obscene consumption—he has recently purchased luxury automobiles and an $18,000 Rolex watch—and income stratification that mark capitalist societies by rehearsing the (African) American Dream: "We living good because we work hard, that's all we do: work hard."

The end of the film provides a parade of images signifying the authenticity of the (African) American Dream. After all the perceived adversity that they faced—Lincoln trailed briefly in a couple of games, Telfair had some foul trouble and the coach acted as if the world was against his team despite visual evidence to the contrary—Lincoln is able to win its third consecutive New York public school championship, prompting Telfair to proclaim: "They wrote in the paper that we wouldn't do it, but we did it!" Then, in case viewers are unable to pick up for themselves on the fact that this is a true-to-life rags-to-riches story, Telfair declares, "We used to go work out and we had no cars and nothing and we just had to go borrow people's cars and go work out, you know what I'm saying.… Well I just signed my Adidas deal and I just bought my brother a 645ci, the brand new BMW." Telfair's charmed story culminates with his selection as the thirteenth pick in the draft, higher even than the family anticipated, leading to an understandable display of euphoria. Ultimately, it is little wonder that *Through the Fire* delivers a straightforward rehearsal of the (African) American Dream given that the film is an ESPN production and the NBA is one of the network's most significant partners. Nevertheless, it is sadly and ironically instructive to note in retrospect that just two years after the film was released, Telfair was cut by his second team, the Boston Celtics, after a weapons possession felony (Celtics severing ties with Telfair, 2007, April 24). Needless to say, there is little room for such an ending to the spectacular narrative of *Through the Fire*.

Perhaps the most famous of verisimilar or documentary films about sport in the last thirty years is Steve James' classic documentary *Hoop Dreams* (1994). The film chronicles the high school experiences of Arthur Agee and William Gates, aspiring young Black basketball players in inner-city Chicago. *Hoop Dreams* offers a scathing critique of the racial and economic injustices of American society and the ideology that legitimizes them. Nevertheless, as we have argued in *Out of Left Field* (Abdel-Shehid & Kalman-Lamb, 2011) and as I will expand upon here, like the other films discussed in this essay, it too ultimately succumbs to an idealistic reassertion of the sanctity and possibility of material prosperity in the United States for African American youth. When the young subjects of the film are first introduced, it is immediately apparent that they live under the spell of the (African) American Dream. Gates tell viewers, "I wanna play in the NBA like anybody else would want to be. That's something I dream, think about all the time, playing in the NBA." Agee echoes his acquaintance: "When I get in the NBA … first thing I'm gonna do, I'm gonna see my momma and buy a house, then I'm gonna make sure my sisters and brothers are okay. Probably get my dad a Cadillac, Oldsmobile." For both boys, the idea of playing professional basketball provides meaning and hope for the future. *Hoop Dreams* is not merely a spectacular rehearsal of the merits of this Dream, however. On the contrary, it demonstrates how cruel, callous, and illusory it can be.

The first example the film provides of the Dream gone awry is William's older brother Curtis. Curtis was the player of the decade at Colby Junior College before moving on to the University of Central Florida, but his career stalled due to altercations with the coach, leaving him without a degree. Curtis informs viewers early in the film that "All these basketball dreams I had, they gone. I see all my dreams in [William] now. I want him to make it so bad I don't know what to do." Curtis demonstrates that the Dream is dangerously deceptive, but also that its allure does not swiftly recede. Even after his own personal failure—or, rather, "failure," for this game is rigged—the Dream continues to captivate Curtis in the form of his new ambitions for his brother. Instead of realizing that the Dream is a myth, Curtis internalizes it and thus blames himself for failing to succeed. In his case, spectacle has succeeded in legitimizing capital.

The film is initially structured around the journey of the two boys to suburban private school St. Joseph's in order to pursue their dreams in the shadow of illustrious graduate Isaiah Thomas. This avenue to success is not as just or seamless as it initially appears. By his sophomore year, Arthur's family is struggling to afford the cost of his tuition. The school is no longer willing to provide the financial aid it had promised them because Arthur has not performed up to the necessary standard on the court. Arthur thus has to transfer, exposing the reality that the rags-to-riches narrative proliferated by major colleges, the NBA, and various media outlets is really just an alibi for the economic exploitation of African American youth. *Hoop Dreams* in no way downplays this bitter truth. After being let go from her job as a nurse's assistant, Arthur's mother Sheila makes it clear that lack of economic opportunity due to structural racism, not a shortage of individual effort, accounts for the harsh conditions in the racialized inner city of Chicago. She consistently confronts viewers with both the difficulty of her family's lives—she reports that surviving month-to-month on state assistance is "very hard"—and the fact that this difficulty has a *structural* cause: "So, you know what the system's saying to me? You know what it's saying to a lot of women in my predicament? They don't care." In other words, Sheila explicitly holds racialized capitalism accountable for the material impoverishment of their lives.

William's career was far more successful than Arthur's at St. Joseph's but takes a serious blow when he critically injures his knee. Soon after, his grades begin to plummet. It becomes evident that the inevitable vicissitudes of life are tragically derailing to the ambitions of an inner-city athlete. Despite what these young men are led to believe, Sebastian Telfair's triumph is the exception, not the rule. In the sectional finals of his junior year, William returns from injury and has a chance to shoot two crucial free throws. He misses. His life is not the rags-to-riches story of verisimilar Hollywood film or neatly packaged corporate documentary. It is, on the contrary, a cruel knee injury and two missed free throws in the most important game of his life. It is poverty. Like Sheila, William's brother-in-law ensures that viewers will not fail to understand this point by condemning "the system" for allowing William to play hurt. After repeated injury-related setbacks, it is small wonder that the young man lacks confidence in his game and his body when he returns for his senior year. The season finally ends in heart-wrenching disappointment, as William is unable to achieve his goal of making the state tournament, or of piquing the interest of more than a couple college scouts. The spectacular American Dream narrative seems almost disconcertingly absent in this moving story.

Yet, in the end that narrative only *seems* absent. The final quarter of the film offers a parade of uplifting moments that suggest that hard work can overcome structural racism. Curtis, after being fired from his job as a security guard, finds work in an Encyclopedia Britannica warehouse thanks to William's relationship with the company's president. Suddenly, it seems like athletic ability may indeed translate into material success. Soon after, viewers learn that Sheila's dream is to become an R.A. nurse and that she has received the highest grade in her nursing class, resulting in certification. She tearfully proclaims, "And people told me I wasn't gonna be anything." Again, the triumphalist way in which this moving moment is framed serves to obfuscate her earlier message about the structural nature of constraint in a racialized capitalist system.

Arthur himself has also managed to rehabilitate his dream at Marshall High School, a public school at which he is one of the star players. Indeed, Marshall's journey through the city and state playoffs, a sequence embellished by a soundtrack of by turns suggestively triumphant and heartwarmingly melodramatic music, functions as the climax of the film. When the team finally reaches the state tournament—a feat that feels almost as inevitable as the ending to *Glory Road* at this point—Sheila articulates the ascendant message of the film's latter stages: "We been the underdog and I'm glad we are because then it just shows you how you can come up and then you beat your opponent." For all intents and purposes, she has now completely embraced the narrative of the American Dream. Even William has an opportunity to end the film on a positive note by achieving the necessary ACT score to qualify for admission at Marquette on a basketball scholarship. This gratifying moment is further spectacularized when we discover that Marquette is the school his brother Curtis had wanted to attend. When Arthur ultimately agrees to attend Mineral City Community College on scholarship, it becomes possible to say that the impossible dream of the NBA technically remains in play for both boys. While the end credits of the film indicate to viewers that William only played two years at Marquette, and that Arthur ultimately made his way to Arkansas State University but remains unlikely to reach the NBA, it is the affective impact of the film's triumphant final stages that lingers for the viewer. The harsh indictment of capitalism and the American Dream found in the initial stages of *Hoop Dreams* functions similarly to the early portrayals of poverty in the other films examined. Each serves only to induce pathos and emotional investment from the viewer so that the triumphant conclusion feels all the more profound. This is a manipulative tactic and a spectacular one, for it exploits the irrational tendencies of viewers at the expense of their critical reason, and in this way is able to legitimize capitalism and elide systemic racism as structural forces shaping American society.

Sports film is an important genre in part because it produces narratives that frame the way in which people understand athletic cultures in the "real world," particularly films that claim to be verisimilar in that they are telling "true" stories or "documenting" the nature of reality. I have argued that verisimilar sport films persistently rehearse a narrative around the (African) American Dream that claims sport is a site of opportunity for racialized, particularly black, Americans as long as they are disciplined and hard-working. This is a narrative that serves the interests of capitalism and denies the continued existence of structural racism by explicitly and implicitly positing a teleology towards a fair and equitable post-racial society in which equal opportunity exists for all. Sport is figured instrumentally as a mechanism for the realization of this fantasy of opportunity. What is largely missing from these fairy tale stories are the concrete conditions of material constraint that continue to obstruct the ability of impoverished and racialized people to live the (African) American Dream. While sport does offer material benefit to a tiny fraction of those who embark on a quest to reach the professional ranks, for the vast majority of aspirants this is an illusory and ultimately disappointing journey. If narrative film about sport is to make a meaningful intervention against structural racism and capitalist exploitation, that is the story that needs to be told. Until it is, this genre of film will remain little more than spectacle in the service of racialized capitalism.

References

Bruckheimer, J. (Producer), & Gartner, J. (Director). (2006). *Glory road* [Motion picture]. United States: Walt Disney Pictures.

Bruckheimer, J. (Producer), & Yakin, B. (Director). (2000). *Remember the titans* [Motion picture]. United States: Walt Disney Pictures.

Celtics severing ties with Telfair. (2007, April 24). *New York Daily News*. Retrieved from http://www.nydailynews.com/sports/basketball/celtics-severing-ties-telfair-article-1.208770.

Debord, G. (1994). *The society of the spectacle*. (D. Nicholson-Smith, Trans.). New York: Zone Books. (Original work published 1967).

Feagin, J., & Bennefield, Z. (2014). Systemic racism and U.S. healthcare. *Social Science and Medicine, 103*, 7–14.

Gilbert, P., James, S., & Marx, F. (Producers), & James, S. (Director). (1994). *Hoop dreams* [Motion picture]. United States: KTCA Minneapolis.

Hall, S. (1997). The spectacle of the 'other'; In S. Hall (Ed.), *Representation: Cultural representations and signifying practices* (pp. 223–290). London: Open University.

Hochschild, J. (1995). *Facing up to the American dream*. Princeton: Princeton University Press.

Hock, J. (Producer), & Christopher, A., & Hock, J. (Directors). (2006). *Through the fire* [Motion picture]. United States: ESPN.

Kalman-Lamb, N. (2013). The athlete as model minority subject: Jose Bautista and Canadian multiculturalism. *Social Identities: Journal for the Study of Race, Nation and Culture, 19* (2), 238–253.

Kalman-Lamb, N. (2015). Deconstructing Linsanity: Is Jeremy Lin a model minority subject?" In N. Hartlep and B. Porfilio (Eds.), *Killing the model minority stereotype: Asian American counterstories and complicity* (pp. 203–218). Charlotte: Information Age.

Layden, T. (2001, October 15). Does anyone remember the titans? *Sports Illustrated*, 72–83.

Lowery, W. (2015, 11 July). Aren't more white people than black people killed by police? Yes, but no. *Washington Post*. Retrieved from https://www.washingtonpost.com/news/post-nation/wp/2016/07/11/arent-more-white-people-than-black-people-killed-by-police-yes-but-no/?utm_term=.2076ca31fdb3.

MacCabe, C. (2007). An interview with Stuart Hall, December 2007. *Critical Quarterly, 50* (1–2), 12–42.

McCallum, J. (2001, February 5). Reel sports. *Sports Illustrated*, 92–106.

McNally, D. (2011). *Global slump*. Oakland, CA: PM Press.

Musick, M., & Wilson, J. (1998). Work, race, and the American dream. *Sociological Focus, 31* (1), 17–30.

Ovadia, S. (2003) The dimensions of racial inequality: Occupational and residential segregation across metropolitan areas in the United States. *City & Community, 2* (4), 313–333.

Probability of competing beyond high school. (2017, March 10). Retrieved from http://www.ncaa.org/about/resources/research/probability-competing-beyond-high-school.

Rose, N. (1999). *Powers of freedom*. New York: Cambridge University Press.

Sugrue, T. (2005). *The origins of the urban crisis: Race and inequality in postwar Detroit*. Princeton, NJ: Princeton University Press.

Rethinking Sports Fetishism in Contemporary African American Art

Daniel Haxall

From the Black Power salutes of Tommie Smith and John Carlos at the 1968 Olympics to Colin Kaepernick taking a knee during the national anthem, iconic images of racial protest have occurred at sites of athletic competition. The visibility of sport and its significance in America's psyche renders it a popular platform for such expressions, yet in addition to athletes, artists frequently employ sport's symbolic power to comment on sociopolitical issues.

This essay examines three contemporary African American artists—Hank Willis Thomas (b. 1976), Rashid Johnson (b. 1977), and Kehinde Wiley (b. 1977)—who engage stereotypes of athletic prowess and cultural identity in sports, particularly the fetishism of the Black body. Utilizing figuration to question the marketing of blackness and challenge our fixation with athletes, these contemporaries reorient the position of the black sporting icon, both within the arena of sports and culture at large. Moreover, these individuals exploit advertising devices, fan behavior, memorabilia and fashion trends, and societal expectations to contest the commodification of the black athlete and historical associations produced by their intersection. The artists counter the fetishism of sports and black athletes in contemporary society with works that expose racial stereotyping, while celebrating the accomplishments of African Americans and redefining black identity in the process.

Hank Willis Thomas, Sports and Marketing Blackness

The concept of fetishism runs throughout the fields of philosophy and psychology yet it remains grounded in visual representation as an association between human desire and physical objects.[1] In many ways, the discourse surrounding racial fetishism corresponds with Edward Said's description of Orientalism as "a battery of desires, repressions, investments and projections."[2] As such, the fetish exists as a form of signification variously constructed upon commercial, racial, and gendered factors among others. The ideologies behind these components prompt artists like Hank Willis Thomas to reconsider athletes as fetishized figures. In particular, he investigates advertising and its strategies for representing the black body, exploring, according to the artist's website, "the ways in which corporate culture is complicit in the crisis of black male identity."[3]

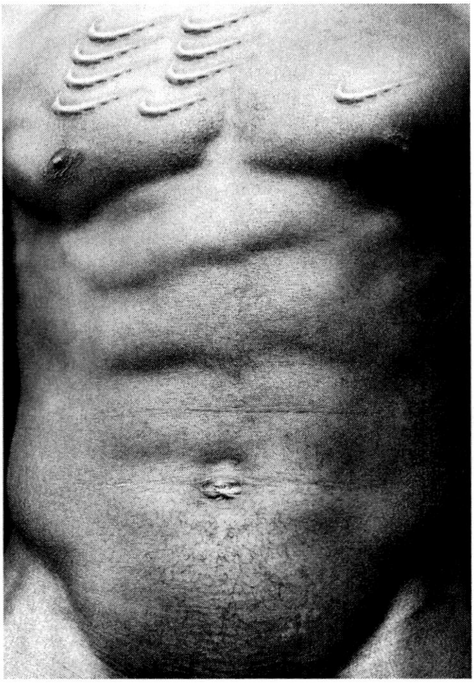

In photographs like *Branded Head* (2003) and *Scarred Chest* (2004, fig. 1), Thomas makes explicit the connection between sports, marketing, and subjugation, with the branding of the Nike swoosh onto dark skin a direct commentary on stereotypes about race and athletic prowess. In both works, the artist digitally applied the Nike logo to photographs of black bodies, imprinting the corporate marque on the head and upper torso, allowing sportswear companies to literally occupy a place on the subject's mind or over his heart. The anonymity of the subjects, produced by cropping the faces out of the images, implies our reverence for these brands, while the accumulation of nine swooshes across *Scarred Chest* evokes sporting accomplishments akin to military insignia or collections of vintage sportswear. This extreme devotion to corporate commodities recalls the recurrence of violence for expensive, fetishized

Fig. 1—Hank Willis Thomas, *Scarred Chest*, 2004. Lambda photograph. © Hank Willis Thomas. Courtesy of the artist and Jack Shainman Gallery, New York.

footwear, where teens are killed for Air Jordan shoes or shoppers riot at malls selling the coveted brand.[4]

In addition to corporate fetishism, the artist addresses the ownership and objectification of the black athlete, a practice he likens to slavery. Thomas admits to being "particularly interested in the commodification of the African-American male body and the fraught connection between this figure and the cotton and slave trade that brought this country so much wealth. Today, African-American sports stars are traded similarly."[5] While these associations in Thomas' work are readily apparent, further readings expose the attributes of racial fetishism that characterize sports and marketing. Through photographs isolating a particular anatomical feature, such as the torso or head, his art exemplifies Jean Baudrillard's notion of the "fetish-beauty," wherein a fetishized object, in this case the body, becomes abstracted into a system of representation. Since the fetish refers to a surrogate, or proxy for that which is desired, the body becomes separated into partial units, a montage of sorts that Baudrillard considers consumable. The divided body loses agency, and stripped of its totality and power, becomes an object safe for ownership or consumption.[6] In this way, the isolated body fragments adopt the properties of fetishes, reducing the black male to a code of somatic activity framed by physique and sports logo. No other trope beyond the Nike swoosh defines the male in these photographs, thus without further contextual references sports branding establishes the sole identity of the objectified body.

This limited framework for engaging black masculinity draws the attention of many critics, particularly the ways in which race and sports overlap in advertising campaigns. Some, like bell hooks, consider marketing "an imperialist colonialism that perpetuates and maintains white supremacist capitalist patriarchy."[7] She further argues that "the contemporary commodification of blackness has become a dynamic part of that system of cultural repression."[8] Accordingly, the use of black athletes like Michael Jordan to sell Nike shoes, for example, limits the aspirations of African Americans while enabling the mechanisms of racial exploitation to remain intact. Thomas recognizes this condition of professional athletes in *Basketball and Chain* (2003), a photograph of a leaping player held down by the manacle wrapped around his ankles. Despite donning Nike high-tops that promise to make him "like Mike," the weight of a ball emblazoned with the name "NBA" prohibits his ascension. Exploited as a token of athleticism and constrained by a singular concept of visibility and success, Thomas' basketball player exposes the fallacy that professional sports provide upward mobility, a notion supported by sociological research.[9]

Critiques of the National Basketball Association appear frequently in Thomas' oeuvre, such as the adding of the league's logo to an 1853 slave advertisement (2004). In the original notice, William Talbott from Kentucky publicized his willingness to spend "$1200 to 1250 dollars for negroes," boasting that he will pay more for slaves than rival agencies. Free market spending like this runs throughout professional sports where record-breaking salaries are established each year. In addition, the monetary value of both slave and athlete increase according to strength and stamina, fetishizing the body by reducing it to metrics of corporeality. While the money offered by Talbott pales in comparison to the transfer fees paid for athletes today, the practice of trading and acquiring sportsmen is often likened to the slave trade, particularly as teams "own" players' legal rights.[10]

Thomas similarly appropriated a famous abolitionist image of a kneeling slave pleading, "Am I Not a Man and a Brother," for the print *First Round Draft Pick* (2004). Where the historical source appealed for compassion from the public, the suppliant of the updated narrative begs to be selected in the first round of the professional basketball draft: "*I know I ain'ts da' only one up fa' draft dis' yea.' But … Lawd, Lawd, Lawd!!! Please let me git picked in da foist round!!! And please, please lemme keep ma' chains!*" Despite the wealth and fame that accompanies this distinction, the athlete remains the property of the team and its owners, a form of enslavement acknowledged by the phonetic spellings and his desire to keep his chains. These artworks undermine the strategies of the commodity fetish, because as Marx and Engels explain, monetary value typically conceals the social character of labor.[11] Baudrillard similarly argued that the commodified body is not only exploited as a productive force, it is formulated into an object both controllable and consumable. Labor, then, becomes abstracted into a system of signification privileging values or types of performance, an act that often results in discrimination.[12] Thomas exposes these facets of commodities and fetishism, challenging professional sports, its treatment of black athletes, and their representations in media and marketing campaigns while recalling the complicated history of sports for African Americans.

In the large-scale photograph, *Cotton Bowl* (2011, fig. 2), a cotton picker lines up against a football player. The athlete assumes a three-point stance for engaging the line of scrimmage, a pose replicated by the farmer who bends down to harvest his crop. The Nike cleats of the athlete oppose the work boots of his counterpart, while a helmet protects the head of the former and straw hat that of the latter. The association between football and slavery is direct, however the work also acknowledges racial prejudice within America's sporting traditions. One of college football's premier bowl games, the Cotton Bowl has been staged annually since 1937. Played in Texas, the Cotton Bowl remained segregated until the 1947 season, when Penn State University was selected to face Southern Methodist University. The Nittany Lions featured two African Americans which compromised the team's ability to compete in the segregated South. Penn State refused to play at the University of

Fig. 2—Hank Willis Thomas, *Cotton Bowl*, 2011. Digital c-print. © Hank Willis Thomas. Courtesy of the artist and Jack Shainman Gallery, New York.

Miami without their black players the previous season, and their undefeated team of 1947 declined bowl invitations unless their entire team could appear. For the Cotton Bowl, held on January 1, 1948, Southern Methodist agreed to play the Nittany Lions in the first interracial college football game in the state of Texas, however Penn State could not stay together in segregated Dallas so they lodged at a Naval Air Base outside of town.[13] While this history is not directly represented in *Cotton Bowl*, narratives of segregation and racially motivated violence remain embedded in the sport's history and Thomas' powerful photograph reminds viewers of this legacy.[14]

　　In the series, *Unbranded: Reflections in Black by Corporate America, 1968–2008* (2005–08), Thomas reveals how advertising portrays football players as intrinsically violent or hyper-sexualized. The artist removed the captions and logos from magazine ads to demonstrate how African Americans symbolically function within marketing campaigns. Several of the subjects were professional football players, such as Terrell Owens and O.J. Simpson, and their representation epitomizes Roland Barthes' critique of mass culture and "what-goes-without-saying."[15] For example, in the *Liberation of T.O.* (2003/05), Owens is portrayed fleeing a scene of urban chaos. Ostensibly a participant in a pickup game of football, Owens' physique and movement suggests what René de Guzman called the "escaped slave motif."[16] No fewer than four sets of hands reach for the athlete in the photograph, several more people race after him, and the majority of those chasing Owens are white. The subtitle of the work reinforces the historic tropes of subjugation for this Nike advertisement: *"I'm not goin' back to work for massa' in dat darned field!"* In addition to referencing slavery, de Guzman observed that setting this scene in Oakland rather than San Francisco, where Owens played for the 49ers, connected the black athlete to a site known for urban violence, thus linking race, sports, and criminality.[17]

In addition to misconduct, the black male has also been framed within sexual potency, an aspect apparent in a Dingo boot advertisement from 1980 featuring O.J. Simpson. Seated while wearing blue jeans and leather cowboy boots, Simpson bears a mysterious third leg suggestive of the fetishized discourse surrounding the black phallus. The original text in the marketing campaign does little to clarify why Simpson carries this extra appendage, identifying the former running back as "a Dingo man down to his feet. And when he starts walkin', people start talkin'. Because he walks in the fast lane, and he's all legs." This slogan reinforces the fetishism of the black male, identifying him as "all legs" and celebrating his capacity for speed. That the marketing of black athletes affirms such stereotypes is further evident in Thomas' *Something to Stand On: The Third Leg* (2007). Here, the artist endowed the iconic silhouette of basketball star Michael Jordan with an elongated extremity providing extra lift to his renowned leaping ability. This maneuver exposes two ways the black male body becomes fetishized, through athletic ability and sexual potency. It bears noting that the silhouetted form asserts only Jordan's propensity for dunking the basketball rather than celebrating his intelligence on the court or success as a businessman away from it.

The fetishism within marketing black athletes extends into seemingly benign products. Thomas calls attention to representations of the black athlete as sexualized specimens in *Gotten* (1996/2007, fig. 3), an appropriated milk poster featuring basketball player Dennis Rodman.

A shirtless Rodman wears the milk mustache characteristic of the advertising campaign, yet his reputation for sexual exploits and rebounding tenacity rehearses clichés about black masculinity. In the original, a caption read: "I'm not the boy next door. I'm the baddest rebounder this game has seen. And my body? It's a temple and milk is the drink of the gods. Three glasses a day give the average man all the calcium he needs. Maybe I should drink six." This statement establishes Rodman as a body beyond the average man, and the Othering of his form remains clear even when Thomas removed the text. In laying bare the initial photograph by Annie Leibovitz, he demonstrates how tattoos, piercings, and dyed hair contribute to the fabrication of an oriental body remarkably similar to Robert Mapplethorpe's erotic framing of

racial difference. Rodman lifts
his arms above his head, exposing his torso, and perhaps more,
to the camera. Clearly posed for
ocular consumption, the image
stops short of Rodman's geni-
talia, yet the appearance of his
navel and hips suggest complete
nudity. Evocative of sexual
taboos while remaining concealed, this image epitomizes
Freud's conception of eroticized
looking,   where   libidinous
impulses are simultaneously
satisfied and unattainable.[18]
This device has been a staple of
racial fetishism, what Kobena
Mercer dubbed an "alibi" and
Homi Bhabha described as "dis-
avowal."[19] Accordingly, the
racial fetish or object of desire
is both indulged and denied,
attributes that connect Thomas'
appropriated imagery to historic codes of objectification.
Removing the ad's text allows
Thomas to expose the activity
of fetishism at work in these
campaigns, focusing our attention on the stereotypical image and its signifying potential.

Fig. 3—Hank Willis Thomas, *Gotten*, 2007.
LightJet print. © Hank Willis Thomas.
Courtesy of the artist and Jack Shainman
Gallery, New York.

Rashid Johnson, Black Masculinity and the Sporting Icon

Where Thomas contests the fetishism of black athletes in advertising,
Rashid Johnson employs the fetishized sports collectible to reconsider Black
History and American values. Several of his works consist of framed, "auto-
graphed" jerseys from two sets of fictional teams devised by the artist, the
Civil Rights All-Stars and *Uncle Tom All-Stars* (2003–06).

The *Civil Rights All-Stars* feature Angela Davis (fig. 4), the activist and
scholar wrongfully incarcerated in 1971 for supplying the weapons used in a

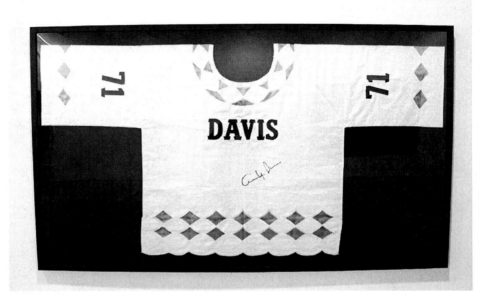

Fig. 4—Rashid Johnson, *Signed Angela Davis "Civil Rights All-Stars" Throw-Back Dashiki Jersey*, 2003. Ink on cloth with embroidery, sew mounted on fabric in a Plexiglas frame. 37¼ × 61½ in. (95.3 × 156.2 cm). Courtesy the artist and Hauser & Wirth.

courtroom shooting. The number "71" appears on the sleeve of her "throw-back" dashiki, a reference to the year of her imprisonment as well as the politicized fashion of Black Nationalism. In a similar way, Johnson commemorated Amiri Baraka, née LeRoi Jones, the celebrated yet controversial writer. His framed dashiki jersey is numbered "64" for the year his *Dutchman* won an Obie Award, the Off-Broadway equivalent of the Tony Awards. Johnson's admiration for Baraka continued beyond his all-star tribute, as he directed the play in 2013, which dramatizes issues of miscegenation and violence in America.[20] Whereas Davis and Baraka assume great prominence as activists in Johnson's tributes, the last work of the series strikes a different note, "honoring" Clarence Thomas with the *Uncle Tom All-Stars Judicial Robe* (2006). His number "91" refers to the year of his appointment to the United States Supreme Court, yet rather than a Civil Rights hero, he is enshrined into a pantheon of racial traitors for his conservative position within the Court.

As a whole, these works reflect the commodification of significant figures from Black History and their subsequent deification. By labeling them "All-Stars," Johnson employs a sporting metaphor to make viewers consider who we value and why. The fetishized dashiki and judicial robe become surrogates for their ideals, with the jersey allowing us to symbolically channel the potency of that individual. In this way, the political leanings of Davis, Baraka, or Thomas are projected onto whomever wears their shirt, a fashionable notion underpinned by the concept of the "throwback." In considering this series, Touré imagined halls of fame honoring Black Power or Slavery All-Stars, noting: "Young Black men used to wear throwback sports jerseys as fashion and I could see the Angela Davis jersey being worn on the street alongside the inevitable jerseys commemorating Malcolm X, Huey P. Newton, Marcus Garvey, Frederick Douglass, Harriet Tubman, Nat Turner..."[21] Yet these jerseys remain problematic because fashion trends might obscure the stories of the all-stars, with their significance lost amidst a "throwback" fashion craze. As Touré astutely notes, Johnson does not critique these individuals "as much as the reverence we have for them."[22] Indeed, the sports memorabilia industry thrives off this reverence, as one of Jesse Owens' gold medals from the 1936 Berlin Olympics sold in December 2013 for nearly $1.47 million, and the shoes worn by Michael Jordan in the famous "flu game" of the 1997 NBA Finals netted $104,765 a few days later.[23]

The reverence bestowed upon sporting icons fueled another work by Johnson, a blue basketball jersey embroidered with the words, "white people love me." Here, Johnson suggests that sports, and specifically basketball, remain the context in which the black male is most appreciated by white America. The jersey frames the black body as a monolithic specimen, a token of physicality fetishized to the point of envy. As Kobena Mercer argued in his critique of Mapplethorpe, the imperial white gaze can become "lost in admiration" of the black body, offsetting stereotypes of violence with an acknowledgment of athletic brilliance.[24] Where the previous series encouraged viewers to fabricate other members of the African American All-Stars, this one prompts reflection upon the black athletes revered by whites: Michael Jordan, LeBron James, and others.[25]

Johnson continued to explore the visibility and acceptance of black athletes in his photographic series, *The New Negro Escapist Social and Athletic Club* (2008–10). Employing the term "New Negro" to refer to the cultural and intellectual achievements of the Harlem Renaissance, the artist paid tribute to this era by creating his own private club. These societies date to the early twentieth century, and for African Americans they ranged from the Sigma Pi Phi fraternity, or "The Boulé," to the Salem Crescent Athletic Club and St. Christopher Club, church organizations that sponsored athletic competitions to instill positive values in children.[26] For his fictional version of the social club, Johnson created portraits of well-dressed men named after famous figures in American history, including Thurgood (Marshall) and Emmett (Till), with the formality of the black-and-white images evoking the celebrated artists of the Harlem Renaissance, namely photographer James Van Der Zee.

Johnson also devised a summer tennis tournament hosted by *The New Negro Escapist Social and Athletic Club*, and for this competition the artist fashioned himself as the *Black Jimmy Connors* (2008, fig. 5) in tribute to one of America's favorite athletes in the 1970s.

While Connors was remarkably successful, establishing the men's record for tournament victories (109), including eight Grand Slams, Johnson's

Fig. 5—Rashid Johnson, *Self-Portrait as the Black Jimmy Connors in the Finals of the New Negro Escapist Social and Athletic Club Summer Tennis Tournament,* **2008. Lambda print. Courtesy the artist and Hauser & Wirth.**

maneuver confronts the racist bias underlying sports and their heroes. Many African Americans have excelled in the sport of tennis ranging from Althea Gibson, the first African American to win a Grand Slam tournament (the French Open in 1956), to Serena Williams, winner of the most Grand Slam titles (23) in the Open Era. Within men's tennis, Johnson did not have to dress as the "Black Jimmy Connors" because he already existed in the form of Arthur Ashe, formerly the world's top-ranked player and winner of three Grand Slam titles, including Wimbledon in 1975 when he defeated Connors. Ashe's significance transcended the court as he protested the apartheid policies of South Africa and later became an advocate for AIDS research, yet rather than Ashe, Johnson seeks the fame bestowed upon Connors, the white athlete. This maneuver suggests how Ashe could not access the same type of adulation directed towards Connors as racial bias clouds fan perspectives. Indeed, the smoky background of these images obscures Johnson's countenance, undermining our ability to see the athlete and removing the anthropological power of the camera in capturing a likeness of the sitter.[27] In this way, the artist subverts the fetishism of the athlete in mass media, particularly the tradition of the photographic poster that lionizes the appearance and physique of the sports star.

Where sports like tennis and golf are commonly framed within whiteness, boxing features prominently in the black sporting landscape as well as Johnson's own life. His father won the Golden Gloves award as an amateur fighter and the artist watched championship bouts with him.[28] Johnson depicted boxing in a range of mediums and formats throughout his career, for example in 2006 he photographed himself lying atop the grave of legendary fighter Jack Johnson. The first black heavyweight champion of the world in 1908, Jack Johnson's success sparked race riots in America and the quest for a "great white hope" to defeat him and restore racial order.[29] Where Jack Johnson triumphed over his opponents, Rashid Johnson sprawls across the funerary monument with eyes closed as if dead, knocked out, or in meditation. This image remains ambiguous because he could be channeling his namesake, a figure significant for his place in history, or simultaneously projecting a supine body defeated in competition.[30] The artist's pose contrasts greatly with how the pugilist was portrayed in *The White Hope* (1921, lithograph), George Bellows' widely distributed print that depicts Johnson's victory over James Jeffries, the former white champion. The upright and triumphant boxer of Bellows seems a far cry from the tombstone holding the artist's recumbent form, potentially reflecting upon the exploitation and fate of the black athlete.

Jack Johnson appeared in another work by Rashid Johnson, the short film *100 Men* (2005). Here, the artist crafted a slideshow of images downloaded from the Internet while contemplating the concept of manhood. The resulting presentation includes headshots of one hundred men selected by the artist, some musicians and politicians and eleven of them athletes. Jack Johnson appears with boxing legends Muhammad Ali and Mike Tyson, and several of these men, including Tyson, O.J. Simpson, and baseball Barry Bonds, remain contentious figures within the history of sports because of legal issues or allegations of cheating. Johnson's collection of icons recalls the collecting of trading cards or posters that hang on the walls of young sports fans, and as viewers, we wonder about the criteria used by the artist to compile this menagerie. Johnson makes us consider how we historicize men, through success or controversy, athletic brilliance or social significance. Ultimately, Uwe Gellner argues that this reflection upon masculine identity serves as a self-portrait, in which Johnson attempts to better understand himself by considering how society defines men.[31]

Boxing references continued throughout Johnson's 2012 exhibition at the Hauser & Wirth Gallery on 69th Street in New York. He named the show *Rumble* after learning the gallery occupied the former townhouse of legendary boxing promoter Don King. King's flamboyant patriotism fascinated yet perplexed the artist, as Johnson explained how King claimed to be "the living attestation of the American dream, the extolment of this great nation…. He was the archetype of a new Negro patriot, which was an unthinkable concept for just about every black person in America at that time."[32] Indeed, King attributes his great wealth to American exceptionalism, and he became legendary in the sports world for staging major international bouts such as the "Rumble in the Jungle," pitting Muhammad Ali against George Foreman in Zaire in 1974. This famous contest inspired not only the name of Johnson's show, but also the pugilistic titles of several artworks in the exhibition: *Rumble*, *Split Decision*, *Rabbit Punch*, *Glass Jaw*, *The Squared Circle* and *The Sweet Science* (all 2011). Most of the art in *Rumble* consisted of abstract paintings without direct references to sport, however Johnson's application of materials, artistic gestures, and references remained loaded with symbolism.

In *Glass Jaw* (2011, fig. 6), the artist created a painting on mirrored tile panels with several built-in shelves holding shea butter, a CB radio, Charles Mingus album, and stacks of hardcover books with the word "negrosis" printed on the spine. The objects cite everything from personal experiences to the history of art, but the wordplay employed by Johnson aptly summarizes his interest in sport as an artistic metaphor. He often uses the word "negrosis" to refer to the "relationship between blackness and anxiety,"[33] and the title *Glass Jaw* refers to a boxer's weakness, appropriate language for an artwork made of fragile mirrors with inscriptions of the word "negrosis" repeated throughout. Ultimately, this work encapsulates Johnson's anxiety about the vulnerability of masculinity and conditions of fetishism that frame black identity within athletic Otherness.

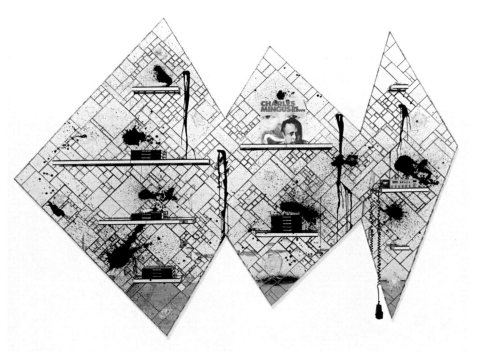

Fig. 6—Rashid Johnson, *Glass Jaw*, 2011. Mirrored tile, black soap, wax, books, shea butter, vinyl album cover, CB radio, oyster shells, and paint. 88½ × 118½ × 12 in. (224.8 × 301 × 30.5 cm). Collection Museum of Contemporary Art Chicago, Gift of Mary and Earle Ludgin by exchange. Courtesy the artist and Hauser & Wirth.

Kehinde Wiley, Throwbacks and the Politics of Sportswear

Like Johnson, Kehinde Wiley addresses the fetishism of sports figures through fashion and throwback jerseys. Wiley initially caught the attention of the art world by recreating famous paintings from art history albeit with African American men replacing the traditional Caucasian subject. He found volunteers for his project while "street casting" in urban settings, and by rewriting the history of art to include anonymous black men Wiley overturns what he calls, "the history of Western European white men in positions of dominance."[34] Many of the individuals in his portraits wear the "throwback" referenced by Rashid Johnson, for example, the jersey of former Dallas Cowboys wide receiver Michael Irvin appears prominently in *Saint Adrian* (2006, fig. 7).

This painting stems from Wiley's "Scenic" series, a body of works inspired by the sixteenth century German artist Hans Holbein the Younger (c. 1497–1543). Here, Wiley borrowed poses from Holbein while deriving floral backdrops from French wallpaper designs popular among nineteenth-century elites. A young man wears Irvin's jersey while holding a sword and

Fig. 7—Kehinde Wiley, *Saint Adrian*, 2006. Oil on canvas, 96 × 84 in (243.84 × 213.36 cm) © Kehinde Wiley. Used by permission.

golden anvil, attributes that refer to Saint Adrian of Nicodemia (died 306 CE), a patron saint of metal smiths and the military who served the Roman army before being martyred for converting to Christianity.[35] The emblems of militarism and athletics seem at odds with the pink hues and floral patterns in the portrait, allowing Wiley to question the conventions of race, gender, and sexuality fashioned by society. Despite wearing baggy jeans and an oversized Cowboys shirt that obscure his physique, the subject conveys physical strength through the heavy objects he holds, his muscular forearms and neckline, and the sporting reference to Irvin, a Hall of Fame wide receiver.

While the painting establishes the popularity of sportswear through the matching Dallas Cowboys hat and shirt, their elevated status via depiction in fine art suggests the social value ascribed to the "throwback," one that extends beyond its value as clothing. The donning of such attire suggests game day rituals in which the shirt denotes allegiance to a team, however it also communicates a status linked to the identity of the athlete associated with said jersey. As such, Wiley's subjects embody Baudrillard's description of fetishism wherein the possession and display of objects separate from their purpose originate from consumer desire and the fetishism of the signifier. In this context, a symbolic value becomes attached to the shirt and its function becomes that of signification rather than usefulness or necessity. Thereby removed from practicality, the jerseys worn in Wiley's paintings maintain currency beyond commodity value and become beneficial as symbols.[36] While this transferal of semiotic power can occur across racial boundaries, Wiley frames the fetish within codes of race by representing black men wearing throwback jerseys of black athletes and modeled after paintings of white men. As Tim Dant has argued, the social value of objects bestows diverse benefits or "capacities" upon those in possession of such objects. For example, sports attire becomes "ostensive" symbols denoting membership to a social group, i.e., the jersey establishes one's fandom, while its throwback reference bestows a separate category of "knowledge" to its user due to the contextual information triggered by the iconography of a number "88" Dallas Cowboy jersey. The physical attributes projected through athletic references might further promote "sexuality," while the shirt also becomes a site of "mediation" where human interaction, perhaps a debate about Irvin's career as an athlete, can derive from the object's symbolism.[37] Ultimately, by immortalizing the throwback jersey through its depiction in the exalted language of fine art, Wiley acknowledges the range of values ascribed to the sporting fetish, including our reverence for star athletes and fabled teams, desires for their success or attributes, fantasies stimulated by its projected performance, and pleasure derived from its possession.

Such capacities enhance the powers ascribed to the fetish, particularly where sporting references are concerned.

For example, in *Equestrian Portrait of the Count Duke Olivares* (2005, fig. 8), Wiley refashioned Velázquez's painting of Spanish prime minister Gaspar de Guzmán (c. 1635) into a representation of an anonymous black man on horseback. Holding a gold staff while leading a horse through the *levade*, a dressage maneuver in which the mount rears at a particular angle with its two hind legs on the ground, the subject conveys mastery of his steed and by extension his environment. In Wiley's portrait, the sitter wears Nike

Fig. 8—Kehinde Wiley, *Equestrian Portrait of the Count-Duke Olivares*, 2005. Oil on canvas, 108 × 108 in (274.32 × 274.32 cm) © Kehinde Wiley. Used by permission.

shoes, athletic pants, and a Negro League sweatshirt unlike the ornate scabbard and saddle in the reference image, with the casualness of his contemporary sportswear distinct from the painting's formal gilded frame and patterned backdrop. To a certain degree Wiley fetishizes Western art history and its subjects, hoping to transfer their symbolic power to contemporary black men. While this mission extends beyond the arena of sports, the prominence of athletics in society affords the most visible means for granting his sitters agency. Derek Conrad Murray notes that the command of the gaze is one device bestowing power to Wiley's subjects. Here, the figure "peers backwards defiantly at the viewer," allowing the artist to "represent distinctively black countercultural codes of street style, elegance, and swagger."[38] Indeed, the potency of this "swagger" becomes amplified by his command of equestrian maneuvers and the projected mastery of sports implied by his sweatshirt. While the logo of the Negro League might stem from a fashion trend equivalent to the decorative stylings of the painting's background, it also establishes baseball as a site of conquest analogous to the battlefield in the distance of Velázquez's original portrait. As suggested within the text of the Negro League emblem, Wiley's subject can "discover greatness" through sport, crafting new histories of empire predicated upon athletic achievement while "empowering an entire underrepresented racial group over any one individual."[39]

One of the most celebrated examples of sport's potential for combatting racism remains Jackie Robinson, the Hall of Fame player who broke baseball's color barrier in 1947. Wiley paid homage to the athlete in *The Investiture of Bishop Harold as the Duke of Franconia* (2004), juxtaposing the Christian iconography of his source material with Robinson's Brooklyn Dodgers jersey. The unidentified man in Wiley's portrait holds a gilded staff over his shoulder as a hitter might carry a baseball bat waiting on deck, while a crucifix necklace flanks Robinson's #42, the only number to be retired by every team within Major League Baseball. The year 1955 is stamped on the shirt, the season Robinson won his only World Series title, and a variation of the fleur-de-lis symbol associated with the French monarchy furthers the connection between Robinson, royalty, and sainthood. Through the popularity of the throwback and his iconographic scheme, Wiley acknowledges the fetishism of star athletes who attain the devotion and prestige traditionally granted only to religious figures.

Perhaps due to its iconic position as "America's pastime," baseball references abound in Wiley's oeuvre. In his restaging of Peter Paul Rubens' *Albert and Nikolaus Rubens, the Artist's Sons* (c. 1624), one man dons a red hooded sweatshirt with the New York Black Yankees logo, a team in the Negro League from 1936 to 1948, while the other character wears Jackie Robinson's jersey. Interspersed among various floral motifs appear several floating "spermatozoa," symbols of a masculine potency distinct from the prepubescent children in the source image.[40] The sperm conjures virility yet also draws viewers into a network of desire that challenges assumptions about the sexual identity of the artist and viewer. While the bodies of the men remain whole and lack the fetishized cropping of Mapplethorpe's photographs or Thomas' advertising sources, the artist's illumination of his sitters' dark skin produces a sexualized sheen. The bodies of these men remain concealed beneath their clothing, yet their sports attire conjures an idealized muscularity, physical attributes suggested by strong jaw lines and the tightly modeled neck. Openly gay, Wiley often acknowledges the sexual attractiveness of his male sitters, an aspect of his paintings that, Murray argues, "skewer very *straight* signifiers of black masculinity."[41]

While Wiley grants agency to previously marginalized subjects and challenges histories of representation that fetishize the black body, his work also frequently targets marketing trends and consumerism. His paintings of African soccer stars commissioned by German sportswear manufacturer PUMA reflect this interest, operating at the intersection of racial, sexual, and economic codes of desire and power. PUMA commissioned Wiley to launch an African-themed marketing campaign to celebrate the 2010 FIFA men's World Cup, the first time the soccer championship had been hosted on African soil. He responded with a series of sportswear designs, including soccer cleats, shoelaces, t-shirts, and jackets. Wiley also created four portraits depicting PUMA's African pitchmen: Emmanuel Eboue from Ivory Coast, Samuel Eto'o from Cameroon, and John Mensah of Ghana.

Three of the paintings represented each athlete individually, while a fourth work, *Unity* (2010, fig. 9), portrayed them standing together with interlocked arms in a monumental 9-feet-by-12-feet canvas.[42] The unique backdrops created by Wiley replicate textile patterns produced in West Africa, while the poses used for each work were inspired by African sculpture. In all four images, rather than the national or club shirts that would establish them as opponents the footballers wear the same PUMA "unity kit," an-African inspired soccer jersey that would serve as an alternate uniform for the twelve African national teams sponsored by PUMA. This jersey, and Wiley's painting, promotes an ideal of togetherness linking African nations, pan-African ideals upheld through soccer and consumerism.

In many ways, the PUMA commission was no different than Wiley's previous work, for it enabled him to graft notions of race and prestige onto the black male body. Much of this endeavor forced him to confront the role of capital and commodity in generating status. In addition to celebrating African textiles, these portraits advertise the PUMA brand and its new "Unity" jersey. The company's logo appears no fewer than six times in *Unity* alone, while the association of PUMA with soccer greatness is implicit in the players' larger-than-life persona and nearly divine status on canvas. The phys-

Fig. 9—Kehinde Wiley, *Unity*, 2010. Oil on canvas, 108 × 144 in (274.32 × 365.76 cm) © Kehinde Wiley. Used by permission.

ical beauty of the African men depicted by Wiley transcendently evokes the divine; an aspect furthered by what Wiley calls the "super-rapturous light" illuminating his sitters.[43] Through the reflective glow of studio flashbulbs, he often casts an ethereal radiance on his subjects, rendering them deific through heavenly brilliance. The privileged position of Wiley's soccer icons becomes even more pronounced through *Unity*'s source image: Benin sculptural groups representing the Oba, or divine ruler, and his attendants. Although Wiley modified the original to suggest equality and partnership among the athletes, his allusion to the revered Oba of Benin elevates the status and power of the African male, and their interlocking arms conjure community and brotherhood. In fact, upon watching Eto'o play in a soccer match, Wiley commented, "Eto'o went from being a human being to being a god."[44]

While these soccer players appear immortal through their idealized bodies, historical references, and large scale, the reflective properties of their painted skin recall more pernicious forms of capitalism, namely the African slave trade. Traders often lathered oil onto slaves to hide scars and beautify their physiques, employing bodily shine as a means of objectifying the human body.[45] Wiley's adoption of bodily shine reverses this history, transforming the African figure from a fetishized commodity into otherworldly fetish. Desire, then, stems not from an impulse to occupy the black body, but from aspirations to attain its beauty, power, and status. Wiley's commission proves ironic because his inversion of history potentially implicates his patron, PUMA, in acts of exploitation and commercial colonization. Simultaneously exposing while profiting from market desire, Wiley reclaims black agency only to repackage it for consumption, reflecting the intersection of different modes of fetishism. This type of reversal runs throughout his work, and here Wiley employs soccer to invert the channels of exploitation that upheld colonial networks by celebrating those who mastered the European sport. In this sense, *Unity* embodies Homi Bhabha's critique of Western imperialism, wherein colonizer becomes colonized.[46] In the case of sports, this certainly seems apt, because as western athletic competition—such as basketball, baseball, and soccer—spread in popularity throughout the world, the foundations of racial Othering were simultaneously redefined and defeated. And as Wiley's work makes clear, visual codes of desire and power remain embedded in the potency of sports and its fetishism, affording those attributes to those who control them.

Conclusion: A "Post-Black" Perspective

In 2001, the theory of "Post-Black" became formalized in the art world through the work of curator Thelma Golden and artist Glenn Ligon. Their conversations about African American culture and identity informed the conceptual framework of *Freestyle*, an exhibition organized by Golden for the Studio Museum in Harlem that defined the characteristics of post-blackness. The title of the show reflected the possibilities available for a new wave of artists born after the Civil Rights Movement of the 1960s. These artists, wrote Golden, "were adamant about not being labeled as 'black' artists, though their work was steeped, in fact deeply interested, in redefining complex notions of blackness."[47] While many debate the currency of post-black following recurring issues of police brutality towards African Americans and the emergence of the Black Lives Matter movement, the term remains useful for contextualizing a generation of artists invested in revising formulaic perceptions of black identity. Hank Willis Thomas, Rashid Johnson, and Kehinde Wiley represent this generation in age and perspective, although great diversity characterizes their approach to art, race, and sexuality. Their efforts to redefine African American identity led them to confront the impact of sports on constructions of blackness, particularly masculinity, while their work unpacks the visual codes that have restricted and objectified African Americans for centuries. They acknowledge complex histories of visualizing race and utilize sports to contest the fetishism of black athletes, and by extension black men, so prevalent in society. Ultimately, these artists redefine black masculinity through sports and the codes of signification perpetuated through athletic systems of race, class, gender, and commercialism.

NOTES

1. Tim Dant, "Fetishism and the Social Value of Objects," *Sociological Review* 44, no. 3 (1996), 496–516.

2. Edward Said, *Orientalism* (Harmondsworth: Penguin, 1978), 8.

3. http://www.hankwillisthomas.com/BOOKS/Pitch-Blackness/1.

4. For a record of murders over Air Jordan shoes during the 1980s, see: Rick Telander, "Senseless," *Sports Illustrated* 72, no. 20 (14 May 1990), 36–49. For two recent episodes, see: Carol Christian, "Man Dies After Shooting Over Air Jordans," *Houston Chronicle* (26 December 2012): http://www.chron.com/news/houston-texas/houston/article/Man-dies-after-shooting-over-Air-Jordans-4146552.php; Frank Heinz, "Frenzied Crowd Rushes Hulen Mall for New Air Jordans," (22 December 2012): http://www.nbcdfw.com/news/local/Frenzy-Rushes-Hulen-Mall-for-New-Air-Jordans-184433261.html.

5. http://hankwillisthomas.com/2011/Branded/1/.

6. Jean Baudrillard, *For a Critique of the Political Economy of the Sign*, trans. Charles Levin (Candor: Telos Press, 1981), 94–97.

7. bell hooks, "Marketing Blackness: Class and Commodification," in *Killing Rage: Ending Racism* (New York: Henry Holt and Company, 1995), 173.

8. *Ibid.*, 176.

9. Robert E. Washington and David Karen, eds., *Sport, Power and Society: Institutions and Practices* (Boulder: Westview Press, 2010); Reuben May, *Living Through the Hoop: High School Basketball, Race, and the American Dream* (New York: New York University Press, 2009).

10. William C. Rhoden, *Forty Million Dollar Slaves: The Rise, Fall, and Redemption of the Black Athlete* (New York: Broadway, 2007); John Hoberman, *Darwin's Athletes: How Sport Has Damaged Black America and Preserved the Myth of Race* (New York: Mariner Books, 1997); Joe Nocera and Ben Strauss, *Indentured: The Inside Story of the Rebellion Against the NCAA* (New York: Penguin, 2016).

11. Karl Marx and Friedrich Engels, *Capital*, vol. 1. trans. Samuel Moore and Edward Aveling; reproduced in *The Norton Anthology of Theory and Criticism*, ed. Vincent Leitch (New York and London: Norton, 2001), 777, 779.

12. Baudrillard, *For a Critique of the Political Economy of the Sign*, 95, 97.

13. Mark Wogenrich, "Penn State's History at Cotton Bowl Stadium Includes Historic Moment for College Football," *Morning Call* (1 January 2012): http://articles.mcall.com/2012–01-01/sports/mc-penn-state-1231–20120101_1_wally-triplett-chima-okoli-joe-paterno.

14. See: Charles Martin, *Benching Jim Crow: The Rise and Fall of the Color Line in Southern College Sports, 1890–1980* (Urbana-Champaign: University of Illinois Press, 2010).

15. Roland Barthes, *Mythologies*, trans. Annette Lavers (New York: Hill and Wang, 1972).

16. René de Guzman, "Nothing Better," in *Hank Willis Thomas* (New York: Aperture, 2008), 96.

17. *Ibid.*

18. Sigmund Freud, "Fetishism," (1927), repr. in *On Sexualities* (Harmondsworth: Penguin, 1977), 96.

19. Kobena Mercer, "Reading Racial Fetishism," in *Welcome to the Jungle*, ed. Kobena Mercer (London: Routledge, 1994); reprinted in Stuart Hall, ed., *Representation: Cultural Representations and Signifying Practices* (London: Sage Publications and the Open University, 1997); Homi Bhabha, "The Other Question," in *Literature, Politics and Theory* (London: Methuen, 1986), 168.

20. Randy Kennedy, "A Play That's Sure to Make You Sweat," *New York Times* (31 October

2013): http://www.nytimes.com/2013/11/01/theater/barakas-dutchman-to-be-staged-in-a-bathhouse.html.

21. Touré, *Who's Afraid of Post-Blackness? What It Means to Be Black Now* (New York: Free Press, 2011), 48.

22. *Ibid.*

23. Darren Rovell, "Jesse Owens Gold Goes for $1.47M," ESPN.com (8 December 2013): http://espn.go.com/olympics/trackandfield/story/_/id/10101684/jesse-owens-gold-medal-1936-olympics-sells-147-million; Darren Rovell, "$104,765 for Michael Jordan's Shoes," ESPN.com (12 December 2013): http://espn.go.com/chicago/nba/story/_/id/10124171/michael-jordan-flu-game-shoes-shatter-record-price-auction.

24. Mercer, "Reading Racial Fetishism," 288.

25. Despite being retired for over a decade, Michael Jordan continues to rank among America's favorite sports stars, placing second in 2014 and 2015 to LeBron James in Harris Polls about the country's best-loved athletes. "Is LeBron James Americans' Favorite or Least Favorite Sports Star? Yes!" *The Harris Poll* (2015 September 24): http://www.theharrispoll.com/sports/Americas-Most-Least-Favorite-Sports-Star.html.

26. While the basketball teams of organizations such as the St. Christopher Club often gained the most notoriety, these associations sponsored a range of athletic competitions. For example, the Salem Methodist Episcopal Church organized the Salem Crescent Athletic Club which became renowned for developing boxers, notably Sugar Ray Robinson (née Walker Smith, Jr.). See: Bob Kuska, *Hot Potato: How Washington and New York Gave Birth to Black Basketball and Changed America's Game Forever* (Charlottesville: University of Virginia Press, 2004); Wil Haygood, *Sweet Thunder: The Life and Times of Sugar Ray Robinson* (New York: Knopf, 2009).

27. Rodrigues Widholm, "The Moment of Creation," in *Rashid Johnson: Message to Our Folks* (Chicago: Museum of Contemporary Art Chicago, 2012), 38.

28. Dorothy Spears, "Fusing Identity: Dollops of Humor and Shea Butter," *New York Times* (5 January 2012): http://www.nytimes.com/2012/01/08/arts/design/rashid-johnsons-show-rumble-a-nod-to-don-king.html.

29. Geoffrey C. Ward, *Unforgiveable Blackness: The Rise and Fall of Jack Johnson* (New York: Knopf, 2004); Randy Roberts, *Papa Jack: Jackson and the Era of White Hopes* (New York: Free Press, 1985).

30. Rodrigues Widholm reads this work as "perhaps channeling the greatness of the indomitable boxer's spirit or quietly meditating on his own mortality and wondering what his legacy will be." Widholm, "The Moment of Creation," 35.

31. Uwe Gellner, "Rashid Johnson. Photographer, Artist," in *Rashid Johnson: Sharpening My Oyster Knife* (Bielefeld/Leipzig: Kerber Verlag, 2008), 19–20.

32. Rashid Johnson, as quoted in press release for *Rashid Johnson: Rumble* (2012): http://www.hauserwirth.com/exhibitions/1168/rashid-johnson-rumble/view/.

33. Jessica Lynne, "Where Anxiety Lives: Jessica Lynne on Rashid Johnson," *The Art Newspaper* (6 November 2015): http://theartnewspaper.com/comment/reviews/exhibitions/where-anxiety-lives-jessica-lynne-on-rashid-johnson/.

34. Kehinde Wiley, as quoted in Sarah Lewis, De(i)fying the Masters," *Art in America* 93, no. 4 (April 2005), 123.

35. Christian Müller, Stephan Kemperdick, Maryan Ainsworth, et al., *Hans Holbein the Younger: The Basel Years, 1515–1532* (Munich: Prestel, 2006), 218.

36. Baudrillard, *For a Critique of the Political Economy of the Sign*, 92–94, 97.

37. Dant, "Fetishism and the Social Value of Objects," 510–512.

38. Derek Conrad Murray, *Queering Post-Black Art: Artists Transforming African-American Identity After Civil Rights* (London: Tauris, 2016), 96–97.

39. Richard Aste, "The Canon in Crisis," in Eugene Tsai, ed., *Kehinde Wiley: A New Republic* (Brooklyn: Brooklyn Museum of Art, 2015), 54.

40. Franklin Sirmans, "Barkley Hendricks, Ordinary People," in *Barkley L. Hendricks: Birth of the Cool*, ed. Trevor Schoonmaker (Durham: Basher Museum of Art, Duke University, 2008), 87; Krista Thompson, "The Sound of Light: Reflections on Art History in the Visual Culture of Hip-Hop," *Art Bulletin* 91, no. 4 (December 2009), 495.

41. Murray, *Queering Post-Black Art*, 94.

42. For a more detailed discussion of *Unity* and Wiley's PUMA commission, see my essay: Daniel Haxall, "From Bank Lobbies to Sportswear: Julie Mehretu, Kehinde Wiley, and the Shift in Corporate Patronage in the Twenty-First Century," in *Corporate Patronage of Art and Architecture in the United States, Late 19th-Century to the Present*, edited by Monica E. Jovanovich and Melissa Renn (London and New York: Bloomsbury Academic, 2019), 225–244. For a reading of Wiley's work through the lens of Négritude and other African influences, see my essay: Daniel Haxall, "In the Spirit of Négritude: Kehinde Wiley in Africa," *Nka: Journal of Contemporary African Art* 41 (November 2017), 126–139.

43. Kehinde Wiley, as quoted in Thompson, "The Sound of Light," 490.

44. *PUMA Presents: Of the Same Earth*. http://www.youtube.com/watch?v=1dECwcd JMXg&feature=relmfu.

45. Thompson, "The Sound of Light," 488.

46. Homi Bhabha, *The Location of Culture* (London: Routledge, 1994).

47. Thelma Golden, "Post…," in *Freestyle* (New York: Studio Museum in Harlem, 2001), 14.

About the Contributors

Stanley Keith **Arnold**, Ph.D., is an associate professor of history at Northern Illinois University, where he teaches courses in sports history, public history and American history. His work has appeared in the *Historian*, the *Journal of Sport History* and the *Journal of American History*. He is the author of *Building the Beloved Community* and is working on a book on African Americans and the first modern Olympic Games (1896–1948).

Travis R. **Bell**, Ph.D., is a multimedia journalism instructor at the University of South Florida. His research focuses on sports media, often at an intersection with race and gender. He has published in the *International Journal of Sport Communication* and *Communication & Sport* and is working on a book on the role of media construction of CTE as a public health issue through the NFL. He has produced four documentary films, including two connected to race and high school football.

Drew D. **Brown**, Ph.D., is an assistant professor of Africana studies at the University of Delaware. His work interrogates race, sports, and culture in the lives of people of African descent, both continental and diaspora, and examines the cultural elements, identity, and oppression of contemporary Black male athletes in the U.S. and in a global context. He spent a short time with the Edmonton Eskimos (Canadian Football League) and went on to complete a master's degree in African American studies at Clark Atlanta University and his doctorate at Temple University.

Akilah R. **Carter-Francique**, Ph.D., is an associate professor at San Jose State University (SJSU) in the Department of African Studies. Her research explores the intersections of race/ethnicity and women in the contexts of sport and physical activity, education, and health. As a former collegiate athlete in track and field at the University of Houston, her work has an emphasis on Black girls and women. She received her Ph.D. from the University of Georgia and served as the 2018–2019 president of the North American Society for the Sociology of Sport (NASSS).

Joseph N. **Cooper**, Ph.D., is the Dr. J. Keith Motley Endowed Chair of Sport Leadership and Administration at the University of Massachusetts (UMass) Boston. His research interests focus on the intersection of race, sport, education, and culture.

Daniel **Haxall** is a professor of art history at Kutztown University of Pennsylvania. A former fellow at the Smithsonian American Art Museum and Institute for the Arts and Humanities, he earned his Ph.D. from Pennsylvania State University. He publishes on diverse topics in contemporary art, including abstract expressionism, collage, installation art, and the African diaspora. His research investigates the intersection of art and sport, and he is the editor of *Picturing the Beautiful Game* (Bloomsbury Academic, 2018).

Bruce Lee **Hazelwood** is a Ph.D. student in the Cultural Studies and Social Thought in Education doctoral program at Washington State University. His research argues that students may learn about social justice issues more critically through their intersections with sport, particularly on college campuses.

Kevin **Hogg** holds an MA in English literature from Carleton University. He teaches English, social studies, and history at Mount Baker Secondary School in Cranbrook, British Columbia. He has contributed articles to 30 reference works and an essay on cultural appropriation for *Identity in Professional Wrestling* (edited by Aaron Horton, McFarland, 2018).

Nathan **Kalman-Lamb** is a postdoctoral lecturing fellow in the Thompson Writing Program at Duke University. He received his Ph.D. from the graduate program in social and political thought at York University. His research focuses on labor, race, multiculturalism, gender, spectatorship, and injury in sport. He is the co-author of *Out of Left Field*, as well as the author of articles on race, multiculturalism and sport in the journals *Social Identities*, *Topia*, and *Social Inclusion* and the edited collection *Killing the Model Minority Stereotype*.

Christina **Kanu** received an MA in African American studies from Clark Atlanta University. Her research focuses on African American male collegiate athletes and examines structural racism in college sports. Her future work will be stationed in both sport management and higher education. She is the CEO of Christina Kanu Consulting, LLC. In 2016 she was recognized as World Wide Women's Group's Women Influencers. She actively mentors more than 25 people across the country.

Charles D.T. **Macaulay** is a Ph.D. student in the Learning, Leadership, and Educational Policy (LLEP) program in the Neag School of Education at the University of Connecticut. His research interests focus on the intersection of sociology, economics, race, culture, and sport.

Michael **Mallery**, Jr., is a doctoral student in the Learning, Leadership, and Educational Policy (LLEP) program in the Neag School of Education at the University of Connecticut. His research interests focus on the intersection of education, race, business, and sport.

Demetrius W. **Pearson**, Ph.D., is an associate professor, and formerly associate chair, in the Department of Health and Human Performance at the University of Houston. His research areas and teaching have focused on the sociocultural and historical aspects of sport. He has conducted research and written about African American involvement in various sport forms, including North American rodeo, as well as their depiction in contemporary sport films. He maintains a repository listing of American sport films from 1930 to 2017.

Fritz G. Polite, Ph.D., is the Assistant Dean for Student Affairs and chair of the Management Science Division and Director of the Sport Management Program at the Harry F. Byrd, Jr., School of Business at Shenandoah University (Virginia). He earned his Ph.D. in sport administration from Florida State University. His research focuses on sociocultural aspects of sport, including leadership, hiring practices, race, gender and diversity. He has more than 30 years of experience in business, sports, management, coaching, and teaching, including 19 years of international experience.

F. Michelle **Richardson**, Ph.D., is an assistant professor of sport management at Coppin State University. Her scholarship focuses on Historically Black Colleges and Universities; the Black female athletic experience, Black student-athletes and Black Greek letter organizations (BGLOs), as well as leadership and organizational commitment. She has written a number of articles including "Black Female Athletic Experiences" in *The Athletic Experience at Historically Black Colleges and Universities* (edited by Billy Hawkins et al., Rowman & Littlefield, 2015).

Jeremai E. **Santiago** is a doctoral candidate in the School of Education and Human Development at Shenandoah University. His research interests include social responsibility and accountability as it relates to constructs of critical race theory.

Derrick E. **White**, Ph.D., is an associate professor of history and African American and Africana Studies at the University of Kentucky. He is a scholar of modern Black history, with an emphasis on intellectual, political, and sports history. White has authored two books, *The Challenge of Blackness* (2011) and *Blood, Sweat, and Tears* (2019). He is working on a book on Florida A&M and the rise and fall of a Black college football dynasty.

Miciah Z. **Yehudah**, Ph.D., is a scholar of Africana and African American studies. His research interests coalesce around two points: (1) the consequences of the erasure of Black narratives from global and local histories; and (2) the development and application of strategies of resistance against such methods of marginalization. He earned his Ph.D. from Temple University's Department of African American Studies and is the founder and executive director of the SBA Center.

Index

Numbers in **bold italics** indicate pages with illustrations; tables are indicated by t.